# TEARS OF HISTORY

EUROPEAN PERSPECTIVES

EUROPEAN PERSPECTIVES

A SERIES IN SOCIAL THOUGHT AND
CULTURAL CRITICISM

**LAWRENCE D. KRITZMAN, EDITOR**

European Perspectives presents outstanding books by leading European
thinkers. With both classic and contemporary works, the series aims to
shape the major intellectual controversies of our day and to facilitate the
tasks of historical understanding.

Dominique Kalifa, *Vice, Crime, and Poverty: How the
Western Imagination Invented the Underworld*

Ernst Jünger, *A German Officer in Occupied Paris:
The War Journals, 1941–1945*

Étienne Balibar, *Secularism and Cosmopolitanism:
Critical Hypotheses on Religion and Politics*

Roland Barthes: *Album: Unpublished Correspondence and Texts*

Marc Augé, *Everyone Dies Young: Time Without Age*

Claude Lévi-Strauss, *We Are All Cannibals: And Other Essays*

Jacques Le Goff, *Must We Divide History Into Periods?*

François Hartog, *Regimes of Historicity:
Presentism and Experiences of Time*

Eelco Runia, *Moved by the Past: Discontinuity and Historical Mutation*

Julia Kristeva, *The Severed Head: Capital Visions*

Georges Vigarello, *The Metamorphoses of Fat: A History of Obesity*

Jean-Louis Flandrin and Massimo Montanari,
*Food: A Culinary History*

Roland Barthes, *How to Live Together:
Novelistic Simulations of Some Everyday Spaces*

*For a complete list of books in the series, please see the Columbia University Press
website.*

# TEARS OF HISTORY

## THE RISE OF POLITICAL
## ANTISEMITISM IN
## THE UNITED STATES

## PIERRE BIRNBAUM

### TRANSLATED BY

### KAREN SANTOS DA SILVA

Columbia University Press  *New York*

Columbia University Press wishes to express its appreciation for assistance given by the government of France through the Ministère de la Culture in the preparation of this translation.

Columbia University Press
*Publishers Since 1893*
New York   Chichester, West Sussex
cup.columbia.edu

*Les larmes de L'Histoire. De Kichinev à Pittsburgh*
copyright © 2022 Editions Gallimard, Paris
Translation © 2023 Columbia University Press
With the support of La Fondation pour la Mémoire de la Shoah

Library of Congress Cataloging-in-Publication Data
Names: Birnbaum, Pierre, author. | Santos Da Silva, Karen, translator.
Title: Tears of history : the rise of political antisemitism in the United States /
Pierre Birnbaum ; translated by Karen Santos Da Silva.
Other titles: Larmes de l'histoire. English | Rise of political
antisemitism in the United States
Description: New York : Columbia University Press, [2023] |
Series: European perspectives : a series in social thought and cultural criticism |
"Les larmes de L'Histoire. De Kichinev à Pittsburgh copyright © 2022
Editions Gallimard, Paris." | Includes bibliographical references and index.
Identifiers: LCCN 2022054115 (print) | LCCN 2022054116 (ebook) |
ISBN 9780231209601 (hardback) | ISBN 9780231209618 (trade paperback) |
ISBN 9780231558020 (ebook)
Subjects: LCSH: Jews—United States—Historiography. | Antisemitism—United
States—History. | United States—Race relations—History.
Classification: LCC E184.33 .B5713 2023 (print) | LCC E184.33 (ebook) |
DDC 305.892/4073—dc23/eng/20221214
LC record available at https://lccn.loc.gov/2022054115
LC ebook record available at https://lccn.loc.gov/2022054116

Columbia University Press books are printed on permanent
and durable acid-free paper.
Printed and bound by CPI Group (UK) Ltd, Croydon, CR0 4YY
Cover design: Julia Kushnirsky
Cover images: Shutterstock

Columbia University Press gratefully acknowledges the generous contribution to this book provided by the Florence Gould Foundation Endowment Fund for French Translation.

# CONTENTS

# PREFACE
# TO THE AMERICAN EDITION

As perhaps many readers will know, since the birth of the United States up through the middle of the twentieth century, apart from the tragic Leo Frank affair, Jews have often been confronted with antisemitic prejudice, with various forms of malevolent behavior, even open hostility, but never the deadly violence that beleaguered their coreligionists in Old Europe. The latter were threatened by endless antisemitic movements that united frenzied mobs, from the 1848 Revolution to the Dreyfus affair. They lived through the incessant pogroms that punctuated the Tzarist empire, all the way up to the Shoah, the culmination of the vale of tears that has defined Jewish destiny since the Crusades.

Nothing of the sort was happening at the heart of American society, which was busy worrying about other problems. Other minorities were perceived as threatening, other social groups were the target of ferocious hate, extreme violence, and endless brutality in the name of religious feuds and racist ideas. Deaths, murders, lynchings, and savage executions were uncountable, from the near-eradication of the Native Americans to the savage lynching of African Americans. To these endless assassinations could be added the racially motivated murders of Chinese, Japanese, Irish, and Italian immigrants. The list is interminable and is evidence of American society's extreme violence against multiple minorities. During the modern period alone, over four thousand Black men and women were lynched. In 1891 eleven Italian men—though acquitted—were extracted from a prison and assassinated in the name of religious rivalries, in the name of economic competition blended with nationalism and populist views, in the name of a true nationalist anti-Catholic "hysteria" and of exacerbated nativism. In 1895, five Italian factory workers were killed by miners; the following year, three Italians were hanged in Louisiana.[1] Throughout the country, Italian, Polish, and Irish immigrants were murdered. Physical violence thus affected a great number of minorities.

It did not however affect the Jews. None of them experienced a similar tragic fate, from the birth of the United States through the twentieth century. No Jew was assassinated due to antisemitism, racism, or xenophobia. From this perspective, compared to the old continent, the exceptionalism of American society is obvious. Things were nevertheless not rosy. Prejudices prevailed: the Christian nation imposed its beliefs and at times rejected the Jews.[2] Despite article 6, section 3 of the Constitution, which states that "no religious test shall ever be required as a qualification to any office or public trust under the United States," Jews remained excluded from public office in North Carolina up until 1868. In the name of the Christian nation, society continued to impose its values and rituals, from the Christian Sunday to the reading of Bibles in public schools, only abolished late into the twentieth century.

Similarly, Jews often faced measures and ideological stances that were hostile to them. From General Ulysses Grant who, in July 1862, mid Civil War, wrote that "no Jews are to be permitted travel on the railroad southward from any point. They may go

north and be encouraged in it but they are such an intolerable
nuisance that the department must be purged of them," to the
racist biological theories expressed by Madison Grant at the end
of the nineteenth century, and to the exacerbated racial Darwin-
ism that dominated the period, Jews were subjected to exclu-
sionary policies. They were targets of antisemitic statements that
brutally affected their daily lives, and questioned the legitimacy
of their place in public life. In the interwar period, this led to
laws that restricted their immigration.[3]

Antisemitic prejudices, anchored in unchangeable traditions—
more often than not Christian—touched their lives in spectacular
ways. People saw in the Jews dangerous exploiters, threatening
Shylocks, malevolent characters eager to dominate the world
through their conspiracies,[4] revolutionaries who advocated anar-
chism, strangers unable to assimilate, immoral beings whose customs could only degrade American society and must be opposed.
Thus, following Madison Grant's example and in the name of the
purity of the Anglo-Saxon race, the aristocrat Henry Adams
declared: "The people of this country won't be starved and driven
to the wall by Jews who are guilty of all crimes, tricks and wiles
that have hitherto been unknown and unthought of by civilized
humanity."[5] Later, Henry Ford would distribute *The Protocols of the
Elders of Zion* to stoke hatred of the Jews.[6]

Amidst this context of deep antisemitic prejudice, in 1877, the
exclusion of banker Joseph Seligman from the Grand Union
Hotel in Saratoga provoked an enormous scandal. There, like at
other resorts, one could find signs that read "Jews are not admitted." Discrimination similarly reigned in the Catskills or at Manhattan Beach. Jews were at times excluded from certain jobs,
such as at the New York Western Union Company or in other
companies where candidates had to be blond and "have straight
noses."[7] Jews were refused access to certain neighborhoods. Their

presence was equally curtailed in private schools and universities, from Harvard to Columbia, which implemented policies to reduce the number of Jewish students. Their nomination to the Supreme Court since Louis Brandeis inspired a torrent of antisemitic statements that recured when Benjamin Cardoso and Felix Frankfurter were both granted access to the highest court in the land.[8] These antisemitic prejudices were manifest in serious practices that threatened the equality of citizens as well as religious pluralism, a foundation of American society. Jews were hit hard by these policies that challenged their integration.[9]

Worse yet, this racism turned violent at times. Indeed, in Louisiana and Mississippi in the 1890s, Jewish farms were burnt. Around the same time, factory workers in New Jersey opposed the hiring of young Russian Jews, resulting in many days of rioting and abuse against them. Similarly, in 1902, the funeral services of rabbi Jacob Joseph instigated a riot in the streets of the Lower East Side, after workers from the Hoe and Company threw various metal and wood objects onto the funeral procession, yelling insults that stoked the anger of the Jews. They in turn invaded the factory, and were held at bay by water cannons. Worse, the local police, primarily comprised of antisemitic Irish Catholics, viciously attacked the Jews. Over two hundred were wounded, others were arrested.[10] Emotions were running high throughout the country.

Antisemitism thus resulted in rare acts of violence without however leading to any deaths. This bears repeating: it seems no Jew was ever killed as a result of antisemitism before the first decade of the twentieth century. As deplorable as this social antisemitism may have been, it did not lead, as in many European countries during the same period, to deadly acts of violence and innumerable pogroms. In this way, we can only agree with the many historians who have stated: "that the Jews were emancipated by general constitutional doctrine, applicable to all white residents, rather than by special legislation, as in western Europe, meant that no counterrevolutionary, antisemitic political movements aimed at revoking aspects of Jewish emancipation were able easily to take roots here." Henceforth, and this is crucial, "while in Europe Jews were traditionally the least protected group in society, in the United States public officials have rarely sided with antisemites in active hostility against Jews."[11] This observation is almost universally shared. For Jonathan Sarna, "if America has not been utter heaven for Jews, it has been as far from hell as Jews in the Diaspora have ever known."[12] Similarly, Hasia Diner considers that "on this side of the Atlantic, no legacy of state-supported exclusion and violence, encrusted aristocracy, no embittered peasantry, or legally established church hierarchy manipulated centuries-old Judeophobia."[13] Diner adds, "however starkly Christian Americans stereotyped the Jews, these words rarely led to action."[14]

These observations are essential. They justify the argument of this book by emphasizing the long absence of any antisemitic movement in the United States, the protective role of the law, the state's rejection of any intervention hostile to the Jews, the low degree of violence they faced, and the importance of cultural and religious pluralism. If social antisemitism is often apparent in the streets, neighborhoods, beaches, clubs, private businesses, and universities, it does not result in extreme physical violence and murder until the turn of the twentieth century.

If we take a leap through contemporary history, events today have taken a different shape. According to the logic that motivates the extremist mobilization of the far right, and following so many antisemitic attacks resulting in the murder of many Jews, tragedy struck on October 27, 2018, when assailant Robert Bowers attacked the Pittsburgh synagogue, killing eleven Jews and wounding many others. This event followed in the wake of countless earlier Aryan discourses defending the white race and hostile to the emergence of a strong state, from Franklin Delano Roosevelt to Barack Obama. It is the result of the violent rejection of a state that has allegedly rejected the Christian right and its traditions in order to better impose the power of the Jews, who have supposedly brilliantly triumphed by occupying the Biden administration, as they had already managed to do with the previous administrations of Roosevelt, Clinton, and Obama.

Today in the United States, we are witnessing the birth of another type of antisemitism, this time in the name not of traditional cultural and social prejudices but of a political idea that we could name political antisemitism. Born in France as a reaction to the admission of Jews into the higher administration of the republic, itself a response against reactionary movements that refused the secularization of public spaces—which was deemed destructive to Christian society—this antisemitism against a universal and meritocratic strong state was unknown in the United States, a decentralized country with a weak state and low institutionalization. This form of antisemitism is equally unknown in other countries with weak states, such as Great Britain, Holland, or Italy. Its targets are states supposedly controlled by Jews.

The far right's nationalistic antisemitism, mobilized against the welfare state put in place by Obama, has resulted in a rejection of the Jewish power that allegedly occupies Washington.

And then we have Donald Trump's triumph, the triumph of a nationalistic and xenophobic populism celebrated immediately

following his entry into the White House by extremist movements, to the cries of "Heil Hitler." It is this far-right mobilization that led straight to the events of Charlottesville.

The next stage was practically inevitable: the mobilization of
the alt-right responsible for the insurrection against the Capitol, led by a coalition of fringe antisemitic groups that toted the
supremacy of the white race. After the attack against the Pittsburgh synagogue, the Buffalo attack—as well as more recent acts
of violence—symbolizes this shift. In Buffalo, in May of 2022,
Payton Gendron, in the name of the Great Replacement theorized by French author Renaud Camus, kills ten African
Americans: in his mind, the Jews are using Black people to
eradicate Aryan society. In a long manifesto sent out over social
media, Gendron answers his own questions:

**"Are you a fascist?**

Yes, fascism is one of the only political ideologies that will unite Whites against the replacers. Since that is what I seek, calling me a fascist would be accurate.

**Are you an antisemite?**

YES!! I wish all JEWS to HELL! Go back to hell where you came from DEMON!

"The elite," "The 1%," "The bankers," "The capitalists," ((((them)))), "The marxist's" they all refer to the same group: THE JEWS!!

When referring to "the Jews" I don't mean all ethnic or religious Jews. Some can be actually decent, and make significant progress to humanity. However many of them are not. Many are born to exploit the goyim and exploit the Earth for capital gain. They control the mainstream media, many government positions, and international and global banking. They advocate for leftist ideology, and spread propaganda among the right. They spread their lies through all forms of media. They want us to divide ourselves by race, instead of goy and non-goy, like they already do. "Remember the 6 million goyim!" The real war I'm advocating for is the gentiles vs the Jews. We outnumber them 100x, and they are not strong by themselves. But by their Jewish ways, they turn us against each other. When you realize this you will know that the Jews are the biggest problem the Western world has ever had. They must be called out and killed, if they are lucky they will be exiled. We cannot show any sympathy towards them again."

This political antisemitism is now fed by new accusations against Biden's cabinet that is allegedly also in the hands of the Jews, as is illustrated by the strange and imaginative table on the following page.

This book proposes to describe the emergence of a political antisemitism in the second part of the twentieth century. This political antisemitism is in full bloom today in the United States, similar to what we might have found in Germany under Weimar or in France in the period spanning the Dreyfus affair to the Vichy government. American exceptionalism, which previously had been immune to this form of antisemitism when its state was weak, when political power was dominated by a WASP establishment from which Jews were for a long time excluded, is now endangered. In a context marked by generalized political violence, as evidenced by the ninety-six hundred threats issued

against members of Congress, as well as attacks against FBI agents, while at the same time recent polls show that almost half the respondents consider it acceptable to use violence against the state, we can expect the worst. We will show that the radical political antisemitism of the alt-right which has been multiplying anti-Jewish attacks, may tip all of American society toward a racist national populism that can only weaken the place of the Jews in what was for a long time a golden America.

# INTRODUCTION

## On American Happiness

When Alexis de Tocqueville arrives in the United States, he cannot believe his eyes. Democratic mores seem to be the rule; violence seems to have been banished; risks of dictatorship and authoritarianism remain nonexistent; the protection of freedoms is a given; love of equality is rampant; the pluralism of groups and communities is assured; religious life is respected by all. A land of plenty. True, he concedes in one dedicated chapter of *Democracy in America*, Black Americans find themselves relegated to the margins of society, humiliated: slaves in the South, exploited in the North. True again, in this same chapter, he describes the dispossession of Native Americans condemned to disappear. These pessimistic considerations do not mar his general view of American society, whose liberalism and individualism remain, for all that, the foundation of this society, anchored in a Protestant cultural code, infinite in its variations, and a protector of each one's conscience and beliefs. No wars of religion, no Saint Bartholomew, and yet no revolutionary rejection of the Church, all the more since the Catholic world embraces democratic ideals with respect for the law that tempers the rule of the majority in a separation of powers that guarantees moderation. Moreover, no Jacobean excesses, no Terror, no revolution comparable to 1789 or even 1830 with its insurrections and its barricades. Finally, no violent challenges against the state, which remains weak, decentralized, devoid of prestige, far from the absolutist monarchic state, or the revolutionary state, or the Napoleonic state; it is a state in which the people, through their participation in the local life of municipalities, remain the source of all power. To such a degree that its servants, almost always elected, are replaceable at will, "have neither palaces nor guards, nor ceremonial uniforms," dress modestly, lead an ascetic life without pomp or regalia, given that "administrative power in the United States offers in its constitution nothing centralized or hierarchical, that is why it remains unobtrusive."[1] The function of high-ranking civil servants remains discreet. They do not presume to single-handedly run the nation and thus attract no jealousy, arouse in their wake no riots, revolts, or revolutionary mobilization.

Tocqueville crisscrossed this country, whose quasi-utopian appearance he fell in love with, though not blind to the risks of authoritarianism, the consequence of an excess of individualism. Nor did he neglect the social injustices that emerged, to such a degree that he dreaded that a new economic aristocracy would manage to seize power. Over the course of his many travels, at times dangerous, on American soil, he met Iroquois, Cherokees, and other members of Indian tribes; he met Black Americans, but never once did he come across a single Jewish inhabitant. Not one paragraph, out of the two thick volumes of *Democracy in America,* mentions the Jewish population, nevertheless present on American soil for centuries, active throughout the country, in the North and the South alike, as well as in the large cities of the Midwest. If the Jews are absent from this great work, so is any allusion to the question of the antisemitism that could have come to light in any particular city or any particular community. The Jews simply do not exist.

It is indeed remarkable that *The Ancien Régime and the French Revolution* similarly ignores their presence on French soil, their role under the monarchy, as well as the process of revolutionary regeneration that fundamentally changed their destiny at the end of 1791 by allowing them to suddenly attain citizenship, turning them into citizens. Tocqueville, a well-informed observer of French society, does not broach, in his narrative of the Revolution, the violent antisemitic maneuvers they sparked in Alsace. He also underestimates, in his *Recollections*, the antisemitic unrest that broke out during the 1848 Revolution and gives no attention to the role of the Jews in the formation of a counterrevolutionary discourse prompted by their emancipation. Strangely, Tocqueville, the father of comparative sociology, remains silent on the Jewish question at the heart of French society, a question that nevertheless gave fodder to the Franco-French wars throughout the nineteenth century and that has imprinted itself upon the framework of a large portion of the period's literature, such as Honoré de Balzac's *The Human Comedy*, which spans 1789 to 1848. Tocqueville neglects the role of the Jews, who were nevertheless quite visible throughout the July Monarchy and the Second Empire. He does not see that they provide the ingredients for a Catholic counterrevolutionary discourse or that they are the privileged target of a utopian socialism, from Charles Fourier to Pierre-Joseph Proudhon or George Sand.

In so doing, his work lacks a non-negligible dimension in his comparison between the United States and France. The Jews are as central to the history of modern France as they are invisible in the American society of his time. Loudly emancipated in France, and prompting a massive rejection from the Catholic world as well as from various social circles, singled out as the instigators of the Revolution, more still as the pillars of capitalism, they are seemingly absent from an American society that emancipated them silently, at least juridically, even before 1791. They therefore flourished noiselessly and remained in the margins of society on its social but also territorial periphery. They evaded involvement with political struggles and did not participate in ideological skirmishes, thus escaping Tocqueville's sharp gaze. Their bliss was palpable as long as they remained invisible to the author of *Democracy in America*, ensconced in their niche far from the center, from the state.

In this way, throughout the nineteenth century, American happiness is different from French happiness. From the beginning, as the French nation rooted itself in Catholicism and then in universal rationalism, the founding 1787 Constitution of American society states, in article 6, section 3, that "no religious Test shall ever be required as a Qualification to any Office or public Trust under the United States." This mean recognizing, from the get-go, the equality of all beliefs, rejecting none, ensuring the implementation of a separation between church and state that protects religions more than it does the state. The happiness of American Jews was seemingly ensured by president George Washington's speech in his response to the congratulations from Rabbi Moses Seixas of the Touro synagogue: "The Citizens of the United States of America have a right to applaud themselves for having given to mankind examples of an enlarged and liberal policy. . . . All possess alike liberty of conscience and immunities of citizenship. . . . For happily the Government of the United States . . . gives to bigotry no sanction, to persecution no assistance." Tocqueville should have had to quote this fundamental text, which alone justifies the vision of an American society based upon a deep liberalism, protector of the religious life of all, refusing to be muzzled either in the name of a French-style Enlightenment rationalism or in the name of the Catholicism that founded a unified French nation. Moreover, the accession to citizenship of American Jews was a given: it required no regeneration, created no controversy. With Washington adding, in this unique text in modern Jewish history,

> It would be inconsistent with the frankness of my character not to avow that I am pleased with your favorable opinion of my Administration, and fervent wishes for my felicity. May the children of the Stock of Abraham, who dwell in this land, continue to merit and enjoy the good will of the other Inhabitants; while every one shall sit in safety under his own vine and fig tree, and there shall be none to make him afraid. May the father of all mercies scatter light and not darkness in our paths, and make us all in our several vocations useful here, and in his own due time and way everlastingly happy.[2]

The image of "vine and fig tree" is borrowed from the Old Testament, a text familiar to the founding fathers of the American nation. We find it word for word in this text that shapes the worldview of these Puritans, so fond of biblical culture: "but they shall sit every man under his vine and under his fig tree, and no one shall make them afraid, for the mouth of the LORD of hosts has spoken" (Micah 4:4). For Washington, the "Jewish nation" fully participated in the life of the American nation. Jewish citizens were not in any way required to give up their collective aspects. There was no fear of maintaining a nation within a nation, given that society was conceived of as being eminently pluralistic. Under its "fig tree," the Jewish nation had nothing to fear from its fellow citizens from other nations. It could peacefully bloom, fearing no pogrom, no violent antisemitic mobilization of the sort that the ancient world had known since the Crusades, the Spanish Inquisition, and the Russian or Ukrainian pogroms.

Admittedly, Thomas Jefferson brought a nuance to this optimistic observation by noting, in a speech given at the Mill Street Synagogue, that beyond the laws that are hostile to "intolerance," "public opinion erects itself into an Inquisition and exercises its office with as much fanaticism as fans the flames of an auto da fe."[3] This Inquisition nevertheless remained entirely relative as long as the nation's culture was sustained by biblical references that shaped daily life. Americans saw themselves as the new Hebrews that freed themselves from Egypt, that is, from the yoke of the British. They also crossed the Red Sea, naming their children Jonathan, Rachel, Ezra, or Daniel. Their preachers sang this new promised land, and the metaphor of the Exodus has persisted throughout all periods of the American nation.

While the terrible Kishinev pogrom had just occurred in Russia in 1903, preceded and followed by so many other appalling massacres in Russia, former president Grover Cleveland celebrated, in 1905, the two hundred and fiftieth anniversary of the arrival of the Jews in the United States, emphasizing that "the Jews among us have in their care and keeping the history and traditions of an ancient Jewish commonwealth astonishingly like our own Republic in its democracy and underlying intention. . . . And we should not close our minds to a conception of the coincidence in divine purpose discoverable in the bestowal, by the Ruler of the universe, of a similar plan of rule, after thousands of years, upon the people of the United States."[4] As terror descended on the Jews of the Russian Empire, as the Dreyfus affair continued to divide a French public opinion overly excited by an intransigent Catholic movement and by aggressive populism, as antisemitism continued to spread throughout German

society, which still excluded Jews from its state, happiness seemed
to be part and parcel of the daily life of American Jews.

True, the emancipatory promise was far from having been
fully kept: various states failed to proclaim their Declaration of
Independence as well as the First Amendment guaranteeing religious freedom. True, in many states, Jews did not have access to
prestigious public careers before the end of the nineteenth century, nor could they even vote. True, during the Civil War, they
were at times faced with, from both camps, hostile attitudes.
True, social antisemitism excluded them from certain clubs and
hotels, and it is also true that they were rebuffed by quotas from
the Ivy League. Finally, it is true that despite the separation of
church and state, the presence of Christianity was strong at the
heart of public institutions, where the reading of the New Testament and the presence of crosses remained a consequence of
the natural order further propagated by an aggressive nativism.
But the Jews enjoyed, despite these prejudices and restrictions,
an almost cloudless happiness within their recesses, in their community. They led a peaceful life and were not confronted by the
same violent hostility as Black Americans and even, at times,
Catholics. They did not occupy, as in France, a central role in
political crises or in the conflicts that brought turmoil to society. They avoided ideological quarrels, and were not considered
scapegoats as in so many European societies. Throughout the
nineteenth century, their presence did not give rise to any national
mobilization, no large-scale "antisemitic moment," given that
during this period they remained confined to the periphery of
society.

From this moment on, John Higham, the great historian of
American Judaism, was able to put forward that "no decisive
event, no deep crisis, no powerful social movement, no great
individual is associated primarily with or significant chiefly

because of anti-Semitism."⁵ Similarly, Dennis Wrong underlines that "anti-Semitism has never in America been politicized as the basis for a right-wing nationalist movement as it has in such countries as pre-Nazi Germany or in France."⁶ The exceptionalism of American society led the Jews to remain a nation at the periphery of society, whereas French exceptionalism pushed them on the contrary to penetrate it. The happiness of French Jews was undeniable, given some of their glorious victories: "Happy like God in France." Their disillusion was not, for all that, less frequent for being a favorite target of so much mobilization. The happiness of American Jews was more peaceful, less flamboyant, more hidden within communities, within collective structures with a strong religious character. As Irving Howe notes, "Tocqueville had seen [voluntary organizations] as distinctively American but [that were], in this context, distinctively Jewish."⁷ The troubling story he tells in *World of Our Fathers* is that of the nuptials between European Jews and those of the new continent, an open and multicultural society.

In this sense, the happiness of American Jews is intriguing, imposing itself as a privileged mode of diaspora likely to attract millions of emigrants to come and join these tiny but vibrant forms of legitimate community life. Like so many other "nations" within the American nation whose cultural code was Christianity, they blossomed under their tree, in their territory, at the heart of their neighborhoods, sheltered from the deadly passions rampant throughout American society that targeted African Americans, Native Americans, and even . . . the deeply Catholic Irish or Italians.

America became the new center of global Judaism at the turn of the century, leaving American Jews alone to embody modern diaspora, the predominant form of the most vibrant exile and an unparalleled source of creativity. Borrowing from the terminology

coined by Albert Hirschman, we could argue that American
Jews long confined themselves to the pursuit of a private happiness by relinquishing public action.[8] They found a way of life
and a form of limitless fulfillment, a type of local happiness that
protected them, separated them from any form of visibility, and
defended them from becoming the scapegoats of popular anger.
They found it through the strategy of community, tailored to an
eminently pluralist society dominated, nevertheless, by a superior white Anglo-Saxon Protestant class, hostile to the emergence of a French-style state. This was not unlike living under
the enormous Russian Empire where so many groups, religions, and nationalities coexisted. Yet here, at the heart of an
empire just as fragmented but also profoundly liberal, democratic, and attached to respect for rights and freedom of thought,
the Jews enjoyed a unique life. Entrenched in their *community*,
their collective and autonomous collective life, their quasi-limitless
fulfillment expressed itself in incomparable creativity. It would
henceforth be on this continent, in this "open" society, according to the Karl Popper's pretty metaphor, that novels, music, and
Jewish studies would flourish, nourished by waves of immigrants,
of scientists fleeing the "closed" societies of Eastern Europe.

Going forth, this society of abundance would have a power-
fully consensual dimension that managed to avoid the torments
and ideologies that ravaged Europe. A kind of end to ideologies
seemed to slowly impose itself at this contemporary period in a
society that was not favorable to intellectuals, that rejected the
"isms" carriers of radical confrontation. This *affluent society* also
favored a social mobility that mitigated the class struggle, broke
barriers and shackles, opened all possibilities: *from rags to riches*.
Like Horatio Alger, an American myth of individual advancement all to himself, of the self-made made man, Jews hoisted
themselves up the social hierarchy. Outside a few periods of

difficult ideological and political tensions, between populist pushes and anarchist attacks, or even McCarthyist episodes where violence, tenseness and prejudices reemerged, often tinged by antisemitism, American society seemed overwhelmingly immune to the great revolutionary ideologies that reach only a small number of intellectual circles and a limited part of the working class (the socialist and communist parties not having managed to take root in them). The question that Werner Sombart asked, "Why is there no socialism in the United States?," retains all of its meaning.[9] Mechanisms of intergenerational mobility as well as territorial mobility have limited confrontation between classes and assured everyone possible integration—with the exception of Native Americans, who remain marginalized, and Black Americans, (still) often excluded because of racial prejudice.

Henceforth the "third generation . . . felt secure in its Americanness and therefore no longer saw any reason for the attitude of rejection. . . . Social radicalism virtually disappeared, and passionate, militant Zionism espoused by groups of American Jews until 1948 became diffused into a vague . . . friendliness to the State of Israel."[10] The "quest for the blessed lost past" dissipated.[11] Far from Europe, and despite a superior white and Protestant dominant class that defended its privileges, Jews, much like their fellow citizens descended from other minorities, with, again, the exception of Black Americans, knew a state of grace that nothing seemed to trouble. Far from the miserable Lower East Side where their grandparents resided after their emigration, and where they at times led difficult strikes, they had become fully Americanized, to the point that they considered their new home the definitive solution to their exile.[12]

# 1

## SALO BARON, THE GOLDEN LAND, AND THE REFUSAL OF A LACHRYMOSE HISTORY

S alo Baron is also delighted to find, in New York, a welcoming land bereft of the feeling of exile. He remains a prime example of those academics who have turned away from the old continent to join the new one, the *goldene medine*, or golden country. Salo (Shalom) Baron was born on May 26, 1895, in Tarnow in West Galicia, at the heart of the Hapsburg Empire. His father, Elias, was a banker and had at his disposal many important revenue streams: an oil field, a mill, real estate, and land. As a member of the municipal council, he played an essential role in the organization of collective activities in which his son sometimes participated. His mother, born Mina Wittmayer, was from a well-to-do family that owned the largest store in the city; she also took part in managing local business, wore different-colored headscarves, and ordered her clothes from the best stores in Paris and Vienna.[1]

Baron's family was religious. His father sported a beard and wore traditional garb, but he professed liberal ideas. President of the Jewish community, he was attracted by Hasidism but gave his son a liberal education. As a child, Salo wore the traditional caftan and black hat, but on vacation he dressed like a European. A brilliant student in primary and high school, he knew Greek and Latin, used German at home, and spoke Polish, Hebrew, and probably French, Italian, and English. He studied the Talmud at Tarnow in a *heder* and thus had a strong religious education.[2] A gifted mathematician and chess player, able to take on the family's business at the age of fifteen, he was primed to be his father's successor at the head of the family company. But starting in his seventeenth year, while still in high school, he began publishing articles in Hebrew in *HaMizpech*, a Galician newspaper. He espoused the ideas of religious Zionism and seemed opposed as much to assimilationist theories as he was to Hasidism. He also condemned the deadly confrontations between Jews who fought in antagonistic armies, imploring them to pursue higher education. He wished to see a reformation of the electoral system such that it would offer better representation and a multiplicity of perspectives whose aims were to preserve Jewish specificity within diaspora, in line with the diasporist theories of Simon Dubnow.[3]

After having studied at the University of Krakow starting in 1913, he left during the summer of 1914 for Vienna, where he was a university student while also attending rabbinical school. There he earned three doctorates, in history (1917), political science (1922), and law (1923), and obtained his rabbinical degree at the Jewish theological seminary, though he would never practice. He taught Jewish history for a few years at the Jüdisches Pädagogium and in 1920 published a scholarly work on Jewish autonomy of action during the Vienna Congress. In 1926, recommended by numerous professors, he was invited to teach at the Jewish Institute of Religion in New York, a liberal institution directed by Stephen Wise in which future rabbis completed their studies. Baron threw himself entirely into his educational activities at this institution, giving courses on the Talmud, as well as on Jews in the Middle Ages, and on the growth of capitalism. He quickly obtained tenure and became the director of graduate studies. In 1928, he was offered a position at the Rabbinical Seminary in Breslau, famous for having once housed the instructors of Heinrich Graetz, the great historian of the Jewish people. He refused, deciding to stay in the United States.

This is when he publishes, on September 8, in the *Menorah Journal*—the most renowned Jewish journal of the period—his now famous article "Ghetto and Emancipation: Shall We Revise the Traditional View?"[4] In it, he means to refute the "lachrymal conception of history" put forth by Heinrich Graetz, and also the perspective of Leopold Zunz, according to which, "if there is an ascending scale of suffering, Israel has reached its highest degree."[5] This view of a history made of tears goes far back in Jewish history. It is illustrated, for example, by Joseph Ha-Kohen, a doctor and historian born in Avignon in 1496, author of *The Vale of Tears*, which already gives an inventory of all the suffering and persecutions Jews were subjected to. In this work, Ha-Kohen tirelessly covers the "cemetery of martyrs" of the Jewish people, this "painful history of the Jewish nation . . . a history of grief and oppression, of immense suffering and limitless bitterness, a history of desolation and despair."[6] For Baron, this tragic and pessimistic vision was propagated in the modern period by Graetz, whom he accuses of neglecting the socioeconomic dimension of Jewish history in favor of the psychological interpretation "of excessive subjectivity" manifested in a "pulsating heart which cries out over the sufferings of his people."[7] And even today this somber vision is shared by a good many Jewish thinkers. Isaiah Berlin, for instance, recalls the words of the famous British philosopher Lewis Namier. When a colleague asked why he studied the history of Great Britain and not that of the Jews, he replied, "There *is* no modern Jewish history. There is only a Jewish martyrology, and that is not amusing enough for me," a proposition that Berlin considers to contain "a certain truth."[8]

For his part, by opposing the two terms, "Ghetto and Emancipation," Baron wishes to propose a general interpretation of Jewish history that challenges the idea of a fundamental and frontal opposition between two commonly accepted ideal-typical stages. For a number of historians, nothing could be further from the ghetto than an emancipation that liberated the Jews from the chains that had long confined, excluded, humiliated them. Oppression was followed by liberation, flourishing, access to equality, education, social mobility, and an integration that provided relief from the constraints of the group.

> Emancipation, in the judgment of Graetz, Philipson, Dubnow and other historians, was the dawn of a new day after a nightmare of the deepest horror, and this view has been accepted as completely true by Jews, rabbis, scholars and laymen, throughout the Western world. It is in terms of this complete contrast between the black of the Jewish Middle Ages and the white of the post-Emancipation period that most generalizations about the progress of the Jews in modern times are made.[9]

Yet what if the Middle Ages were not in fact such a dark period? he wonders. What if, on the contrary, emancipation was not devoid of suffering and unhappiness? What might become of this ideal-typical interpretation of a Jewish history all too easily embraced by almost everyone?

Baron wishes to invert the terms of a history that is regularly presented through an evolutionary lens, as an evolution from suffering to liberation. In his view, Jews experienced a more dreadful fate with the start of emancipation than they did in the heyday of the ghetto during the Middle Ages; he thus observes that a comparison between the loss of life by violence in the two eras—pre- and post-Emancipation—would probably show little improvement since the French Revolution. Between Chmiel-nicki and Human, the two great pogrom movements of earlier East European Jewish history, more than a century intervened, whereas three major pogrom waves have swept Eastern Europe between 1880 and 1920, despite the coming of Emancipation.[10]

A lachrymose view of history would thus be less relevant for the period of the ghetto and the premodern period than for emancipation. Besides, up until that point, Jews were not concerned by wars since they were not conscripted into the army: "During the continuous wars of the sixteenth, seventeenth, and eighteenth centuries, when even the non-combatant Christian felt the curse of religious conflict, the Jews were neutral and suffered few losses. If they had been combatants they might have lost more than in all the pogroms."[11] In contrast, after the French Revolution, at different times, Jews were incorporated into rival armies and sub-jected to the horrors of successive wars in which they sometimes confronted one other. For Baron, "despite minor attacks, peri-odic pogroms and organized campaigns of conversion, the num-bers of Jewry during the last centuries preceding Emancipation increased much more rapidly than the Gentile population."[12] This means evaluating the period of the ghetto as being more benefi-cial than that of emancipation, given that the Jewish population, far from the wars that devastated Europe, experienced consid-erable growth, more than its non-Jewish neighbors.

In order to dismantle this dominant evolutionary and irenic view of Jewish history, so long taken for granted, Baron means to rely on socioeconomic analyses and somewhat neglects the religious or idealist foundations of Jewish history. He accuses Graetz of "interpreting the history of Jews in the diaspora almost exclusively in terms of a 'history of suffering and scholarship' and hence paid little attention to economic and social history,"[13] though they are at the origins of Jewish happiness. For Baron, the Jews of the Middle Ages benefited from better living conditions than non-Jews: as servants to the king, they were less exploited than the serfs, who were subject to the good graces of their master, the local lord, whose power was unrestrained by norm or tradition. Relying on observations by Jean de La Bruyère, Baron emphasizes the extreme poverty of the peasants compared to the social situation of the Jews.[14] Excluded from working the soil and from a number of other professions, the Jews found themselves confined to business and moneylending, trades from which they acquired large benefits that eventually shaped the beginnings of capitalism. Baron especially underscores how the Jews, unlike the serfs, could move about freely from one land to another. Their status was thus radically different from that of the serfs, who were sold according to the whims of their masters, to whom they were bound by innumerable financial and legal ties. Finally, unlike serfs, male Jews could marry the women of their choice without the approval of their master and had access to their own tribunals that handed down judgments according to their own laws.

In his provocative rehabilitation of a ghetto that others unanimously condemned at the time, Baron is looked upon as an iconoclastic author when he suggests that the Jews deliberately confined themselves to ghettos in order to preserve their social and religious cohesion. In his view, the ghetto favored the protection of both the Jews against their enemies and their autonomy. From then on, the ghetto appears to have been an essential factor in the "preservation of Jewry as a distinct nationality." True, he emphasizes, the Jews are then devoid of any political rights: "no one had them," outside of "the nobles and the clergy."[15]

This shows the extent to which the ghetto, at least in its origins, represented a place where the Jew could paradoxically flourish, more so maybe than during the period of emancipation, during which the Jews faced, often alone, the greatest dangers: popular violence the king could not restrain, challenges to the privileges linked to their corporations, subjection to common law and the loss of their own legislation, the unpredictability of assimilation, and, finally, the military service that came with their newfound citizenship. In this way, for Baron, we cannot oppose the "blackness" of the Middle Ages to the "whiteness" of emancipation. It is urgent to "revaluate radically our notions of Jewish progress under Western liberty. . . . If the status of the Jew (his privileges, opportunities, and actual life) in those centuries was in fact not as low as we are in the habit of thinking, then the miracle of Emancipation was not so great as we supposed."[16]

Thus, from the very first words of this essential text, Baron directly confronts the French Revolution that grew out of the Enlightenment and supposedly "opened up the gates that shut [the Jews] off from civilized life."[17] He straightaway opposes Heinrich Graetz, the first great historian of the Jewish people, citing these words that he means to challenge: "The Revolution was a judgement which in one day atoned for the sins of a thousand years. . . . For the Jews, too, the most abject and despised people in European society, the day of redemption and liberty was to dawn after their long slavery among the nations of Europe. . . . What Mendelssohn had thought possible at some distant time . . . was realized in France with almost magical rapidity."[18] Since he intends to present a fundamental reevaluation of Jewish history that will leave its mark on a generation of historians, Baron, from his American haven, rejects a French-style centralized state, established by the triumph of the absolute monarchy, which little by little reduced to nothing the cultural and social particularisms of the Middle Ages. In his view, "the medieval drives toward national unity, most clearly exemplified in the struggle of the French Crown with its feudal vassals, operated in the direction of ethnic exclusivity and national sovereignty. The former played an enormous role . . . in underscoring the 'alien' character of the Jewish minority and in the ultimate quest for its total elimination via expulsion, conversion, or extermination."[19]

Baron also targets the assimilationist perspectives exposed by Mendelssohn that the French Revolution would, though after many false starts, implement. This reversal of the doxa rests upon a reevaluation of 1789. It is formidable, for it leads inexorably toward a reexamination of emancipation conceived of as the inheritor of a French universalist Enlightenment. Many years later, Arthur Hertzberg, one of Baron's favorite doctoral students, pushed this logic to its extreme: he published a work radically opposed to the process set in motion by 1789, going so far as to see in the French Revolution the origin of all the totalitarianisms and misfortunes that Jews would face in modernity.[20] In the minds of Baron and some of his students, France represents the territorial and spiritual unification par excellence between the *Ancien Régime* and the revolution: agreeing with— though without citing—Alexis de Tocqueville, he elucidates the specific consequences this would have on Jewish destiny. And as for Tocqueville, there begins to appear an opposition between this assimilationist France and American pluralism, for which he will become, again like Tocqueville, the eulogist.

Baron thus seeks to "reevaluate" the benefits of 1789, anticipating, in the United States, a central thread in a political theory that is hostile to this major event, heavy with authoritarian excesses, accused still today of the wrongs that have undermined cultural pluralism. This charge against the French assimilationist model, moreover, is driven, at the same period, by Jewish American intellectuals such as Horace Kallen who rejected a French notion of citizenship and advocated a hyphenated identity based upon multiple identities that are not mutually exclusive. In the *Menorah Journal*, where Baron published his famous article, Kallen rejects the process of the melting pot, of a French-style assimilation proposed by Israel Zangwill, who also contributed to the *Menorah Journal*.[21] Kallen invented this notion of a hyphenated identity, a nomenclature that continues in the anglophone social sciences. He published in 1924, four years before "Ghetto and Emancipation," *Culture and Democracy in the United States*, a work in which he theorizes American cultural pluralism. In his view, the *oneness* of nation-states such as France is opposed to the *manyness* of American society, whose weak and decentralized state favors a connection to *localness*.

Contrary to Zangwill, Kallen considers, like Baron, that the United States is, at least in the way Lincoln meant it, "a government of the people, by the people, for the people." "The American people however are no longer one in the same sense in which the people of Germany or the people of France are one. . . . They are a mosaic of peoples, of different bloods and of different origins. . . . In essence, therefore, Democracy involves, not the elimination of differences, but the perfection and conservation of differences."[22] Did Kallen meet Baron, who subsequently rejected the concept of the melting pot?[23] Similar to Baron in his interests and career, he founded the Boston Menorah Society and became the vice president of the Jewish-American Congress. He taught—although at the other end of Manhattan—at the New School for Social Research, where Baron's friend Hannah Arendt joined him. This shows how similar Baron's and Kallen's interests and preoccupations were, how they accessed similar social circles, rejected the idea of the melting pot, and did not share Zangwill's harsh critique of the ghetto as he exposed it in his book *Children of the Ghetto*.[24] Did they both exchange ideas with Mordecai Kaplan, who, at the same time, joined their fight in favor of a community pluralism hostile to the state? In 1934 Kaplan publishes *Judaism as a Civilization*, an essential text for contemporary American Judaism, in which he considers that by perverting the true goal of national feeling, the state has often betrayed the individual, and salvation is only possible through community.[25] Yet this work, fundamental to the conceptualization of American Judaism, is published in New York soon after *Culture and Democracy in the United States*, and specifically between "Ghetto and Emancipation" (1928) and Baron's first three of many more volumes published in 1937, *A Social and Religious History of the Jews*. Following Dubnow, in whom Baron often finds inspiration, but also Ahad Ha'am, who maintains that the French Revolution turned the Jews into slaves by forcing them to renounce their culture at the price of assimilation into the nation, Kaplan, similarly to Kallen and Baron, wishes to provide a pluralist and local foundation for American Judaism.

This striking similarity among the three authors, who lived between the end of the 1880s and the 1980s, from Poland (Baron), Lithuania (Kaplan), and Silesia (Kallen), all geographically close regions, all three rabbis or sons of rabbis, seems to be largely unrecognized by commentators on Baron's work. He himself seems to be unaware of Kallen's work and mentions only in passing Mordecai Kaplan's many books—though they quickly became famous—even those that concern American Judaism, such as *Judaism as a Civilization*.[26] Today, in line with Kallen's ideas, to which he often acknowledges his debt, Michael Walzer defends ideas that are close to Baron's. Like him, he denounces Stanislas Marie Adélaïde, count of Clermont-Tonnerre's famous speech, the Jacobin regeneration that it presupposed as well as the radical state control that was essential to its implementation. In opposition to any form of tolerance, he considers that France, a nation-state if ever there was one, "intensifies pressure on minorities and immigrants: assimilate or leave!" following the example of other nation-states, in the name of its own "ethnic identity."[27] And, in continuation of Kallen's perspective but without referencing Baron, Walzer shows in *What It Means to Be an American* the extent to which Jews find a haven of peace on American soil: a joy of living, creating, and flourishing, far from the state.[28]

The parallels among these thinkers, who show great admiration for American Judaism, are plentiful. Mordecai Kaplan, like Kallen, Baron, and Walzer, means to reject the French-style state paradigm and to strengthen American Judaism according to its roots in community living by moving away from Orthodox practices, opening the Jewish world to the surrounding world and immersing it in global society, all the while reinforcing the role of the community as a bearer of its own culture. To this effect, Kaplan,[29] like Baron, wishes to extend Dubnow's heritage in the decentralized and pluralist context of American society, the latter recognizing explicitly that in this context "minorities are largely ignored by the state, but Jewish communities carry on their public functions."[30] Moreover, both look to the social sciences to understand the specificity of Jewish life in the American context, a discipline that, precisely during the interwar period, underscored the vital nature of community and of belonging to a group as a key factor of socialization. Kaplan followed Franklin Giddings's teachings at Columbia University, where Baron had been teaching since 1930. Giddings, the famous sociologist, much like his contemporary sociology colleagues Albion

Small and Charles Cooley, wanted to avoid the excesses of individualism as well as state control over forms of sociability anchored in community; in this spirit, for Kaplan as for Baron, the *kehillah* protects its members and ensures cultural continuity at the heart of America's pluralist society.[31] It is, in other words, a contemporary version of the ghetto.[32]

Returning to the Middle Ages, Baron furthermore offers in "Ghetto and Emancipation" an observation that promised to have a long-term influence even today. According to him, the peasants were, from the perspective of civil rights, serfs, the property of their master, while the "Jews were *servie camerae* (servants of the Treasury)." For him, they were serfs

in public law and as such belonged to the ruler as representative or embodiment of the State, and they were inherited by his successor in office through public law. . . . Now we ought not to forget that even today we are, in effect, serfs of the State in public law, notwithstanding all theories of personal rights, natural rights of citizens, and the sovereignty of the people. . . . This situation, expressed in medieval terminology, is a serf relationship applying to all citizens. The Jew then, insofar as he was *servus camerae*, was in substantially the same position all modern free citizens are in. . . . But in general it was a profitable theory, for the Emperor often did provide the protection for which Jewry paid.[33]

These "privileges" from which the Jews benefited during the Middle Ages no longer subsist alongside the modern state. With the "new citizenship" and the revolution that brings "the equality of rights," they abandon their autonomous structures and no longer form a "nation within a nation."[34] They thus find themselves forced to neglect their collective religious identity in order to assimilate completely into the national values of society.

According to Baron, with the advent of the French Revolution, which secularizes public spaces, Jews turn away from the beliefs that shape their own national identity, from the very idea that they are a people. They are encouraged to abandon the study of the Talmud, so rich in the diaspora, in favor of the Bible in order to live a "normal life." The proof of this in his view is the birth of a reformed liberal Judaism "eager to widen the breach with the past."[35] Reducing the contribution of emancipation—the access to all professions, the greater social mobility, the admission to public spaces and to citizenship, the right to vote, the possibility to apply for state jobs, the gains brought about by the implementation of secularism, so many key factors that drastically change Jewish destiny—Baron goes so far as to write that "it is clear that Emancipation has not brought the Golden Age."[36] And his final sentence reverberates like a clap of thunder: "It is time," he writes, "to break with the lachrymose theory of pre-Revolutionary woe, and to adopt a view more in accord with historic truth" that rehabilitates the Middle Ages.[37] For Baron, even during this period, Jewish history was not a result of anti-semitic threats or of the suffering they brought about: in his view, it is important to fight this emollient and passive vision that minimizes the Jews' own will to shape their destiny by establishing, as they did during the Middle Ages, trade relations with their non-Jewish neighbors or even with the authorities that allow them to survive and fully participate in the civilization of their time.[38] According to him,

> It would be a mistake, however, to believe that hatred was the constant keynote of Judeo-Christian relations, even in Germany or Italy. It is in the nature of historical records to transmit to posterity the memory of extraordinary events, rather than of the ordinary flow of life. A community which lived in peace for

decades may have given the medieval chronicler no motive to mention it, until a sudden outbreak of popular violence, lasting a few days, attracted widespread attention. Since modern historical treatment can no longer be satisfied with the enumeration of wars and diplomatic conflicts, the history of the Jewish people among the Gentiles, even in medieval Europe, must consist of much more than stories of sanguinary clashes of governmental expulsions. . . . Normal relations between Jews and Christians were generally amicable, or at worst characterized by mild mutual suspicion.[39]

This provocative reevaluation of the compared advantages of the Middle Ages and of emancipation, published by a young historian as yet unaffiliated with a major university, was for many reasons troubling to the thinkers of the time. The rehabilitation of the Middle Ages was shocking to the upholders of a Jewish history who, following Heinrich Graetz, saw in the French Revolution the advent of a beneficial modernity, a liberation from the chains of servitude, a golden age of their history, the end of their Jewish suffering. Yet following Salo Baron's disconcerting logic, Jewish happiness may be more certain in the shade of the protective ghetto than during the Enlightenment: emancipation is a lure bringing only misfortune, exacerbated violence, deaths due to the numerous wars among states, a demographic regression, an assimilation that abolishes the very idea of a Jewish people, and a secularism that empties Judaism of all of its creative richness. The accusation is heavy, devastating, shattering any hope of a shared universalism, a fraternal harmony founded on reason.

Innumerable quarrels and debates resulting from Baron's position, often understood reductively, have continued up until today. Indeed, in 1937, Yitzhak Baer published in the Israeli journal *Zion* a long critical review in which he underscored that if *"galut* (exile) is not so terrible . . . the fact remains that Jewish history in the Middle Ages *was* an unending series of persecutions."[40] Many are those who, even today, accuse Baron of minimizing the acts of violence between the Middle Ages and the eighteenth century, the dramatic circumstances surrounding the evictions that occurred in waves throughout Europe from Spain to Poland, the forced conversions, the massacres that targeted Jewish communities, and the resulting traumas for the survivors: tragic events that challenge his view of a peaceful coexistence between Jews and Christians. Others, more numerous even, wishing to refute his analysis, paint the modern period essentially in terms of adaptation, happiness, and a peaceful life free of tears. In reality, Baron, on the one hand, defends the idea of a Middle Ages less dark than they have been described, though he knows many instances of violence, and, on the other hand, he presents the emancipatory period as equally punctuated by acts of violence whose intensity is often infinitely greater. For him, Jews in modernity have faced a series of misfortunes— pogroms, crises, constraining assimilationist processes, leading up to the utter tragedy that was the Shoah—all of which are testimonies to the fact that it is out of the question to paint this period with cheerful colors. From then on, "he did not call for complete exclusion of references to the sufferings of Jews in all periods or for relegating the moments of crisis in the Jewish past, especially after the revolution, to the background."[41] In this way, when one argues that "the dichotomy that Baron drew between normalcy and persecution, which allowed him to downplay the signification of violence and antisemitism as factors in the historical process, was too sharp," and that "in almost every time and place, Jewish societies found themselves dealing with difficult and troublesome issues of persecutions and its after-effects. These shaped their view both of their history and place in the world, and of their status in non-Jewish society and relations with their neighbors,"[42] which contributes in a way to the logic of Baron's own analyses, not so much refuting as confirming them. As a result, it is difficult to grasp the true impact of his criticism of the lachrymose conception of history that claimed, at first in "Ghetto and Emancipation," to clearly separate the two periods in history.

There remains the question of the state and the royal alliance that supposedly protected the Jews in the Middle Ages by preserving their security, a guarantee of their happiness.[43] Baron studied with passion the *Shevet Yehuda*, Salomon Ibn Verga's work that exposes this logic. Baron held on to the model Ibn Verga developed of a vertical alliance between the king and the Jews intended to protect them from the populace, from neighbors, and from mass antisemitic mobilizations. He subscribed to this vision of the royal alliance, all the more since it seems to confirm the privileged status of the Jews during the Middle Ages, a unique status that they lost after the French Revolution since all citizens finally gained access to this same alliance with the state. Baron remains loyal to this alliance, which provides a powerful argument for his reevaluation of the Middle Ages. He prefers not to take notice of the indifference of kings who for centuries abandoned the Jews to their tragic destiny during mass antisemitic eruptions, though Ibn Verga underscored these behaviors himself by deploring that "the good king" Manuel let excited crowds behave with impunity.[44]

Baron wishes to maintain, in spite of everything, this favorable view of the Middle Ages, which contrasts with, according to him, the political future of Jews after their emancipation. In 1937, he observes that the government has always attempted to protect the lives of Jews. Unlike czarist Russia, there was no medieval government that ever provoked pogroms.[45] For him, everything is in favor of the Middle Ages. On the one hand, the Russian Empire whence he came continuously gave free rein to the pogrom perpetrators. On the other hand, the modernity of postrevolutionary societies has annihilated the previously privileged status of the Jews, who then lost the protection of the royal alliance, as the state now only recognizes the equal rights of all citizens. In Baron's view, a radical change occurred rendering the royal alliance null and void. Henceforth, all citizens find themselves *servi camerae*, servants of the treasury, tied to the state, and equally protected by it. He thus confirms in 1937 his intuition in "Ghetto and Emancipation" when he remarks already that "even today we are, in effect, serfs of the State in public law, notwithstanding all theories of personal rights, natural rights of citizens, and the sovereignty of the people. . . . This situation, expressed in medieval terminology, is a serf relationship applying to all citizens. The Jew then, insofar as he was *servus camerae*, was in substantially the same position all modern free citizens are in."[46] The Jews thus lost their specific royal alliance with the advent of a universalist state that no longer pays particular attention to them, while their access to citizenship, their entrance into public spaces, their fusion within the nation-state undermines their cultural and juridical autonomy, eliminates the protective barriers of the ghetto, and leads to their integration within the nation, symbolized by conscription. What will happen when the Jews have disagreements with their fellow citizens? How will the state settle them, given that the state is now tasked with protecting all citizens equally? Can we from now on claim that the royal alliance forged in the Middle Ages, assuring their relative happiness, faded away after emancipation?

In 1960, Baron continues to denounce the "dark" description of the Middle Ages as opposed to the more "luminous" presentation of the emancipatory period inaugurated by the French Revolution.[47] He forcefully underscores that during the Middle Ages the Jews were the only ones to benefit from royal privileges, which disappeared once the "modern state," also the "democratic state," reduced all forms of corporatism and imposed, from Holland to the United States, and despite some restrictions, equality among citizens.[48] Baron shows that this new equality is not a beneficial generosity granted to the Jews by altruistic rulers but an exchange between a former status considered obsolete and a new status from which the state can profit. For Baron, "old Jewish tradition reinforced this conception" by focusing too much on ancient "suffering," compared to an emancipation seen solely in a "messianic" light. From then on, Baron repeatedly accuses Graetz of having thought of the Middle Ages as a "lachrymose conception of Jewish history."[49] More than thirty years after his famous article "Ghetto and Emancipation," he tirelessly uses the same arguments to belie this view of the past, noting that "the picture of the medieval and early modern Jew living in constant dread of attack, and obsessed with fear for his life and possessions, has been decidedly exaggerated."[50]

Baron wants to remain confident, and he condemns, in 1942, the "hysterical" reaction of American Jews in response to Hitler's discourse, underestimating the magnitude of the Nazi threat by predicting its decline. As Robert Liberles notes, an optimist above all, "he maintained his fallacious predictions concerning the Nazis for many more years. . . . He opposed the mentality of persecution with such ardor, he failed to detect the real and imminent threats of the time" during the Second World War.[51] In this way, despite the nuances he brought to his analyses over the years, despite the unimaginable catastrophe of the Shoah that reinforces this history of tears, he remained loyal to his general thesis, hostile to a lachrymose vision.[52] Less than twenty years after the end of the Shoah, which of course took place during modernity, Baron implores the Jews not to succumb even further to desperation but to build, create, and dedicate themselves to their community rather than despair over the future. However, paradoxically, in 1961 on the occasion of his testimony during the Eichmann trial, in order to better help understand the exceptional nature of the Shoah, he states that, previously, "only a minute part of the Jewish people suffered destruction. Generally speaking this is true of all the disasters and all the suffering the Jewish people endured throughout the generations."[53] In this dramatic context, it is as though he repudiated his own theory by recognizing the suffering of some of the Jews since the beginning of time, including, consequently, before the period of emancipation.

The example of Nazism is alone proof of the possibility of a sudden disappearance of the royal alliance at the heart of a democratic society in which some citizens violently target their Jewish fellow citizens. During his testimony at the Eichmann trial, Baron evokes the Kristallnacht (Night of Broken Glass) in 1938 and declares that "the government itself, instead of protecting the synagogues, caused their destruction. This was an unusual step, since there had been nothing like it throughout the history of the darkest Middle Ages and throughout modern times."[54] Nazism thus differed radically from the Middle Ages:

> there were violent disturbances in the Middle Ages, many disturbances, and Jewish blood was shed, and this was very frequent. But on no occasion was it possible to bring evidence to the effect that some government or other, whether of a king, emperor, or cardinal, or one of the elders of the city, a member of the ruling authority organized the disturbances, these pogroms. The "Crystal Night" was perhaps the first time, apart from precedents in

Czarist Russia, where the government itself organized the disturbances against the Jews. And again, this was not a return to the Middle Ages, but a complete innovation.[55]

Indeed, a modern state can, in one moment, abandon some of its citizens and, worse even, take it upon itself to organize the pogroms that have punctuated the modern era. The royal alliance, fragile but frequent during the Middle Ages, collapsed immediately. The state, now metamorphosized into a Nazi power, was the one to initiate the hounding of Jews who had placed all of their trust in it.

It is the entire vision, hostile to the lachrymose theory of history, that the Shoah seems to belie. Baron is conscious of this after the Eichmann trial and writes in 1963:

> All my life I have been struggling against the hitherto dominant "lachrymose conception of Jewish history"—a term which I have been using for more than forty years—because I have felt that, by exclusively overemphasizing Jewish sufferings, it distorted the total picture of the Jewish historic evolution and, at the same time, it served badly a generation which had become impatient with the "nightmare" of endless persecutions and massacres.
>
> However, just as we must not misunderstand the true realities of life and psychology among the still predominant orthodox and traditionalist east-European [*sic*] masses during the nazi [*sic*] era, so we must not overlook the inherent tragedies of Jewish life during the two millennia of the dispersion.[56]

Abruptly, the evolutionary model built upon the famous 1928 article seems to collapse. Faced with this sudden awareness of the magnitude of the Shoah, mockeries of the lachrymose theory fade away, and any previously denied suffering is now unavoidable. Not only is the royal alliance revealed to be a myth, but the massacres that the Nazi authorities implemented are henceforth inserted into the continuity of the tragedies inherent to Jewish life in exile . . . for two millennia, in other words, during a long period that includes the Middle Ages previously celebrated! Although in work after work Baron praises the merits of Jewish life in diaspora, in this article he not only casts a more than critical eye on exile but also abandons any dichotomizing analysis of Jewish history, since the Middle Ages is included in the long period of suffering whose reality he previously denied.[57]

Is it to extricate himself from these contradictions that Baron turns henceforth toward a comparative analysis of the emancipation of the Jews, in order to shed light on the merits of the American example compared not only to Eastern Europe but also to some countries of Western Europe such as France, going so far as to oppose Great Britain to the United States? For Baron, the contrast between the new continent and old Europe proves considerable. In his view, modern nationalism, initiated by the French Revolution, led to a rapid unification of society that eliminated Jewish particularism, according to the count of Clermont-Tonnerre's logic in his famous speech. Opposed to the Jews constituting their own nation, he added that, should they refuse, "Let them be banished!" This formula aroused the ire of many American thinkers, from Baron to Walzer and others: on its own it proves, for Baron, that "the traditional medieval solution of the Jewish question through conversion or expulsion was here modified only by the secular alternative of national assimilation or banishment."[58] Ceaselessly, the French Revolution is accused of all evils, as "the modern egalitarian State could no longer tolerate the existence of a self-governing corporate body."[59] One year after Eichmann's trial and his becoming conscious of the immensity of the tears caused by Nazism, Baron still blames the French Revolution, but also the rationalist Bolshevik Revolution that, paradoxically in the wake of the czarist regime of the nineteenth century, in turn persecuted the Jews: for him, Jews did not "foresee that, even under the totally changed social structure, the anti-Semitic feelings of the Russians could assert themselves."[60] In this way, as David Engel justly emphasizes, Baron "viewed modern European Jewish history, unlike the history of European Jewry in the Middle Ages, as a story of continuous upheaval engendered by ubiquitous deep ruptures in the fabric of Jewish society, culture, and relations with others. . . . Such a perspective permitted him to produce works on the modern period that were hardly free of lachrymosity as he defined it."[61]

Henceforth, Baron implicitly renounces his arguments in "Ghetto and Emancipation" by recognizing that the Middle Ages, and even more so the emancipation of modern times, appear to be tragic periods where tears flowed abundantly as well. He then resolves to magnify the American solution that knew neither the Middle Ages, previously thought to be peaceful, nor European modern times continuously darkened by tears. The United States, the *goldene medine*, this golden land, this dream society where abundance reigns,[62] this promised land is adorned with all the virtues. Here, the Jews are not subjected to expulsions, the Crusades of the Middle Ages, or the persecutions, pogroms, and worse yet, the Shoah that besmirched modernity in the old continent. Baron underlines that, starting with the eighteenth century—as the Jew Bill was rejected in Great Britain—in the American colony, despite some restrictions, Jews have had free access to their rights. They benefit from the right to vote and can join patriotic militias.[63] Thus, for the first time in presenting his refutation of a lachrymose theory of history, Baron references the American example to emphasize the freedom that Jews enjoy here and a happiness that can respect their traditions. The United States represents a continent devoid of internal unifying nationalism, a society that respects pluralism, a haven of peace where the lachrymose theory of history is even less applicable than in the Middle Ages.

A noteworthy modification nevertheless took place in Baron's reasoning: neglecting the negative aspects of American society, the individualism that is destructive to forms of collective sociability, the cult of money, the social inequalities it leads to, or even the racist traditions that haunt its history, Baron became a eulogist of American democracy, which, according to him and previous to emancipation, is as free from any lachrymose theory of history as was the royal alliance. "In love with America," Baron sees himself as part of America's destiny. He sheds light on its radical newness, which favors the fulfillment of Jewish life, now autonomous from the state, whereas previously the community "served it."[64] The Jews are fully at home there; pogroms are unknown; the royal alliance seems almost anachronistic because nothing threatens them. The American model can thus not be understood through the lachrymose theory of history: for him, "American Jewish history, unable to produce a succession of riots and discriminatory laws, could hardly fit into this traditional pattern."[65]

This time, we witness a true reversal of Baron's theory: if Baron limits the application of his lachrymose theory to the Middle Ages to contest its reality, if he comes to show that "tears" truly flow during the time of emancipation, this time the American turning point leads him to exclude the United States from the field of application of the lachrymose theory. He does so even if, on one occasion, in the course of an article written in 1956 following the end of an aggressive McCarthyism not without antisemitic dimensions, he recognizes that once in a while American society experiences antisemitic eruptions. He adds (radically turning his back on his optimism): "nor must one completely discount the danger that, if an avowedly antisemitic party were to seize the reins of government over the United States or even over one of the individual states, the existing laws might not be able to prevent discrimination against Jewish citizens in certain practical areas,"[66] as happened during the overthrow of the Weimar Republic, though it was also protected by its constitution.

If political modernity generated, according to Baron, severe consequences affecting Jewish destiny, between assimilation, exacerbated antisemitism, and "tears" more abundant than those shed by Jews during the Middle Ages, for him, American-style emancipation differs from both the ghetto and the period of European emancipation: in this nation of "pioneers" that is the United States, the Jews, within their communities, are at home. The theory of a vertical alliance undergoes a radical transformation given that the American model implicitly puts an end to it. Valid in part for the monarchies preceding emancipation and no longer relevant to the relationship with the Jews at the heart of their national state societies before the revolution, inasmuch as the relationship now applies to all citizens, it loses all function in the context of a society that was constructed from the bottom up, that did not birth a strong and centralized state taking charge of the destiny of its citizens. It is now Baron's turn to recognize the exceptionalism of American society that had so struck Alexis de Tocqueville.

On this point, he is in agreement with Hannah Arendt, who, from 1943 on, celebrated the United States as a country whose federal structure offers a more sustainable solution to the Jewish question.[67] Abandoning Europe and its nation-states focused on nationalist and cultural unification, fleeing Nazi terror and the persecution of the Jews, Arendt also took refuge in New York.

Familiar with Tocqueville's work, which often inspired her, she praised the American Revolution founded on the spirit of free-dom, the rejection of political domination, a constitution that limits the concentration of power influenced by Montesquieu, and "Madison's discovery of the federal principle for the foun-dation of large republics" that favors political participation and the actions of citizens and ensures public happiness.[68] Similarly to Baron's American passion, she welcomes the fact that the "constituted bodies" through which Americans "were organized in self-governing bodies" preserve "their own authority intact" when "held together solely by the strength of mutual promises."[69] In her eyes, "America [was led] away from the European nation-state. . . . By the same token . . . America was spared the cheap-est and the most dangerous disguise the absolute ever assumed in the political realm, the disguise of the nation."[70] America thus avoids, according to Arendt, artificial unification, homogeniza-tion, and makes way for pluralism. Again, not unlike Salo Baron, she accentuates the contrast between an authoritarian French Revolution and an American Revolution on which she in turn projects a "rosy" picture that minimizes violence, conflicts, and racial injustices.[71] She knows that America is familiar with "the biblical story of the exodus of Israeli tribes,"[72] and that, unlike Europe, it is characterized by a certain protective feeling of philosemitism.

Following a number of Jewish thinkers who sought refuge in the United States, Arendt, like her colleagues who fled the old con-tinent, found the same haven of peace that Baron found at Columbia at the New School for Social Research, an identical happiness in this exile, immune from totalitarian atrocities but also from the unifying or nationalist tendencies that came out of the French Revolution. Her first article, solicited by Salo

Baron and published in the journal he created, was about the Dreyfus affair, considered to be the first instance of nationalist intolerance, which never could have occurred in the United States.[73] Her encounter with Baron and their subsequent friendship (temporarily strained only much later by her comments on the supposed passivity of the Jewish people as well as on the role played by the Jewish councils leading up to the concentration camps during Eichmann's trial) are essential to understanding her own evolution,[74] her revelation of the "cosmopolitanism" that she sought and thought she found in the United States. She also agreed with Baron as far as denouncing the lachrymose conception of Jewish history and refused to view the latter as passive. For her, the Jews are endowed with will, they are active beings, political actors, not simple victims subjugated to persecutions. Like Baron, she rose up against the statement that "in sharp contrast to other nations, the Jews were not history makers but history sufferers, preserving a kind of eternal identity of goodness disturbed only by the monotonous chronicle of pogroms and persecutions."[75] In this sense, the theoretician of the *vita activa* finds in Baron enough to justify her preoccupation: push the Jews to act, yesterday as an autonomous Jewish army fighting against Nazism, today as a minority making their voice heard at the heart of the American democratic and pluralist public space.[76]

We can understand that, appointed to the Department of History at Columbia University as the first chair of Jewish history ever created, Baron finds himself in an awkward position. Wanting to attract students who might choose the exceptional nature of American Judaism as a thesis topic, he remembers that he "found it very difficult twenty, fifteen or even ten years ago to persuade graduate students to choose dissertations in this field because they did not find it 'interesting' enough."[77] He thus confirms the judgment of Oscar Handlin, who deplored the "low status" of "those who devote their work to the study of Jews in America."[78] Baron concentrates his efforts on creating a school of historians who, within the university, could take charge of the history of American Judaism so unjustly denigrated. In 1953, he becomes president of the American Jewish Historical Society, dedicated to archival research on American Jews, and he succeeds by the 1960s in launching the careers of many specialists, hired in turn at prestigious universities. Through this rediscovered history of American Jews, it is more their culture than their religion, more their social forms than simply the study of the great texts from the period of the ghetto, that sheds light on their exceptional destiny in the new continent. In Baron's view, "the underlying assumption was that, in order to be meaningful, American Jewish life would have to be based upon a knowledge of Hebrew and Yiddish letters more or less equal to that of our ancestors. . . . Roughly speaking, we have equated Jewish culture almost exclusively with that developed in the ghetto era of Jewish history. . . . American Jewry, I am certain, will also give unprecedented, pioneering answers to its present challenge of creating a novel American Jewish culture" that will flourish in the general context of "cultural pluralism," turning its back on the atheist rationalism of the French Revolution.[79] We can thus put forward that "Baron increasingly saw American Jewish history as an ideal research site for his theories on the mutual influence of social and religious trends in Jewish history."[80]

Henceforth, returning to his great 1928 text, Baron reconsiders his adulatory conception of the period of the ghetto, which alone escaped a lachrymose vision of history. Doing a complete about-face, he now sings the praises of American exceptionalism and its modernity, though this is also a product of the emancipatory Enlightenment. For him, "the entire Jewish historiography of the Middle Ages and early modern times consisted of chronicles recording dramatic events, mostly persecutions, massacres or expulsions" while "American Jewish history . . . could hardly fit into this traditional pattern."[81] True, he estimates in passing that even in the United States, in the 1930s, "antisemitism became a serious public issue with threatening implications for Jewish survival."[82] True also, in 1942, he observes that in the United States "we have witnessed in recent years disturbing manifestations of a new spirit of intolerance and discrimination,"[83] but they nevertheless do not challenge the joy of living in American society and could never be compared to the antisemitic violence then spreading throughout Europe. In this way, like the Middle Ages, the United States appears to represent a moment of economic well-being, of enrichment, of demographic growth, many factors that, as previously, command Baron's attention.

The "ghetto" transposed from the Middle Ages to the United States finds an identical resilience in this context: the sociologist Louis Wirth in fact writes his famous book, *The Ghetto*,[84] after having attentively read Baron's works. He also publishes reviews of Baron's work in *Historia Judaica* and considers that his book, *The Jewish Community*, so close to his own interests, confirms the "very high level of Jewish studies in the United States."[85] In the meeting between Baron and Wirth, we witness a connection between Jewish history and sociology to which Baron seems particularly attached. For one as for the other, the American-style ghetto as a form of community ensures the transition between unique forms of sociability and assimilation.

Henceforth, counter to both the period of the ghetto and the modern period of emancipation so favorable to the most dreadful massacres, American exceptionalism is alone evidence of the limited dimension of suffering and of persecution in the history of the Jewish world: it justifies the legitimacy of the diaspora and attributes to exile a definitive foundational role, an appreciation shared also by Simon Dubnow and Israel Zangwill.[86] With this in mind, Baron rejects the analyses of the great historians from the Jerusalem school, such as Yitzhak Baer, resolutely hostile to the galut, to an exile that is necessarily in their view a "political enslavement."[87] For Baron, these historians attribute disproportionate importance to antisemitism and suffering to justify the return to Zion. In his mind, the American exception from this point forward belies the inevitable and timeless nature of those "tears" that abusively shape the Zionist project. Following Dubnow, Baron is recognized as a thinker of the diaspora, of a diaspora that eschews the iron rule of the state, of any centralized state that undercuts the cultural pluralism crucial to the survival of Jewish culture. He takes as his own Dubnow's proposed perspective of a "nationalism without a nation-state" by minimizing its radically nationalist aspect and considering the American world the best possible realization of a transnational and transterritorial Jewish world that allows for an autonomous life though integrally immersed in American society, participating fully in its future—perhaps more than Dubnow would have wished, as he remained a supporter of a kind of cultural autonomy that Baron rejected.[88] Despite profound differences with Dubnow's diasporic model, Baron adopts, in the United States, a conception of community as the locus of Jewish life beyond the state.

As a result, while he shows himself attentive to the creation of Israel, remains profoundly attached to its existence, and does not hide his sympathy, he remains nevertheless opposed to any nationalist project that confers upon the state a stranglehold over the culture and its citizens.[89] In his view, if Israel is vital, the United States embodies the new center of a diaspora where Jewish existence can happen peacefully in all its richness. In this way, his childhood within the empire, his familiarity with the extreme pluralism of its structures, cultures, and languages, and its attachment to supranational juridical forms, steer Baron away from any form, even national, of state servitude. For him, "America was like the old Habsburg monarchy. It had many ethnic groups who possessed an American political identity and espoused American patriotism but who still retained a strong ethnic consciousness."[90] Salo Baron thus espouses the American dream that belies both the lachrymose vision of history in exile and the Zionist logic for the construction of a Jewish state or even a state for the Jews. He now turns his back on his article "Ghetto and Emancipation," in which he had welcomed the status of Jews as public servants, tied to the state and in a certain way better protected by it than the serfs depending on the good will of their local protectors. The American model with a "weak" state challenges the theory of the royal alliance that Baron was the first to describe in the modern era: like a vast empire, non-authoritative and pluralist, this new center for Jewish history further stresses horizontal alliances as a source of protection, the invention of reciprocal ties with other social groups, immersion in the cultural universe of neighbors from whom we do not dread violence erupting, as in old Europe. The absence of vertical alliances that accompanies a strong state does not endanger the Jews, who do not fear horizontal antisemitic mobilizations.

In an irenic vision of American society that pushes him to renounce his earlier fears, Baron becomes the propagator of an optimistic vision of a new center unconstrained by the state. Nor does he fear, as he did before, the logic of a devastating democratic individualism capable of wiping out cultural attachments and solidarities favorable to the preservation of a unique history that fully acknowledges the importance of community belonging. The presence of the "modern state," whether protective or menacing, fades away and frees creative energies that favor the blossoming of collective forms at the heart of a pluralist democracy able to contain the kind of rampant individualism that threatens community belonging. For Baron, Jews' long history can only take place in its own "emancipation vis-à-vis the state and of territory,"[91] in its distance from the state and its nationalist aims. The royal state of the Middle Ages is no longer represented, as it was in 1928, as protective of the Jews, who were endowed with a unique status according to public law. At the dawn of modernity and emancipation, of a state that relentlessly nationalizes and unifies its nation, Jews can survive and blossom much better if they escape its grip. This shows the extent to which his encounter with the United States with its weak state led Baron to profoundly modify his views on the protective (or on the contrary, alienating) function of the state. As Ismar Schorsch emphasizes, Baron "toned down the redemptive rhetoric on emancipation" and in so doing became an "avowed critic of the modern nation-state."[92]

Far from "Ghetto and Emancipation" and from his negative vision of emancipation, the many works of Baron after the Second World War and the Shoah are proof of his clear engagement in favor of the new American center that picks up, in Jewish history, where Spain, Italy, Holland, and Germany left off.[93] Baron henceforth uses an "apologetic tone," rejects any "critical perspective," and becomes a "spokesperson" and "guardian" of American-style democratic emancipation.[94] The dream of the Bund, of a renaissance of a culture and a microsociety in diaspora, did not materialize at the heart of the Russian Empire but in the context of American society. Dubnow's lost battles of a Jewish Eastern European world that rejected both emancipatory assimilation and nationalist Zionism finally crystallized far from the Russian Empire. Renouncing his previously positive view of the period of the ghetto, during which the state protected the

Jews and imposed their inclusion in flourishing communities, Baron, in a "dramatic turn," becomes an advocate for American liberalism, for voluntary and noncompulsory membership in local community, for spontaneous affiliation, a source of unlimited cultural wealth.[95] He is convinced that, far from the protective royal alliance, "whatever shortcomings we may find in the modern democratic state, it . . . leaves the decision to the Jews themselves."[96] Even if he is conscious of the low rates of true voluntary membership in Jewish American community structures, despite recurrent doubts, he now holds the model close to Alexis de Tocqueville's heart as the way to salvation for the Jewish diasporic world. One has to accept that "roughly speaking, we have equated Jewish culture almost exclusively with that developed in the ghetto. But it represents a way of life of the past and not of the future."[97] From now on, long live a community in its American multicultural form, which peacefully coexists with other collective forms of social solidarity of the most diverse sort. That "cultural pluralism is and has been greatly enriching American culture," a "factor working for mutual toleration within the Jewish group as well,"[98] and protects from an authoritarian orthodoxy. There is thus no reason to "despair,"[99] since for the first time, in this new center, "the Jews are no longer a minority like in Egypt, Babylon, Spain, Germany or Poland, but are part of the majority itself."[100]

This "rosy" presentation of American society coincides in many respects with that of his friend and rival Cecil Roth,[101] published four years after "Ghetto and Emancipation" in the same *Menorah Journal* and titled "The Most Persecuted People?" Both comfortably settled in Anglo-Saxon universities, one at Columbia and the other at Oxford, do they share a tendency to avoid darkening Jewish history by becoming the heroes of the liberal and pluralist Anglo-Saxon world?[102] Can this pacified view stand up to the reality of British history, which has hardly been always "rosy" for the Jews?[103] Is this view confirmed by the history of today's United States as a new center for a Jewish diaspora definitively immunized against secular persecutions, benign during the Middle Ages and violent with the advent of emancipation? The most devastating reply came from Jerusalem. Let us not forget that Yitzhak Baer, in 1938, published a biting critique of "Ghetto and Emancipation" rejecting the optimistic vision of the diaspora formulated by Baron. For him, from the Middle Ages to modernity, Jewish history is really and truly the history of suffering. That is because two years previously, in 1936, Baer had just published a little book in German—which could not be more different from the perspective of Baron's 1928 article and, up front, is radically opposed to the spirit of Baron's three-volume *Jews and Judaism: A Study in Social and Religious History*, published the following year, 1937—as a continuation of his article in the *Menorah Journal*. One cannot imagine a worse refutation of Baron's optimism than this little book, *Galut*, full of vitriol, by the eminent Jerusalem professor. According to Baer, "for the Jews of the Middle Ages, any feeling of having a home had disappeared in exile." His representation of this era so dear to Baron is resolutely negative. More generally, as Baer hammers it home, "all modern interpretations of exile lack any understanding of the extraordinary tragedy that it was."[104] For him, "exile is and continues to be what it never stopped being: a political enslavement that must be completely abolished."[105] It is the very idea of galut that is challenged, as much in old Europe as in the United States, meaning, in exile: according to this view, diaspora, life outside of Israel, is harshly condemned. We can discern in this affirmation a response to Baron's 1928 article that foreshadows his ruthless critique in 1938. From antiquity to the Middle Ages, from the splendor spanning Spain to Germany in the 1930s, for Baer, "the suffering of the diaspora" is such that "the Jews became a persecuted group everywhere in the world."[106] The Middle Ages, a period of prosperity for Judaism according to Baron, is perceived by Baer as a long procession of "massacres," "expulsions," and "martyrdoms" that herald the violent acts of the Nazi period.

This short work published in 1936 acts as a warning: as though predicting the coming of the Shoah during the victorious years of Nazism, Baer implores the Jews to abandon their illusions of the mere possibility of a happy and peaceful life in diaspora. Baron's name is never mentioned; it nevertheless seems to exist between the lines, in the background, before emerging explicitly two years later in his radical accusation published by the journal *Zion*. Baer denounces diasporic life as a deadly attack on the life of the Jewish people. For him, "the Jewish question in Spain in the fifteenth century teaches the modern observer the horribly inevitable nature of the historical conflicts that, manifestly, can only be reproduced under eternally new forms." Alerting German Jews while Baron still shows himself optimistic, he writes, evoking the Inquisition, "this process happens with the tacit or explicit approval of a cultured Europe, accompanied at the most by some occasional and ambiguous shows of compassion."[107] A word to the wise!

Baron, "theoretically, at least, was a diaspora-oriented historian. . . . In an age of intensified anti-galut trends, he became one of the authoritative spokesmen of a pro-galut philosophy . . . and he also declared galut a permanent feature of Jewish existence and destiny."[108] On the opposite side, Baer is persuaded that "everything that we have accomplished in foreign lands was a treason of our own spirit,"[109] thus condemning in advance any and all diasporas, including that of American

Jews who, just like their predecessors, consider themselves "home" in America. Salvation demands the end of exile, the saving return to Zion. One cannot imagine a more radical opposition than between Baron the diasporist and Baer the Zionist who sets off warning bells for the threatened German Jews, as for the Spanish Jews before them—while Baron continues to show confidence in the resilience of all diasporas, convinced that even the German Jews, particularly exposed by the rise of Nazism, will find the means to preserve their lives as well as their spiritual wealth. In response to *Galut*, likely reacting indirectly to Baer's vehement critique,[110] Baron publishes in 1942, during the worst of the Shoah that radically belies any optimistic Baronian diaspora, his three volumes of hymns to the community, sung as though a protective and creative force for all times that—despite all of the suffering endured in diaspora—justifies happiness in American exile. Baron is far from having lost this ferocious battle against Baer. Many rise up, with him, against this irreparably negative view of exile, of life in the diaspora, and especially at the heart of American society that has become, with Israel, the center of Jewish life. For Michael Walzer, for example, "the establishment of a genuine liberal and pluralist society in the United States and of a Jewish state in the land of Israel mark the end of exile. But they only make possible, they cannot guarantee, our release from the politics of exile."[111] For Walzer, the negative view of exile according to Baer is nearing its end when the place of exile itself is metamorphosed into a legitimate "home" that feels good to inhabit.

In 2000, Yosef Hayim Yerushalmi, Baron's most brilliant student, is chair of Jewish studies at Columbia University. He writes a long preface to the French translation of Baer's vehemently critical work, whose attitude toward Baron's implicit ideas is hardly charitable. A staunch New Yorker whose entire existence has been in diaspora, he reveres his master Baron. While he confesses his admiration for Baer's incontestable erudition (Baer authored a masterful study of Jews in Spain), it is to Baron's posterity that he remains faithful. Yerushalmi does not hide his irritation.[112] Author of the fabulous *From Spanish Court to Italian Ghetto*,[113] he does not understand the depreciation of the Middle Ages in Baer, who knows more than anyone else the splendor of the Spanish Jews at this time, on which he is the most renowned specialist. On several occasions, Yerushalmi considers his rejection of exile "excessive," which leads to a "feeling of unease" due to the "absence of balance in the proposition,"[114] all the more given that "the majority of Jews still live outside" Israel. He nevertheless concludes his text with this strange question: "'The questions raised by Baer have not lost their relevance—'galut' or 'diaspora?' What are the relationships between diaspora and center?"[115] This final question picks up Baron's interrogation but reverses it, since for Baron the United States has become the new center, whereas for Baer only Israel can act as a center given the illusions of diaspora and its misfortunes.

These questions are at the very least surprising coming from Yerushalmi, whose work, unlike Baron's, remains practically silent concerning the modern era. Yerushalmi in particular, unlike his mentor, has deliberately ignored the unique history of American Jews, considering it unfruitful. On this point he moves away from Baron, all the more because he does not participate in community Jewish life or in its philanthropic organizations, considered vital by Baron, and thus voluntarily neglects this society that he does not find particularly favorable to the study and enactment of sacred texts. Baron bitterly criticizes him for it. As Yerushalmi browbeats a student working on an

American Jewish thinker by exclaiming: "Why do you work on the history of American Judaism? Is the history of American Judaism so crucial in the eyes of Europe, Asia, or even Africa?" Baron replies: "You are talking about the biggest Jewish community in the world."[116]

We are left with a mystery that we only wish to mention. Yerushalmi, just like Baron and Baer before him, studied the logic of the *Shevet Yehuda*, Salomon Ibn Verga's major work. Baron found in it a confirmation of his description of the Jews as *servie camerae*, servants of the treasury, of the state, protected in a way by this unique tie to the royal state, which never initiated pogroms. For him, the state, having become almost absent, loses its protective function in an American society that is based on a pluralist and liberal democracy where Jews constitute one community among others, a community whose survival no longer depends on the state, but indeed on its insertion into this "nation of nations." From then on, for Baron, the royal alliance whose merits are overly praised by Ibn Verga becomes obsolete with the emergence of a type of horizontal alliance unique to American society. The Jews abandon their status as servie camerae and take advantage of the happiness of American society. The Spanish model loses its function in a society that, unshaped by the state, ignores any unifying nationalism and gives way to peaceful relationships among neighbors.

Baron's student Yerushalmi remains silent on this point. He has spent his life drawing all possible conclusions from Ibn Verga's work, closely following the meanderings of his thought, and has so hesitated to see in the royal alliance a simple myth empty of any reality that he hardly commits to this point. Far from the sociological and comparative approach used by Baron, he sticks to a meticulous study of the great texts that punctuate Jewish history and only addresses the modern period through brief allusions, without undertaking a comparative analysis of the implementation of a kind of royal alliance in today's societies. He refrains from any empirical analysis of the sort Baron introduced through his use of a traditional history of the Jews between old Europe and the United States. He wonders: does the royal alliance retain its logic and preeminence in the context of a weak state, of the pluralist and liberal society with diverse communities in the United States, a quasi-empire similar to the former Austro-Hungarian Empire, so profoundly decentralized? Are the Jews better protected from antisemitism even if they cannot entirely count on the benevolence of a weak state? Is their happiness better ensured here, as long as they prefer their local alcove to an active presence at the top of the state?[117]

The analogy, or parallel, between the Spanish model or even the French model and the unique case of American society, sheds light on diverging paths that Jews follow in opposite governmental contexts. Loyal to Baron's thesis, Yerushalmi validates in his way the complex vision of Jewish history put forth in 1928 in "Ghetto and Emancipation." In his tremendous and definitive *From Spanish Court to Italian Ghetto*, written under Baron's mentorship and for which the latter curiously wrote a preface without much enthusiasm,[118] Yerushalmi follows step by step the exceptional life of Isaac Cardoso, who hoisted himself, as a *converso*, to the top of the Spanish state by imposing himself as an official doctor, enjoying all the attributes of power. A high-ranking official benefiting from his public status, Cardoso singlehandedly embodied these "Servants of Kings and not Servants of Servants"[119] whose role at the heart of the absolute monarchy Yerushalmi theorizes. In this way, Cardoso anticipated the exceptional destiny of these state Jews who, in Spain but even more so in France—whose state is so strong—put all of their energy into serving the state by occupying a preeminent position at its core.[120]

But contrary to these Jews who devoted their life to the state and identified with its rationalist logic, Cardoso, against all expectations, suddenly left his position serving the state to take refuge in Verona's ghetto and become a doctor for the poor. It was as though, to validate Baron's perspective, his immersion behind the protective walls of the ghetto prevailed over the glory of serving the state; as though, like the American model celebrated by Baron at the same time as Yerushalmi is writing his dissertation, the ghetto, or local community, revealed itself to be more suitable to a fulfilling Jewish life, as much in Italy, whose state was weak, federal, and decentralized, as in the United States, with an equally weakened federal state. As though, finally, in Spain's monarchy just like in France's republic, or even in the Austro-Hungarian Empire, access to preeminent roles for Jews could only be fatal for them, to the point that the American situation of insertion into ghetto communities that has long prevailed was much more advantageous than having access to federal politico-administrative structures.

It was as though, to conclude on this point, Spanish, French, or Austrian Jews were deaf to the threat that Stefan Zweig issued in 1936, then again in 1938, at the exact moment that Baron published his first three volumes of *A Social and Religious History of the Jews* as a development of his "Ghetto and Emancipation": "There is nothing that has stirred the anti-Semitic movement as much as the fact that the Jews made themselves too visible in various countries, in various aspects of political life, and all too often as leaders." Zweig does not want Jews to participate in politics in a "leadership position" and advises them to adopt a "certain reserve," to make do with "serving while staying at the second, fifth, or even tenth rank, and to never take the top position, the most visible."[121] Baron, concerned that the Jews stay within their local communities, can only approve this recommendation, just like Yerushalmi, who recounts Cardoso's destiny, preferring the ghetto to the splendors of the state. Is Zweig familiar with Heinrich Graetz's ideas? Has he read Baron's books or articles, his 1928 text, the three volumes that have just appeared in 1936, the same year that he expresses his opposition to the presence of Jews in preeminent positions within the state? When he considers that "the feeling of insecurity and inferiority lies in wait for the Jewish people, always surrounded by hostility, always oppressed, always on the defensive," he is situating himself in Graetz's current of thought and implicitly embraces the lachrymose theory of Jewish history, denounced by Baron, but adds the decisive element that this hostility is stirred by the presence of Jews "at the forefront" of the state. Neither Baron nor Yerushalmi supports such a proposition, namely that the royal alliance that ties the Jews to the state and pushes some among them, such as Isaac Cardoso, to occupy a preeminent position within the state inevitably provokes antisemitic hate. When Cardoso rises, thanks to his competence, to a function that confers upon him high visibility, he does not trigger, according Yerushalmi's analysis, any violent antisemitic hate. Be that as it may, after having risen to the top of the state while hiding his true identity as a practicing Jew, Cardoso flees this Spanish state that mutilated his personhood to take refuge in the Verona ghetto, where he finds protection by returning to a soul-saving Judaism. This is evidence that the royal alliance is hardly synonymous with happiness, that it can reveal itself to be, as Zweig emphasizes, dangerous.

Under the influence of Baron's ideas in praise of the medieval ghetto in which Jews, though benefiting from public status, had hardly any access to the state that protected them, Yerushalmi hesitates. Cardoso proves both the functional nature of the royal alliance that allows his social ascent and its ultimate failure. In Yerushalmi's mind, happiness does not lie at the end of a strategy that ultimately and decisively reveals itself to be a myth, a lure facilitating all tragedies, as shown by the Nazi example— only mentioned indirectly, even less frequently than in Baron— all the while remaining weary, like Baron, of a lachrymal history. Nevertheless, loyal to the historical perspective traced by Baron, Yerushalmi believes that the vertical alliance, despite its fluctuations, its inconsistencies, the royal infidelities, and the Jews' erroneous beliefs, only had merit in the premodern period, during which it avoided as best as possible tears and suffering. Furthermore, when all is said and done, Yerushalmi doubts even more than Baron its functional nature, given how Manuel, the "gentle king," preferred to ignore antisemitic violence, an observation that also ruins the optimistic view of the Middle Ages that Baron defends tooth and nail. Paradoxically, one might even argue that, against his will, Yerushalmi turns away from his Baronian inheritance by justifying the lachrymose view of history, including during the Middle Ages—a prosperous period in the eyes of his mentor. Yerushalmi is more than skeptical as to the protective role of the royal state. Even in this period, happiness seems to reside more in the margins, in the return to the ghetto. Also, in the modern era, at the heart of the Upper West Side of New York, a kind of broad and peaceful urban community that escapes antisemitism is untouched by the grip of the state or by the question of a vertical alliance, a kind of Verona ghetto transposed to the *goldene medine* that meets Baron's and Yerushalmi's expectations.

From then on, Baron's solution becomes more prudent: stay on the sidelines, do not lay claim to the glory of serving the state in a society where it no longer plays the ambiguous role that it did under absolutist Spain. Consciously or not, Baron and Yerushalmi seem to heed Stefan Zweig's advice. For them, in the United States, the royal alliance loses its historical function, and Jews return to their civil society, their community, and abandon the summits of the state. According to this logic, the long quasi-nonexistence of state Jews in the United States prevents the eruption of political antisemitism. By staying away from power, by preferring to be locally rooted, American Jews preserve a "happiness" devoid of glory but shaped by a joyful and fecund community life, favorable to "knowledge," devoid of "tears," and unaffected by the political antisemitism that so severely affected the Jews in French-style states, or even, as in previously, their colleagues in the Austro-Hungarian Empire.

# 2

# THE LEO FRANK AFFAIR

## The Lynching of a Jew

Baron is deeply convinced that history is not a torrent of tears, and American exceptionalism is absolute proof of it. As a new society, it has not experienced the Crusades, the torments of the Middle Ages, the misfortunes of the Inquisition, the pogroms of Eastern Europe. It has dodged the worst: the deportation of European Jews. Baron is persuaded that the United States alone belies the lachrymose version of history, even if a logical or ill-intentioned reader might, with a bit of irony, retort that the exception confirms the rule. It has been said that "if the United States, has not been utter heaven for Jews, it has been as far from hell as Jews in the Diaspora have ever known."[1] Besides, "prior to World War I there were no significant American ideologists or popularizers of anti-Semitism comparable to Dühring or to Marr, Barrès or Drumont, Pobiedonostsev or Krushevan."[2] In this way, in the New World, "anti-Semitism has never in America been politicized as the basis for a right-wing nationalist movement, as it has in such countries as pre-Nazi Germany or in France."[3]

When Baron becomes enamored with the American example, he is merely reproducing the optimistic vision of Alexis de Tocqueville who, at the end of his long journey throughout

American society, in which he had carefully visited many regions, always opening a dialogue with the inhabitants, strongly criticized the racism that victimized Black folk, but without ever once pronouncing the word *antisemitism*. As he did not encounter any Jews during his travels across America, he perceived no signs of antisemitism, to the point that he did not broach this question, as we noted earlier, in his two thick volumes of *Democracy in America*. Although it is an open, pluralist society, one that is attentive to cultural differences and a dream for so many immigrants, the United States has a history forever marred by the systematic massacre of Native Americans and by the violent racism that Blacks endured: nearly 4,400 lynchings between 1877 and 1950 (4,084 in the southern states alone, with Mississippi, Georgia, and Louisiana having the highest numbers), a quarter of which were the result of accusations of sexual violence.[4]

American history, however, avoids, according to Tocqueville and, later, Baron, antisemitic violence. For three centuries, from the beginning of the seventeenth century to the end of the nineteenth, while the old continent was experiencing so many assassinations, pogroms, and blood libels, though wild views about Jews abounded—each more far-fetched than the next—and led to their condemnation, most often in the name of Christianity, no Jews were being put to death in the United States. The values of ancient Judaism have been celebrated since the foundation of American democracy. The Puritans that fled England saw themselves as the new Hebrews who crossed their Red Sea when they navigated the Atlantic. The metaphor of the Exodus was so often used in sermons and speeches that Benjamin Franklin wanted Moses parting the Red Sea to be placed at the heart of the American official seal.

From one century to another, American Jews lived their lives without any major incident, and their insertion into the "nation of nations" aroused no reprobation. True, social antisemitism still cropped up—a constant at the turn of the twentieth century—through exclusions from housing, clubs, some hotels, and even some Ivy League schools (Harvard, Yale, Princeton) where quotas against them remained in place for a long time. True again, at various moments, antisemitic imagery appeared in speeches and utterances, the "Jewish invasion" was represented in newspapers or comics, a sign of protest against Eastern European immigrations. Ordinary antisemitism surfaced and affected Jewish life without, however, giving rise to violent persecutions comparable to those in Europe in the same time period. A history without tears lulled the daily life of American Jews, almost exclusively confined by prejudice.[5]

As the sound and fury of the old continent echoed in the New World, when American Jews learned about the Kishinev pogrom the shock was all the greater for the fact that this form of collective hate had become foreign to them. What an incredible contrast between the deadly violence of Kishinev (facilitated by the nonintervention of the ferociously antisemitic Russian authorities, though they were hostile to this wave of violence,[6] which turned 1903 into a fateful moment in Jewish history) and the pacifying words of the former American president Grover Cleveland in 1905, confirming the identical project of the American people and the Jewish people by emphasizing the peaceful symbiosis between American and Jewish life![7]

For Jews around the world, the Kishinev pogrom in a way marked the beginning of the twentieth century in its most tragic aspects. On April 19 and 20, 1903, to the sound of the bells signaling the end of Passover and following a new blood libel, a savage crowd attacked the Jewish population, comprised of over fifty thousand souls, without any police intervention. Forty-one Jews—men, women, and children—were brutally massacred;

hundreds of others were critically injured; shops and homes were burned down.[8] In April, the Yiddish poet Shimon Frug published, on the front page of Saint Petersburg's daily newspaper *Fraynd*, an immense poem on the "torrents of blood and the rivers of tears" that have punctuated Jewish history to finally arrive at Kishinev. Vladimir Jabotinsky called for self-defense, whereas Simon Dubnow, a diasporist and a proponent of indispensable self-organization, advised the Jewish populations, in this dramatic context, to quickly emigrate to the United States or even to Palestine, which they ultimately did en masse following the pogrom.[9] Finally, Ahad Ha'am, the theorist of cultural Zionism, also condemned the pogrom and advocated the refusal of servitude in diaspora, a source of so many misfortunes. The stands taken by the most important Jewish thinkers in Eastern Europe illustrate this crucial moment in Jewish history, which has left its mark on the minds of Jews throughout the nations of the world. As for Theodor Herzl, when confronted with Kishinev, he proposed a Jewish emigration to Uganda and declared at the Sixth Zionist Congress taking place in August: "Kishinev exists everywhere that the Jews suffer physical and spiritual torture." Also invited by the Sixth Convention of the Federation of American Zionists taking place in Pittsburgh, a city marked by so many antisemitic plots up until the emblematic 2018 massacre, Israel Zangwill declared that "the Kishineff [sic] massacre has brought home to the blindest the need of a publicly and legally safeguarded home for our unhappy race."[10] Though he spoke in favor of Palestine in this speech, he was already thinking of the United States as the site on which to build his utopian *Melting Pot*, the play that will know such immense success in 1908 that it will be performed from New York to Los Angeles, Pittsburgh, Boston, and Baltimore. Zangwill celebrated the United States where all ethnicities combine in a vast melting pot, in every way opposite to Russia and its pogroms.[11]

Everyone sees in this "turning point" that is Kishinev the confirmation of a lachrymose history of the Jews, forever consecrated by Hayim Nahman Bialik in his poem "In the City of Slaughter."[12]

> Get up, go to the city of slaughter and you will come to the
> courtyards,
> And with your eyes you will see and with your hands you will
> touch the fences
> And the wood and the stones and on the plaster walls
> The congealed blood and the hardened brains of the fallen.
> From there you will come to the ruins and you will pass over the
> breaches
> And you will cross over the perforated walls and the demolished
> ovens,
> Into a place where the smashing deepened and crushed, widened,
> enlarged the holes,
> Uncovering the black stone and exposing the burnt brick,
> And they appear as open mouths of wounds mortal and black
> Which no longer have a remedy nor will have a cure . . .
> The sun shone, the acacia bloomed and the slaughterer slaughtered.
> And you will flee and come to a courtyard and in that courtyard
> a mound—
> Upon this mound are beheaded two: a Jew and his dog.
> One axe beheaded them and on one dung-heap were they thrown,
> And in the mixing blood of the two, pigs scratch and roll
> themselves;
> Tomorrow will the rain descend and wash it away to one of the
> wasteland streams—

No more will the blood cry out from the gutters and from the
   dung-heaps,
For in a great deep will it be lost or irrigate a thornbush to
   abundance—
And everything will be as naught, and everything will return as
   though it never was. . . .[13]

"Kishinev will forever symbolize abandonment, solitude,
indifference towards Jewish tears" and, "pogroms would thus
enter the lexicon of Jewish life as little less than a contemporary
analogue to Egypt's biblical plagues . . . the worst Jewish history's catastrophe including the destruction of the temple of Jerusalem."[14] Translated into Russian by Vladimir Jabotinsky who
"Nordaulized" its symbolism,[15] Bialik's poem becomes a call to
action for "muscle Jews" to arm themselves for their defense.[16]
For American Jews, but especially for the seven hundred thousand Jews who fled the Russian Empire soon after Kishinev to
find refuge in the United States, Kishinev is an immense shock.[17]
Their emotion is great. Jews of German or Russian origins unite
to protest and hold numerous meetings, assembling in public
spaces.[18] They have no doubt as to the meaning of Kishinev for
a Jewish future: "east-European Jewry suffered a disaster unparalleled since the Chmielnitsky massacres in the midseventeenth
century" committed by the Cossacks.[19] Large sums of money are
immediately collected: the Yiddish press, such as the *Jewish Daily
News, Di yidishe Gazen, Forverts/Forward*, and many other newspapers launch subscriptions; plays depicting the pogrom are
immediately produced, with the proceeds sent to the victims;
eminent Jewish personalities like Louis Marshall or Oscar Straus
lead demonstrations and donate large amounts of money. Pro-
grams are implemented to facilitate immigration to the United
States for the Jews who survived the pogroms, while Zionist

organizations endeavor to direct them to Palestine. In Great Britain as well, English Jews from emigrant neighborhoods, often close to their American coreligionists, are stricken by the Kishinev pogrom.[20]

In 1906, in order to collectively organize their protest, Jewish leaders create the American Jewish Committee, which will speak on behalf of Jewish American opinion for many years to come. Their emotion is shared by the highest authorities, even though Theodore Roosevelt hesitates to speak out officially, fearing that the Russians will in turn condemn America's lynching of African Americans. He nevertheless wants to show his solidarity by attending a performance of Israel Zangwill's *The Melting Pot* in Washington in 1908. The play's hero, an orphan, violinist, and victim of Kishinev, manages to escape the violence and settle in the United States.[21] It is in this context of national mobilization against Kishinev that Seth Low, New York City's mayor, declares during a massive meeting: "The Jew is a quiet, orderly, and industrious citizen; and . . . if treated with kindness instead of cruelty, he becomes a source of strength to the nation and not weakness. It also entitles the citizens of New York to protest vigorously against such horrors as those of Kishineff. . . . This is a meeting called under Christian auspices—that in the name of our religion we grieve that such a stain should have been cast upon it." President Cleveland denounces: "As members of the family of mankind and as citizens of a free Nation we are here to give voice to the feeling that should stir every true man and every American worthy of the name. There is something intensely horrible in the wholesale murder of unoffending, defenseless men, women, and children, who have been tacitly or expressly assured of safety under the protection of a professedly civilized Government."[22] The *New York Times* publishes long investigative reports on the massacre. William Randolph Hearst, elected to Congress, suggests in the *New York Journal-American* that America declare war against Russia, while the *Atlanta Journal* advises "that we think that the time has come when civilized people everywhere, Christians and Jews, should unite in one voice of disapproval against the Czar and his ministers for these shameless crimes. It is not a few ignorant ruffians in Bessarabia who are on trial today. It is a national government. The criminals who have been hauled before the world's bar of justice are from St. Petersburg as well as from Kishineff. The verdict is made up; and already we hear on every lip the word 'Guilty.'"[23] Kishinev, as well as multiple other pogroms that follow, tips the scales in favor of massive Jewish immigration from these devastated regions.[24]

Kishinev, the culmination of lachrymose history that single-handedly embodies, as much in the past as in the present, the reality of Jewish misfortune, represents absolute distress for American Jews accustomed to centuries of peaceful life. This pogrom "managed to push the Dreyfus Affair to the margins and it dominated the headlines of American newspapers for weeks. The Jewish press would lead with it for months."[25] More recent still, as of 1998, the *New York Times* considered "that before Kristallnacht there was Kishinev."[26] This goes to show the place that such an event occupies in the history and memory of American Jews, suddenly faced with the unimaginable. In Russia, Kishinev represented the pinnacle of incessant pogroms culminating between 1903 and 1906, only to resume their dramatic course between 1919 and 1921.

If the number of victims, from that same region, whether from Odessa or from Kiev, reveals itself to be infinitely greater than at Kishinev, if we can count hundreds of victims throughout Russia, from Minsk to Vitebsk,[27] it is nevertheless Kishinev that stupefies American Jews. In 2018, following the Pittsburgh synagogue massacre, the question remains, with the utmost urgency, whether the time has come to take up arms so as to avoid the tragic fate of the Kishinev Jews, who would have certainly let themselves be slaughtered without defending themselves, according to Bialik's famous poem "In the City of Slaughter," which continues to resonate across contemporary Jewish history. This memory is so vivid that some Jewish commentators have put forth that today "in the context of the long debate on Jewish self-defense, Donald Trump, the president of the United States, is not Bialik. If anything, Trump is more like Tsar Nikolai II, ruler of the Russian Empire at the time of the Kishinev pogrom, often accused by world rulers of inciting inter-ethnic animosity in his own country in order to keep his reign."[28]

Truth be told, far from the large metropolises of the Northeast or even the Midwest, Dixieland Jews, deeply integrated into the American South, only seemed to perceive a dim echo of the Kishinev pogrom. As a recent specialist observed, "here we will find no equivalent of Russian's settlement laws, pogroms, Doctor's Purge or current bars against emigration; France's Dreyfus Case; Spain's Inquisition . . . to say nothing of the Nazi horror."[29] The Jewish population that settled in the South came from various points of origin: first there were the Sephardim in the seventeenth centuries, fleeing Latin America where the Spanish Inquisition raged anew, coming to seek refuge in these regions; they were joined, between 1820 and 1870, by numerous Ashkenazi Jews from Europe, mostly from Germany or Alsace, who settled here and there between Memphis and New Orleans. Finally, at the turn of the twentieth century, following the Russian pogroms, other Jewish emigrants leaving those violent lands settled in these regions. Cohabitation was established between Orthodox, Conservative, and Reform, despite their social differences and their diverse rituals.

A priori, there is a great contrast between those Jewish populations whose professions are often tied to commerce, given the restrictions heaped upon them in the old continent, and an

American Southerner who remained profoundly rural and hostile to the business world, to modernity, and to all forms of wandering that affect the lives of Jewish emigrants, used to traveling through countries according to the whims of persecutions. The South showed itself to be more than ambivalent toward these foreigners, considered nonwhite, who at times had passed through regions of the Northeast of the United States, a region whose egalitarian structures—but also capitalist mentality—the South rejected. Against all expectations, the meeting between evangelical Protestantism that dominates in the South and various Jewish emigrants saw no major clashes, given the extent to which both share similar biblical values. A narrow cooperation was even established, solid friendships were formed, and a kind of cultural closeness was created between people who valued family ties and who were both marked by a feeling of deep solitude and even exile. In this way, the Jews found a true home in the South that might have otherwise seemed so foreign to them. They became integrated into the local culture, sharing its values, appreciating the local cuisine, participating in hunting, duels, and card games, to such a degree that non-Jews deplored their too rapid assimilation.

The fact remains, and we will return to this, that these connections were all the easier that Jews and non-Jews found themselves on the other side of the racial divide that separated them from African Americans, to the extent that numerous Jews who now strongly identified with Southern values looked unfavorably upon any challenge to this hierarchy, especially given that some of them also owned slaves.[30] It is true that others did not hide their Reform opinions and appeared to be respectful to African Americans, providing them with products that white Christians refused to sell them. Friendships were forged between Jewish bosses and their Black employees, who spoke Yiddish to each other.[31] This ambiguous triangulating dance between Jews, white Christians, and Blacks was further complicated and unpredictable due to the fact that many Blacks shared the latent antisemitism of white Christians,[32] while simultaneously the powerful rise of the Ku Klux Klan and of the radical Christian right was becoming worrisome to the Jews.[33] From then on, to prove their patriotism and loyalty to the South, many Jews enlisted in the Confederate army during the Civil War, fighting to maintain a caste system based on race, of which they were also the beneficiaries, without necessarily always agreeing with its reasoning. Many became officers, distinguished themselves during bloody battles, while rabbis justified these heroic acts in fiery sermons in which they were opposed to the Northern armies that contained other Jews.[34] Yesterday, as today, "the law of the land is the law."[35] This is demonstrated by the fact that Judah P. Benjamin, owner of a hundred or so Black slaves, after having been the senator to Louisiana, was appointed Confederate war minister during the clash between the North and the South.

This complex picture should not hide the tensions and rejections—some more, some less painful—that persisted despite everything. During the Civil War, North and South alike often exhibited strong anti-Jewish prejudices. In many regions of the South, Jews were accused of treason against the Confederates, while the antisemitism of the Northern armies was at times virulent: at the end of 1862, General Ulysses Grant wished to expel all the Jews and only renounced his aim after an intervention by President Abraham Lincoln.[36] In the South, a true Jewphobia emerged, in Tennessee and in New Orleans, for instance. A newspaper expressed the wish that "all Southern Jews ought to be exterminated."[37] In Georgia, as in Tennessee, people denounced the Judas, traitors to the Confederacy. Jews were described as the new Shylocks, like locusts ravaging the country;

in North Carolina, all misfortune was blamed on Jews, and the Jewish soldiers in the Confederate army were subjected to all manner of insults. The promotion of Judah Benjamin to the rank of officer was considered a "blasphemy" by the *Richmond Enquirer*.[38] During this time period, many states, particularly in the South, prevented the Jews from accessing their political rights by rejecting the very principles established by the American Constitution, whose reasoning only applied on the federal level. North Carolina was thus the second-to-last state to a accept, in 1868, their access to public jobs.[39] Similarly, South Carolina's Supreme Court considered, until the middle of the nineteenth century, the United States to be a Christian nation. It forbade Jews from working on Sunday as a show of respect for this day of rest, a decision ratified until 1892 by the Supreme Court of the United States, which ruled that it is indeed a "Christian Nation."[40]

In many Southern states, and in Georgia in particular, birthplace of the Ku Klux Klan, Jews also remained excluded from the most select clubs of the Christian elite. They rejected these Easterners whose whiteness was suspect. Jewish doctors and lawyers struggled to find a place to practice. In the press, Jews found themselves frequently and grotesquely caricatured, mocked for their physical appearance and their accent. They were not readily accepted in certain residential neighborhoods or popular beaches, while universities, such as Emory in Atlanta, or the University of North Carolina, Chapel Hill, imposed quotas limiting the admission of Jewish students. Similarly, marital strategies were often used to avoid any form of misalliance with these Jewish newcomers, despite their rapid social ascension. Open antisemitism seeped into the region: violent demonstration erupted in Louisiana in the 1880s; in Mississippi, Jewish farms were burned at night; in Tennessee, as in many regions of the

South, parents took their children out of school where two Jewish students had been admitted.[41] In 1868, again in Tennessee, Samuel Bierfield, a Jewish shopkeeper living in the small town of Franklin, was attacked by masked men who shot and killed him, a brutal execution that some considered to be a lynching, an assassination committed for obscure—perhaps financial—reasons. It is thought that he was executed by members of the Ku Klux Klan, created right near Franklin in 1866, but whose antisemitic motives were not explicit.[42]

Despite these incidents, despite this strange murder, the South seduced many Jews. Already in 1840, the first two who came over from Germany, Jacob Haas and Henry Levi, settled in Atlanta, attracted by a city in full economic expansion and situated on a railway junction. Others headed for that big city and, like them, crossed the Mississippi Delta, from one plantation to another, offering their services as traveling salesmen, hawkers, and merchants. Between 1840 and the turn of the century, they were followed to Atlanta by Jews from Poland and other Eastern European countries. They became tailors and cobblers, opening small businesses and quickly ascending to the middle or even upper class of Atlanta, despite rampant antisemitism and fierce prejudices.[43] During the first decade of the twentieth century, Sephardic Jews from Turkey and the island of Rhodes were the next wave of immigrants to settle in Atlanta. The city experienced a renaissance of many synagogues with different rites, fraternal societies, political organizations, clubs, and even a Jewish press.[44] In 1875, the *Atlanta Daily Herald* wrote: "We congratulate ourselves because nothing is so indicative of a city's prosperity as to see an influx of Jews who come. . . . They make good citizens, pay their obligations promptly; never refuse to pay their taxes and are law abiding."[45]

In 1931, Atlanta was the city to see the fastest growth of its
Jewish population, becoming the biggest in the South. At that
time, there were 2,250 Jews from Eastern Europe, 1,250 from
Western Europe, and 50 from Turkey. Between 1887 and 1910, 4
Jews became the presidents of the 4 big banks of Atlanta, and 9
others were appointed as directors of these essential institutions.
At the turn of the century, many factories making paper, furni-
ture, cotton, and mattresses were also run by Jews. Certain activities saw Jews associate with non-Jews, such as the law firm
founded by Benjamin Philips with which the governor of Georgia, John Slaton, collaborated, or the law firm created by Walter
Visanska with the mayor of Atlanta, Courtland Winn.[46] This
shows that despite frictions, despite an antisemitism that was at
times perceptible in conversations—particularly against Russian
Jews—the Jews of Atlanta managed to climb the social ladder
and integrate into the upper class, creating social ties with non-
Jews. This is also evident in the fact that at the beginning of the
twentieth century the two most well-known Jewish figures both
lived in the most residential neighborhood of Atlanta. Many
Jews of this high socioeconomic status were elected to the Municipal Council of Atlanta at the turn of the century and remained
for many years seated on various committees, one of whom
remained for eighteen years in a row on the Water and Sanitation
Committee. Others headed the education system of Atlanta.
Still, the most select clubs remained closed to them: no Jews
could be found at the Piedmont Driving Club, the Capital City
Club, the Atlanta Art Association, or the Atlanta Athletic Club.

Nothing was sufficient. German Jews pushed their assimilation
into local society to the extreme, to the point that they reconsidered many of their religious rituals, though in vain. Reform
was in full swing in this environment seemingly open to the Jews,

but nothing could sway the strongholds of prejudice. They persisted in a context marked by a strong push of nativism, deeply tinted by racism, rising xenophobia against all foreigners, and in particular against Italian Catholics and Russian Jews. The nativist mobilization reached its apogee in these regions precisely at the beginning of the 1910s, when hysterical mobs attacked foreigners and Italians were hanged.[47] Henceforth, on March 11, 1913, as the film *Shylock* was met with great success in Atlanta, the newly elected president of the Masonic Lodge of Gate City decided to create a review committee in order to examine the complaints against anti-Jewish caricatures that were becoming increasingly common in the city. His name was Leo Frank.

Leo Frank had no idea that a few days later, on April 27, the sky would fall on his head. He would become the star of the most dramatic episode of these years at a time when hatred of the Other was a raging tide. An unbelievable tragedy erupted, an accusation so unimaginable that, in this peaceful society never troubled by a pogrom, it was as though suddenly Kishinev were knocking at its door. Born in Paris, Texas, into a Jewish family originally from Germany, Leo Frank has mostly lived in New York. He was a student at Cornell University, where he obtained his degree. At the age of twenty-four, in 1908, he moved to Atlanta, where he was appointed director of a crayon factory, of which his rich uncle was one of the primary shareholders, and in which Leo himself owned stocks. On November 30, 1910, he married Lucille Selig Frank, the rich daughter of an Atlantan manufacturer, and became part of the city's Jewish elite. They resided near Washington Street, the most privileged part of the city, an old neighborhood surrounded by magnolias where the most notable Jews of the city lived. The couple seemed happy, everything pointing to a kind of bliss, a joy of living in this privileged environment, liberal, tolerant, and lacking in any prejudice.

David Marx, who presided over the synagogue of this deeply assimilated bourgeois neighborhood, pushed Reform to the extreme, putting an end to bar mitzvah ceremonies, no longer imposing the kippa, moving the Sabbath to Sundays, allowing both men and women to mingle during services, and rejecting all forms of Zionism. Confirming his integration and notability, two years later, Leo Frank was elected president of the B'nai B'rith Lodge of Atlanta, boasting over five hundred members at the heart of secular Jewish life in this large city, and it is in this capacity that he launched, on March 11, 1913, an inquiry into the persistence of antisemitic prejudice.

April 26, 1913, was supposed to be a glorious day, between the military parade celebrating Confederate Memorial Day and the evening concert of Arturo Toscanini. In the morning of April 27, emotion overtook the city at the announcement of the murder of a young fourteen-year-old girl, Mary Phagan, from a family of farmers, who spent her adolescence in Marietta, twenty miles from Atlanta. She was discovered lying down in the basement of the factory in which Frank was the manager, likely raped, her body bloody and covered in garbage. Near the body, the police discovered two illegible notes written on white paper ripped out of a ledger:

"He said he would love me, lay down play like the night witch, did it, but that long, tall black negro did boy hisself."

"Mam that negro fire down here did this I went to make water and he push me down a hole a long tall negro black did [had] it I write while play with me."[48]

If a parallel can be drawn between Atlanta and Kishinev, between two cities in full growth with open urban areas that attract a number of Jews, it is with Kiev, as Albert Lindemann notes upon learning about this murder.[49] We are reminded of Kiev, with these overly excited mobs of ten thousand people assembled to lament, in an almost religious frenzy, the death of "Mary of the people" of "Little Mary Phagan." Suddenly, a rumor spreads. The murderer has been found: it is the Black night watchman of the factory, Newt Lee. But he, despite the brutalities heaved upon him by the police, denies all responsibility for the crime, claims his innocence, and maintains that he found the body in the morning during a round, that he got scared and called the police. The police next cast their suspicion on a young man, more or less Mary's fiancé, who is quickly exonerated.

It is then Leo Frank's turn to be the perfect suspect. Besides, the Saturday of the murder, he was at the factory. He had supposedly exhibited inappropriate behavior toward the young women who made up the factory's staff. One of them assures the police that Frank had attempted to touch her chest, another that Frank had offered to come visit her: "I told him to go to hell." The wildest rumors quickly begin to circulate: an innumerable number of young women of the factory claim to have complained of his behavior toward them. Frank was said to be a pervert who orchestrated, at the heart of the factory itself, sexual relationships. He was also allegedly frequently seen in a neighboring brothel with another man, worse even, his sexuality was said to be "immoral," that of an "abnormal" man who preferred oral sex. He was even allegedly recently caught in the woods with a young woman engaged in activities that carried the severe sentence of death in Georgia. A young factory worker swears that she saw Frank put his arm around Mary's waist and offer her a ride to Paradise. Indisputable proof of his guilt is found: hairs as well as traces of blood supposedly belonging to Mary are discovered in the office next to his.

Even if the majority of these "indisputable" proofs are quickly abandoned, Leo Frank is now squarely at the heart of the tragedy and of popular vindication. The police come to his home, interrogate him, find his responses dilatory, hesitant, and contradictory. Frank's attitude is strange: he hedges, considers that only a Black person could engage in such a brutal act, starts by saying he did not know Mary before admitting the contrary, and adding that he did not know her name. Frank confides to the police that after having given Mary her pay a little after noon, he returned home around one o'clock. Yet another employee who also came to get her pay immediately after Mary's supposed departure entered into Frank's office. It was empty, whereas Frank claimed to have stayed there for a while longer before returning home for lunch. How can he explain this contradiction? What was he doing during this time period, about which he provides no explanation, other than a trip to the lavatory? Where was he at the time of Mary's murder, shown by the autopsy to have occurred between noon and one? Why did he call Lee, the night watchman, many times that night, before the body was found, to check if everything was OK, which he did not usually do? His explanations are hardly convincing when he suggests that he wanted to get news on an employee that had just been fired or that he wished to check that there was no fire.

Frank's personality itself raises many questions. Some perceive him in photographs as a perverse being, a true sexual predator that allegedly harassed the young female workers of his factory. His physique is in all ways different from the white Southerners. Not seductive, weak, small, with bulging eyes behind thick glasses, he "looks Jewish." His mannerisms also cast doubt on his sincerity: he is awkward, not sociable, entrenched in his beliefs, and does not attempt to explain himself. As a symbol of Yankee capitalism, he arouses little sympathy, nor does he seek it out. Although the autopsy of Mary's body shows that she has not been raped and the doctor who examined her testified that he found no sperm, there is still evidence that her hymen has been displaced, likely in a violent manner. Everything is in place for the Frank affair to take on a catastrophic scale. Mary's funeral happens almost immediately, with more than ten thousand mourners to accompany the casket. Frank is present throughout the entire ceremony, after which he returns home surrounded by his wife and some prominent Jews who have come to show their support.

On Monday, the city awakens in shock. All the newspapers feature the murder on their front pages and dedicate multiple columns to the tragedy. The *Georgian*, recently bought by the Hearst empire, offers a reward of $500 for any credible information and sensationalizes the event. The national news contributes by urgently dispatching its reporters to the city. In an attempt to outbid the *Georgian*, the *Constitution* offers $1,000. During this time, the investigation moves forward. It alleges that the murder occurred right next to Frank's office, that the body was then dragged to the basement. Everything seems to point to Frank, the last person to see Mary alive. That same Monday, the police arrest him for Mary's murder. Led to prison, Frank has just enough time to declare, in front of the sinister building: "I am not guilty. Such an atrocious crime has never entered my mind. I am a man of good character and I have a wife. I am a home-loving and God-fearing man. They will discover that. It is useless to detain me."[50] Having come with him, Lucille proclaims Leo Frank's innocence and collapses in tears.

Accused by the police of Mary Phagan's murder, Frank is presented before a jury who, despite his protestations and those of his lawyers, charge him. Frank is imprisoned, and Hugh Dorsey, the public prosecutor, prepares the indictment. A graduate of the University of Georgia and the University of Virginia School of Law, he is a man of the people, solidly rooted in the city, friends with many Jews, such as his law firm associate, a middle school peer whose room he shared, and now his son-in-law. He is as much at ease with farmers as with the city elite. He braves the *Georgian* as well as the national press, which both consider the affair to be greatly tainted by antisemitism. The grand jury meets on May 23 at 11 a.m. It is comprised of four Jews and many city businessmen.

Another player enters the scene and complicates Dorsey's mission. James Conley, a Black man working at Frank's factory, was seen cleaning the floor on the second story of the factory where Frank's office is located. He has already been arrested multiple times for drunkenness and disorderly conduct. The historical context following the defeat of the Confederacy has incited increased violence toward the Black population. Lynchings are on the rise, and mobs violently assault their fellow citizens of color whom they bar from accessing public spaces. The pinnacle is reached just prior to the Frank affair, in Wilmington, North Carolina, on November 10, 1898, when rioters—ex-Confederates accompanied by their children—anxious to prevent Blacks from voting, start a violent pogrom in the name of a white supremacy threatened by ex-slaves whom they view as degenerate rapists. The cadavers of at least sixty African Americans are counted throughout the city, while cries of victory and orchestral Dixie music ring out.[51]

In Atlanta, the situation for Black folk, at the heart of Jim Crow's segregationist laws, has turned the city into one of the most hostile in the United States. They are excluded from restaurants, bars, trains, cars, hair salons, etc. The city is renowned

for its animosity toward its Black population. In September of
1906, following the rape of a white woman by her Black friend,
almost eleven thousand angry whites, often armed, take it out
on the African Americans they encounter in the city. The day
following this riot, another wave of assaults is led against Black
folk who defend themselves with guns. In the end, twenty-five
Black people as well as one white person are killed. A torrent of
violence, a real American pogrom, is unleashed against Black
people. Oddly, while many Jews confronted by the Leo Frank
affair evoke Kishinev, Black folk also draw parallels between the
lynchings their people are subjected to and the Kishinev massacres. As the *Cleveland Gazette* notes in 1903, "the terrible massacre of the Jews last week in Kishineff, Russia, and the horrible
outrages perpetrated, are only what have taken place many times
in the south with the Afro-American as a victim,"[52] The same
goes for the racial riots in August 1908 in Springfield, during
which over five thousand white people attack African Americans, a massacre that is also compared to the Kishinev pogrom.
In 1971, when a racial riot erupts against African Americans in
St. Louis, it will again be compared to Kishinev, both cities being
described as "twin cities."[53] The lynching of Frank will force
Blacks and Jews to "recogniz[e] that both identifiably separate
groups were profoundly affected by their marginal status in the
society. . . . [The Frank] affair precipitated an upsurge of Jewish
interest in blacks."[54]

   In this recent context of exacerbated violence against African
Americans, the interrogation of James Conley is strained: the
police accuse him of having written the two notes that were
found; Conley protests that he is innocent, swears he did not
write these texts, and finally, at the moment that the jury charges
Frank, he announces: "Chief, I wrote those notes." He recounts
that Frank asked him to come to his office, inquired as to whether

or not he could write, dictated the words to him, and offered him money, asserting that he knew wealthy people in Brooklyn. During his deposition, Frank's mother will deny having a rich family in Brooklyn, and stresses that the family is of modest means, that "Frank has no rich relatives in Brooklyn."[55] The following day, May 29, during another interrogation, Conley tells a completely different story: having met Frank in the street, the latter allegedly led him to the factory up to his office, asked him if he could write, gave him money with which he bought beer before returning home to drink, eat, and sleep. Then Conley remembers that Frank told him: "I want to be with this little girl and she refused me, and I struck her and I guess too hard and she fell and hit her head against something. Of course you know I ain't built like other men; have seen him with women lying on the table in the factory room and in his office with women with their clothes up."[56]

During yet another interrogation lasting four hours, Conley changes his narration again. This time, when, on Saturday the 26th of April, he returned to the factory, Frank offered him a way to make quick money. He allegedly revealed that he had brought a girl; she had fallen and injured her head. He offered that Conley move her to the cellar using the elevator. Conley carried her; she slipped from his shoulder; Frank helped him, holding her feet while Conley held her shoulders. They both descended to the basement where Conley put her on the ground. Frank allegedly said, "Wow, what tiring work." They returned to the second floor, Frank washed his hands, and at that moment asked him to write the two notes. He supposedly instructed Conley to be quiet and "he pulled out a little roll of greenbacks and said: Here is two hundred dollars. I took the money." Over the course of many successive interrogations, Conley declares, "can't read and write good. Can't read the newspapers good; can't get any sense out of them. There is some little letters like 'dis'

and 'dat' that I can read; other things that I can read; other things
that I don't understand; can spell 'dog' and more simple little
words like that. Can spell 'day' but not daylight; can spell 'beer'
but not 'whiskey.'"[57] Conley confirms his final deposition, and
he is asked to write one of the notes found next to Mary, which
he does but modifying it: *"Dear mother, a long black negro did this
by himself."*[58]

The next episode involves Frank's cook, accused of lying about
the time at which Frank returned home. Arrested and pushed
around, she refuses to sign any deposition in Frank's favor. Furi-
ous, Lucille Frank writes a long declaration published on the
front page of Atlanta's three newspapers: "My husband and my
family and myself are the innocent sufferers now, but who will
be the next to suffer? I suppose the witnesses tortured will be
confined, who will be the next one accused . . . forced to sign
false affidavits? . . . It is hard to believe that practices of this
nature will be countenanced anywhere in the world outside Russia."[59] Russia thus spontaneously reemerges under Lucille
Frank's pen as the place of torture and massacre par excellence.
The memory of pogroms and violence endures. At the heart of
the Deep South, Kishinev, Odessa, and so many other pogroms
flood the memories of American Jews persecuted by the police,
a people whose memory of age-old lachrymose history is reborn
intact. Again and again, the old continent and its massacres are
brought up as soon as unbridled crowds, acts of violence, or injustices, emerge in this otherwise welcoming land. Lucille Frank
joins the battle, publishes long precise analyses in the press in
order to demonstrate the errors of the procedure, the contradictions, and the manipulation of witnesses.

This is when a piece of the envelope from Mary's paycheck is
found in the factory, leading to the hypothesis that the motive
for the attack was a robbery that ended in murder. This time,

the focus is on Conley. A new witness appears, another Black man who played and drank heavily in his company the Saturday of the murder: Conley allegedly told him that he was going to take her money when she went to Frank's office. He tried to prevent Conley, but he left so as not to be mixed up in this incident. The next day, he learned of the young woman's death, and it was indeed the woman who had come down the stairs. Another person confirms that Conley, after having drunk, confided in him that he had killed the young woman.

It is to no avail. The jury does not charge Conley. Frank's trial begins on July 28 in front of an angry courtroom. A long procession of witnesses resumes the accusation, still convinced of Frank's guilt. It is oppressively hot and tensions are high. Suddenly another reversal: interrogated by the prosecutor, Conley adds new details to his deposition. He supposedly saw Frank in a position that "I haven't seen any other man that has got children. I have seen him in the office two or three times before Thanksgiving and a lady was in his office, and she was sitting down in a chair, and she had her clothes up to here, and he was down on his knees, and she had her hands on Mr. Frank."[60] He again accuses him of legally reprehensible sexual practices. Frank allegedly gave him two hundred dollars in hush money.

Equipped with four depositions from Conley, Frank's lawyer, Luther Rosser, begins the cross-examination. To everyone's stupefaction, Conley confesses that he has constantly lied, before repeating endlessly, "I don't remember."[61] The defense then begins to refute the evidence supporting the accusation: it denounces the police's violent behaviors; under cross-examination, the detectives confirm that Conley had never brought up these sexual descriptions; some witnesses retract their testimony: Frank was never seen in a brothel, never seen in the woods with a woman, did not court this or that factory worker, never showed

THE LEO FRANK AFFAIR CR 77

himself overattentive with Mary, etc. A doctor asserts that Frank is physically normal, implicitly belying the accusation of homosexuality: "I have examined the private parts of Leo M. Frank and found nothing abnormal; he is a normal man sexually."[62]

At the end of another interrogation, Frank again denies all the accusations and explains his initial nervousness as caused by the shock of the early arrest and the brutal news of the murder. He reveals that his wife immediately wished to be imprisoned along with him. Finally, he says: "Gentlemen, I know nothing whatever of the death of little Mary Phagan. I had no part in causing her death nor do I know how she came to her death after she took her money and left my office. I never even saw Conley in the factory or anywhere else on April 26, 1913. . . . Gentlemen, some newspaper men have called me 'the silent man in the tower' and I kept my silence and my counsel advisedly, until the proper time and place. The time is now, the place is here; and I have told you the truth, the whole truth."[63]

The atmosphere is tense. Nearing the end, a giant nervous crowd restlessly waits for the verdict on Frank's indictment. Antisemitic murmurs can be overheard, while others claim that if Frank had not been a Jew he would not have been charged. In a final effort, Frank's lawyers accuse Conley of having killed Mary, likely after having raped her. One of them, in his closing argument, turns toward the prosecutor Hugh Dorsey and states: "Enough with these lies of perversion, with these rumors, with your misleading evidence." Another lawyer cries out: "Here is a Jewish boy from the North. He is unacquainted with the South. He came here alone and without friends and he stood alone. He is defenseless and helpless. He knows he is innocent and is willing to find the murderer. God, all merciful and all powerful, look upon a scene like this!"[64] He then takes it out on Conley, "a dirty,

filthy, black, drunken, lying nigger. Alcoholic nigger." Another
lawyer adds: "a smart negro, that Conley. And you notice how
the state bragged on him because he stood up under the cross-
examination of Colonel Rosser. Well, that negro's been well
versed in law. Scott and Black and Starnes drilled him; they
gave him the broad hints."[65] Arnold, Frank's lawyer says, "I will
tell you right now, if Frank hadn't been a Jew there would never
have been any prosecution against him. I'm asking my own people to turn him loose, asking them to do justice to a Jew, and I'm
not a Jew, but I would rather die before doing injustice to a Jew."[66]
Completely surprised that one could believe the testimony of an
African American and disregard the word of a white man, this
lawyer adopts outrageously racist language that will do a disser-
vice to Frank's cause and reflect the often-antagonistic relationships at the time between Jews and African Americans.

The national press reinforces this racist view of Conley. The
*New York Times* blames the "black monster," the *Baltimore Sun*
wonders how the members of the jury could "[take] the word of
a vicious, lying degenerate negro as against that of a white man,"
while the *Washington Post* notes, early in the public controversy,
those "characteristic of a drunken ignorant negro," while it is
evident to the editorial writer "no intelligent white man would
do such a thing." Many observers consider, on the contrary, that
a Black criminal is being sought out at all costs, that the Jews
intend to blame African Americans for Mary Phagan's murder,
given how inconceivable it is in the mindset of the time to
condemn a white man. They are not the only ones to exhibit
deeply rooted racist prejudice against Black folk: even New York's
rabbi, Stephen Wise, a nationally known liberal who worked
closely with the National Association for the Advancement of
Colored People, does not hesitate to propose that "our race is

innocent of all crimes against women," thus pointing to African Americans as the only imaginable assassins.[67]

The Black press, on the other hand, denounces the racism of Frank's supporters and accuses major newspapers of seeking an African American scapegoat. The *Chicago Defender*, shocked by the racism of Frank's allies, considers that he has forgotten the treatment his people underwent in Russia. The *Chicago Tribune*, for its part, bluntly editorialized that "the life of a white man at the disposal of a disreputable negro reveals a complete revolution in ordinarily prevailing sentiments." And, as it turns out, a jury comprised of twelve white men will in fact trust "the testimony of a negro,"[68] proof, if proof is necessary, of its convictions, or its impartiality, which is completely incomprehensible given the time, but that casts doubt on Frank's innocence even today.

Cut to the quick by the rumors accusing him of antisemitism, prosecutor Dorsey, whose daughter married a Jew and whose associate in his law firm is Jewish, begins to pay homage to the pantheon of great Jewish politicians such as Disraeli and Judah Benjamin, secretary of defense of the Confederacy. He emphasizes that he has never used the word *Jew* in his deposition, that "Frank's race is as good as ours, but not better," that Jews, like Blacks or Christians, are equal before the law. All the while challenging the idea that Jews could not have committed such criminal acts, he concludes: "they rise to heights sublime, but they also sink to the lowest depths of degradation."[69]

The crowd awaits the verdict, and the *Augusta Chronicle* fears that "the real reason the trial of Leo Frank was abruptly adjourned Saturday was a fear of the same element which brought about the great Atlanta riot of 1906, the lower element, the people of the back streets and the alleys, the near-beer salons and the pool room. The Saturday night crowd in Atlanta, beer drinking is not an assemblage loving law and order. A verdict that displeased these sansculottes of Marietta Street might well result in trouble." The crowd applauds prosecutor Dorsey who, one last time, proclaims Frank's guilt to the jury, repeating multiple times "guilty, guilty, guilty!!!!"[70] Solemnly questioned by the judge, the jury declares Frank guilty. As Frank proclaims his innocence one last time, "I am as innocent of this crime as I was a year ago," the judge sentences Frank to be hanged on October 13, 1913: "Leo Frank shall be executed by the Sheriff of Fulton County between the hours of ten o'clock and two p.m. That he be hanged by the neck until he is dead and may God have mercy on your soul."[71]

When contacted, the famous lawyer Louis Marshall, who led the protests against the Kishinev pogrom, and the most eminent Jewish personality of the United States presiding on the American Jewish Committee, said that "the case is almost a second Dreyfus affair."[72] Immediately following the verdict, Rabbi Marx travels to New York to garner support for Frank and declares: "I would like to enlist your assistance in what is without doubt an American 'Dreyfus' case that has just developed in Atlanta," but he prefers to act indirectly: "it would be unfortunate if anything were done . . . from the standpoint of the Jews. Whatever is done must be done as a matter of justice and any action that is taken must emanate from non-Jewish sources."[73] This time, beyond the memory of Russian pogroms, the Dreyfus affair prevails in the memory of many American Jews, stunned that such an event, such a denial of justice, could come to light in the United States for the first time in its history. But intent on avoiding a fall into irrationality, the "nightmare of perversion" happening in France, the *New York Times* qualifies this parallel by stating that in France the Jews are in danger of "destruction."[74]

American Jews are not done being disappointed. On October 22, the court rejects the appeal filed by Frank's attorneys and refuses to grant him a new trial. The affair takes a different turn, now explicitly, with the Jewish question at its center. A few days following the rejected appeal, a small group of the most influential Jewish leaders of the country meet in New York, at the famous Reform synagogue Temple Emanu-El. In addition to Marshall, also present are a Chicago judge, Harvard administrators, and Jacob Schiff, associated with the influential bank Kuhn, Loeb, and Company. Adolph Ochs, director of the *New York Times*, who previously had refused to act as a Jew, joins their campaign to save Frank.[75] This meeting immediately arouses the condemnation of part of the national press. Indeed, the *New York Sun* entitles its article "The Jews Fight to Save Frank," considering that "the anti-Semitic feeling was the natural result of the belief that the Jews had banded to free Frank, innocent or guilty. The supposed solidarity of the Jews for Frank, even if he was guilty, caused a Gentile solidarity against him." On February 17, in a four-two decision, the Georgia Supreme Court refuses to overturn the ruling, considering that it is not reflective of any prejudice. Frank is going to be hanged on April 17, 1914. He has tried, again in vain, to defend himself, proclaiming his innocence and denouncing the false rumors, the "virus," that has penetrated even judicial institutions.

Frank returns to prison. On March 4, the *New York Times* argues that "if Frank had been the son of a reputable Gentile, he would never have been arrested."[76] But events take an even more dramatic turn with the sudden appearance of the populist Thomas Watson, whose newspaper, the *Jeffersonian*, will launch a violent explicitly antisemitic campaign, though it does not manage to engender a national movement, given widespread sympathy for Frank.[77] On March 19, Watson, "Georgia's hero" writes: "Does a Jew expect extraordinary favors and immunities *because* of his race?"[78] He concludes that any person who has read New York newspapers has become aware of the efforts made all the way from Atlanta to convince the Hebrews that Frank is the victim of his race.

Watson will relentlessly lead the battle against the *New York Times* and the prominent Jews who have hired a famous detective to come to Frank's rescue. Repeatedly, he accuses "Big Money" of protecting crime. He accuses Frank of every base action. In his vew, "the Blacks act bestially but never commit sodomy. The Black will never take the female in an unnatural way. The brutal negro can act like a beast but it is the degenerate product of money and culture that resorts to sodomy."[79]

After multiple judicial attempts that all fail in Frank's despairing case, after failed verdict reversals, Frank's lawyers consult with Oliver Wendell Holmes, the famous liberal judge of the Supreme Court, whose reputation is prodigious. To their disappointment, Holmes, after having examined the progress of the trial in Georgia, pronounces himself (despite all of the incidents, the pressure of the mob, Frank's absence during the verdict announcement) bound by the judgement of the Supreme Court of Georgia and considers that Frank had access to a fair trial, even though he said that "mob law does not become due process of law by securing the assent of a terrorized jury." On November 30, Frank's supporters present the same case to the United States Supreme Court. Marshall has written the defense memorandum. Fearing a reversal, in early December Watson attacks the national press, "the conspiracy of Big Money against the law, against the courts, and against the poor little victim of hellish passion" that support Frank's cause. He scorns these "Jewish newspapers" that reject the testimony of an African American and adds: "Yet in the Frank case, the great point emphasized by the World and the other Jewish papers is, that a witness against Frank was a negro. It seems that negroes are good enough to kill our ballots, make our laws, hold office, sleep in our beds, eat at our tables, marry our daughters, and mongrelize the Anglo-Saxon race, but are not good enough to hear testimony against a rich Jew!"[80] And Watson adds:

> Here we have the pleasure-loving Jewish business man
>> Here we have the Gentile girl
>> Here we have the typical young libertine Jew. . . . Jews of this type have a utter contempt for law and a ravenous appetite for the forbidden fruit—a lustful eagerness enhanced by the racial novelty of the girls of the uncircumcised![81]

On December 7, a few days following these brutal remarks, the United States Supreme Court rejects Frank's final appeal, which had been based on a procedural error. It considers the error insufficient to question the judgment of the court of a federal state. Marshall perseveres and manages to convince the Supreme Court to accept an appeal. It meets on February 25, 1914, hears Marshall defend the idea of an unfair trial held in front of a hostile audience whose murmurs can be heard even within the tribunal. He also laments Frank's absence during the verdict. After having heard the representatives of the State of Georgia, the court takes its time to deliberate, and on April 19, in a seven to two decision, announces the *Frank v. Mangum* decision: it considers that Frank did get a fair and just trial, that the jury was normally constituted, that the appeals were legally rejected, and that as a consequence it could only approve the decisions arrived at by previous judicious instances.[82] The judges Oliver Wendell Holmes and Charles Evans Hughes write the minority opinion, a vigorous challenge rejecting any judgment taken under the pressure of the "law of the mob." They accused "a savage mob" of having influenced the jury and "declared that lynch law as little valid when practiced by a regular drawn jury as when administered by one elected by a mob intent on death."[83]

Frank's fate is now hopeless. Many of his lawyers offer to implore a pardon. Frank begins by refusing, proclaiming that "my vindication will eventually come, I feel certain; Whether I will live to see it, I cannot tell. I am human enough to want to live to see it, for it is my right and my duty. But I may not; I may suffer death. Still one thing is sure. The truth cannot be executed." He is nevertheless convinced to write this request, which will give his defense more time. Waiting for his execution, Frank reasserts his innocence, pointing out that his execution would not avenge Mary Phagan's death, that he would suffer for another's crime, and that the future would bring his absolution. The ultimate decision is John Slaton's, the governor, for whom the decision is entirely dependent on Frank's guilt. Should he not be guilty, then he ought to be saved from becoming a victim of injustice on the basis that he is a Jew. He does not want to give the impression that the governor of Georgia cannot provide justice to a Jew, reiterating that his own feelings toward Jews may be judged from the fact that his law partner of nineteen years is a Jew.

Petitions in favor of Frank's cause circulate throughout the United States, signed by two million people: they are addressed to John Slaton. The vice president of the United States, many senators, governors, and heads of the biggest newspapers also implore Governor Slaton to pardon Frank. On May 27, Watson publishes a menacing text in the *Jeffersonian*: "If the Prison Commission or the Governor undertake to undo—in whole or in part—what has been legally done by the courts that were established for that purpose, *there will be almost inevitably the bloodiest riot ever known in the history of the South.*"[84] Hundreds of men and women, all opposed to any form of clemency, from the outskirts of Atlanta, gather outside the prison. They quickly number over a thousand, and chant "lynch him." On July 6, there are twenty-five hundred protesting against clemency. After a vote of two to one, the commission for clemency has rejected the pardon, and thus the final decision rests on Slaton's shoulders. He takes his time, shuts himself away at home to reflect, and comes to determine his final position as serenely as possible. His house is protected by the armed forces. He spends the day reflecting. His spouse asks him, "Have you made a decision?" "Yes," Slaton replies, "this could mean my death or worse, but I have decided to commute the sentence." He adds: "The performance of my duty under the Constitution is a matter of my conscience. . . . I cannot stand the constant companionship of an accusing conscience which would remind me in every thought that I, governor of Georgia, failed to do what I thought to be right." His spouse leans over and replies, "I would rather be the widow of an honorable and brave man than the wife of a coward."[85] The *New York Times* adds: "Had Georgia sent Frank to the gallows, would the good name of the State would have been blackened and its people have been under reproach? Governor Slaton has saved Georgia from himself. He has made his name illustrious."[86]

Slaton refuses to have Frank's blood on his conscience, and in his eyes the guilty party is Conley. A few days later, he adds: "a good two thousand years ago, another governor delivered without hesitation a Jew to the mob. For two thousand years, the name of this governor has been cursed. If today another Jew is put in his grave because of my inability to fulfill my duty, I would have been guilty of murder. I can plow and hoe and live in obscurity if necessary but I could not afford not to commute him."[87] In this atmosphere of latent violence, law enforcement quickly comes to grab Frank to protect him and take him by train outside the city to another establishment in Milledgeville, given the uproar immediately upon learning of the pardon. Over five thousand people mobilize for vengeance. Slaton is hanged in effigy with signs saying "King of Jews" and "a traitor to Georgia." The angry mob goes to his house and the entire fifth regiment has just enough time to intervene and place itself between the governor and his wife and the demonstrators who seek his death. While the national news welcomes Slaton's brave decision, Watson, whose newspaper sales increase every day, going in just a few weeks from twenty-five thousand to eighty-seven thousand issues sold daily, cannot hide his rage:

> Jew money has debased us, bought us and sold us-and laughs at us. Bought and sold! Cried off the auction block and knock down to Big Money!
>
> ONE LAW FOR THE RICH, AND ANOTHER FOR THE POOR! . . .
>
> The Haas Finance Committee and its cooperative organizations do not intent that rank shall be punished at all, for the rape and murder he committed on the Gentile girl!
>
> In their eyes she was legitimate prey: and with their Unlimited Money and Invisible Power, they have established the precedent in Georgia that no Jew shall suffer capital punishment for a crime committed on a Gentile"[88]

A militia comprised of around five hundred men, calling themselves the Knights of Mary Phagan, intends to "have Slaton and Frank." An organization called the Vigilance Committee of Marietta puts up signs on stores owned by Jewish merchants:

"You are hereby notified to close up this business and quit Marietta by Saturday night. Or else stand the consequences. We mean to rid Marietta of all Jews by the above date. You can heed this warning or stand the punishment the committee may see fit to deal out to you." Post cards written in red ink are sent to non-Jewish city dwellers, inviting them to only buy from stores owned by Christians, in order to "show their true American blood." Watson demands that "Slaton's blood flow."[89]

Responding to Watson's call, a group of men from Marietta, comprised of some of the same men that belong to the militia, meet and organize with the goal of secretly going to Frank's new prison, about 150 miles from the city, kidnap, and hang him. Among them is the mayor of Marietta, a judge, many lawyers, one of whom has a seat in the Senate—Joseph Brown, once governor of Georgia—ex-officers, a group of prominent locals surrounded by officials in charge of road infrastructure, as well as men capable of leading the operation: mechanics, electricians, phone specialists, doctors, and a few henchmen. Twenty-five men leave for war.

In this atmosphere, Watson's latest editorial ignites a powder keg:

> The question is
>     Do the rich Jews want to create among the Gentile of this country the same deep dislike which they have created everywhere else?
>     There must be some general cause for the universal feelings against the Jews in Spain, in France, in Russia, in Poland, in Hungary.
>     What is that cause?
>     Why is it that all Caucasian races, in the Old World, are "prejudiced" against the Jews. . . . ?

If they continue their rancorous and villainous abuse of the people who wanted Leo Frank punished for his awful crime, they will raise a tempest which they cannot control.[90]

On July 13, the group of avengers sets off, but the alarm was sounded. Troops surround the prison, and the militia does not manage to reach Milledgeville that night. Saturday, July 17, inside the prison, a fellow inmate approaches Frank's bed in the night and stabs him. Deeply wounded, Frank's condition is worrisome. On July 22, the *Jeffersonian* runs the headline: "the butcher-knife used had been in operation during the day killing hogs. Kosher!!!" The tension continues to rise in the city and its outskirts. On August 12, the *Jeffersonian* writes: "Let the rich Jew beware. The next Jew who does the same that Frank did is going to get exactly the same thing that we give to the negro rapist."

On August 16, the group of twenty-five men silently leave the city. They are armed with pistols and rifles and they manage to reach Milledgeville at night without incident, cut the telephone lines, and, with the help of accomplices inside the prison, enter the building, grab Frank, and disappear into the night without encountering any opposition. It was decided that he would be lynched above Mary's grave, but it is ultimately at Frey Gin, two miles away from Marietta, that Frank is hanged from an oak tree. Having repeated many times that he was innocent, calm, Frank dies without fear and, according to his assassins, with great dignity.[91]

The following day, the press runs headlines of Frank's kidnapping by an angry mob. Starting at 8 a.m., as the *Georgian* tells it, it is "like a religious ceremony." Thousands of people rush to see the lynching; it resembles a pilgrimage. People yell "Murderer! Sodomite! Jew! Yankee!" pushing toward the disarticulated

body of Frank, exposing his intimate parts, proof for this mob
of his degeneration. The body is beaten. People take photos of
each other, enjoy themselves, buy postcards showing Frank's
hanged body. They buy pieces of the rope, and many wealthy
inhabitants offer $250 for the tree in which he was hanged.[92]

Taken to New York by train, Frank's casket, surrounded by
his wife and some prominent Jews who defended him, is buried
in Queens. The Georgian press, like the national news, laments
this tragic end that, as the *Chicago Tribune* writes, constitutes "a
reproach and a danger to the American Republic." A crowd of
over twenty thousand Jews, many recent immigrants, crying,
stunned that the persecutions they knew in Ukraine or Warsaw
could occur in the United States, accompany his body. As many
assemble at the intersection in front of Cooper Union in New
York City. People lament, applaud a speaker who evokes the fate
of Captain Dreyfus in France, "a nation less advanced than ours,"
but where Dreyfus was declared innocent before being reinte-
grated into the army, whereas in the United States, the country
of freedom and of freedom of religion, Frank knew a dreadful
fate. And, spontaneously repeating the words of Bialik in "In the
City of Slaughter," they wonder: "isn't it because American Jews
are not organized? They are wusses!!!! Go on! Come together!"[93]
The Jewish press laments the relative inaction of the federal state
in halting lynchings, those of African Americans as well as that
of Frank, which cannot be left to the goodwill of the authorities
in the South, comparing this inaction to the czar's attitude during the pogroms.[94]

Watson does not back away: in September, he takes it out on
the Golden Calf, denouncing "the libertine Jews who abuse our
sisters," and warns: "The assassination of myself would be a signal
for a bloody outbreak against the Jews. The outbreak would not
be confined to Georgia. This country has never had riots against

Jews, as all European countries have had but the same causes, if they exist here, will produce the same results as elsewhere." This is reflected in the coming months by the rebirth of the Ku Klux Klan, which resumes its racist battle against African Americans but also against the Jews. It is also reflected in the number of Jews who opt to leave Atlanta, and finally by the birth of the now essential civil rights organization, the Anti-Defamation League. Another consequence is the triumphant election of prosecutor Dorsey as governor in 1916, a position he would hold until 1921, and also that of John Wood, who was part of the lynching expedition and would hold a seat in Congress lasting several mandates. In 1955, Wood no longer in Congress, President Eisenhower wishes to appoint him to a national committee for subversive actions, but is faced with the determined opposition of prominent figures who accuse him of antisemitism and of still being a Klan member. Finally, and more symbolically, Watson is elected to the United States Senate, an incredible triumph for this antisemitic tribune who will acquire national glory, receiving an official government funeral in Atlanta upon his death in 1926, on the occasion of which the Ku Klux Klan will send a cross of red roses in his homage. His statue is still now raised facing Atlanta government buildings. The story does not end here. The Frank affair does not disappear from memory: in 1961, a white supremacist group claims that "Leo Frank was part of a project to 'mongrelize' Southern white womanhood" and that the true goal of the 1954 *Brown v. Board* ruling that imposed desegregation of schools was to "get revenge for the lynching of Frank."[95]

In the 1980s, things picked up speed. In an unexpected turn of events, in December of 1983, an eighty-year-old man publicly confessed that he had seen, with his own eyes, Conley murder the little Mary Phagan. He had spoken about it to his mother at the time, and she had told him to keep quiet out of fear of retaliation. A first request for a posthumous pardon on Frank's behalf was then put forward and rejected. Faced with this possibility, the Ku Klux Klan marched in their robes through Marietta. But in 1986 the commission finally granted the pardon, taking into account that Frank did not benefit from his constitutional rights by not being protected from the mob in prison.

The story could have ended there, with Frank's guilt or innocence still unknown. In 2013, on the centenary of Frank's arrest, the question was taken up again without any definitive answers acceptable to everyone.[96] The controversy returned yet again in 2015, on the centenary of Frank's lynching. The relative silence surrounding his lynching is then compared to the public's silence in matters of social justice that gave rise to the Black Lives Matter movement. Conversely, the antisemitic and nationalist alt-right attaches great importance to this distant event, which it mentions constantly. Indeed, the man responsible for the Intelligence Project of the Southern Poverty Law Center declares that "the Leo Frank case is interesting in that you're never going to meet a Nazi who doesn't know about it."[97] It seems to "galvanize the white supremacy community" since it retells "accounts of Jewish blood libel, myths of Jews using the blood of gentile children in sacrifice rituals, in medieval Russian villages." We reconsider this tragedy, finding in it lessons to help us understand the *fake news* that are turning many of today's American citizens "crazy."[98]

Such was the lightning strike that the Leo Frank affair symbolized in the American sky, a tragedy about which Salo Baron remained strangely silent. It is because this event alone challenged American exceptionalism and the innocent view of pluralism so lauded by Tocqueville. It is true that Tom Watson was

not Édouard Drumont, even if he shared his unbridled antisemitism. He did not benefit from the support of the same powerful antisemitic leagues that were rampant in France. Nonetheless, he did have the support of the Ku Klux Klan to carry
out his antisemitic campaign, which in many respects recalled
Europe's tearful history. And thus suddenly emerged the antisemitic torments of the old continent, the Russian or Ukrainian
pogroms, the blood libels, making a resurgence in the memory
of American Jews, but also in that of Frank's murderers and
their contemporary successors. We are no longer talking about
exclusion from selective clubs, prohibitions against entering
certain hotels, prejudices voiced more or less loudly, but about
the actual brutal lynching of a Jew by a mob drunk on antisemitic literature.

It is true that the execution of one Jew is in no way comparable to the Kishinev pogrom,[99] in which the number of victims,
dead or wounded, lay in the hundreds. Nevertheless, many play-
ers at the time spontaneously mentioned the period of the Russian pogroms, so taken aback were they by Frank's murder at the
hands of this savage mob of antisemites responding to the call
of a populist leader, explicitly inspired by the Russian pogroms,
to put an end to the power of degenerate rich Jews. And, indeed,
the references to Kishinev during Frank's trial were endless: in
1915, the *Washington Observer* stated that Georgia could help
organize a pogrom, given how much more efficient cars were
than the ponies on which the Cossacks traveled. That same year,
the *Toronto Mail Empire* considered the citizens of Atlanta "to
have about the same opinions of Jews as the people of Kishinev."[100]
In the context of the Frank affair, Zangwill's immensely popular *The Melting Pot* aroused an unforeseen parallel between the
pogroms and the Atlanta tragedy. In the end, the American melting pot, so admired for its supposed merger of all ethnicities,

turns out to be an illusion. And as the *Chicago Defender* wondered, "it must follow as the night the day that as yesterday a
negro was lynched, what is to prevent a white from being lynched
tomorrow? And if one white man, why not another?"[101] As for
the rabbi Henry Berkowitz, his 1914 Philadelphia sermon compared Frank's fate with the 1911 blood libel made against Mendel Beilis in Russia.[102] In other words, it was suddenly the suffering endured by Russian Jews that haunts recently emigrated
American Jews.

On the scale of the United States, of a society that had never
before been confronted with this degree of antisemitic violence,
the Leo Frank affair was a source of worry and trouble in American Jewish circles, becoming a long-term part of Jewish memory, serving as a warning and a threat that they would not forget,
that they still remember today, a kind of "talisman."[103] The fact
remains that, in reality, there are radical differences between
Atlanta and Kishinev. For starters, law enforcement obeyed the
authorities and did what it could to protect Frank, whereas the
same cannot be said for Russian pogromists. Once the decision
to pardon him was known, local law enforcement, like Federal
troops, attempted to avoid the worst: they stood guard in front
of Slaton's home and sought to avoid Frank's lynching by moving him quickly to shelter. Moreover, part of the local press, as
well as the national news and public opinion, did not hide their
enmity toward the way Frank's trial unfolded. Nothing of the
sort occurred in Russia. Governor Slaton, friends with many
Jews, courageously took Frank's side, despite the threats weigh-
ing over him.

Besides Kishinev, American consciousness was also marked
by that other important event whose resonance is global: the
Dreyfus affair.[104] Many of the protagonists of the tragedy that
befell Leo Frank also spontaneously recalled this tragic event,

which had only recently concluded with the acquittal of Captain Dreyfus in 1906. Frank himself, upon learning that a journalist from *Collier's Weekly* had decided to join the battle on his side, exclaimed, "I trust that you may prove to be my Zola."[105] The protagonists of this tragic event showed detailed, though at times inaccurate, knowledge of the affair. Thus, the head of the populist movement against Frank, Watson, writes:

> Does anybody in this country know what was true about Dreyfus, the French officer who was convicted of treason and, at first, sentenced to death?
>
> Nobody does. All we know is what the newspapers told us; and it leaked out, long afterwards, that the wife of Dreyfus abandoned him, as soon as he was turned loose.
>
> Presumably she was Jewess, but, like the other Hebrew champions of Dreyfus, she dropped him as soon as she had accomplished her purpose.
>
> One of the Rothschild banking houses exerts a powerful influence over French finances; another in Frankfort, another in Vienna and another in London, have often stood together to control the policies of European government; if they insisted upon the liberation of Dreyfus, the French Republic—beset by royalists, socialists and clerical, was in no condition to resist the demand.
>
> The peculiar thing and the sinister thing, is that secret organization existed which could permeate the whole European world and the United States, also, with the literature which clamored for Dreyfus.
>
> The French officer, Ricard, who was the staunch champion of Dreyfus in every one of the investigations turned against the Jew after he himself was given a position in the War Office and learned the truth from indubitable evidence.

Has the menace of a secret organization, of an Invisible Power
and of cynical defiance of law, revealed itself, in the Frank case?[106]

Obviously, everything—or almost—is inaccurate in this narration. Lucie Dreyfus never left her husband; quite the contrary,
she passionately defended him. Picquart (and not Ricard) did not
discover the documents used to accuse Dreyfus, nor was Dreyfus condemned to death. This supposed secret organization is but
a fabrication that announces the creation of the *Protocols of the
Elders of Zion*, etc. Yet this imaginary narration was used to
denounce the role of New York and Chicago Jews who tried to
save Frank. It was a call to a populist mobilization against the
international Jewish committee that sought to save one of their
own. It confirmed the place of the Dreyfus affair in the memory
of those who interpreted it the way they wished to in accordance
with their own view of the Frank affair. As ultimate proof of the
way in which his words are a confirmation of his view on the
Dreyfus affair, Watson quotes at length Bernard Lazare's book
on antisemitism,[107] a hostile anti-Jewish pamphlet that Lazare
himself regretted publishing.

Reuben Arnold, one of Frank's attorneys, believed on the contrary that this violence against Frank evoked "the savagery and
the venom of the Dreyfus Affair."[108] For many, Frank was an
innocent "American Dreyfus."[109] In September of 1913, Louis
Marshall received letters from many anxious Jews. One of them
wrote: "I would like your help in what is without a doubt a Dreyfus Affair that has just occurred in Atlanta," and another insists
on the fact that it is "a second Dreyfus Affair."[110] And, as we have
already mentioned, it is the example of Captain Dreyfus that
immediately comes to Louis Marshall's mind, stunned as he is
by the unimaginable events in Atlanta.[111] Similarly, when Louis

Brandeis wrote a letter to the jurist Roscoe Pound, he emphasized that "in talking with Felix Frankfurter this morning about
the Frank case and Justice Holmes' memorandum, he told me
that you were convinced that Frank had not had a fair trial and that
he was not guilty, and that this was another Dreyfus case."[112]
Three of the greatest jurists of the time also shared this belief, two
of whom were about to become members of the United States
Supreme Court.

Many are those who, with varying degrees of accuracy, evoke
the precedence of the Dreyfus affair. Thus, closely following after
Frank's burial, a New York City official said during the course
of a meeting: "In France, not as far advanced as our country,
Dreyfus had ultimately been exonerated of spying accusations
and restored to his military rank." Why is it so? Because "the
Jews of America are not organized. They are weaklings. Come,
rise!"[113] Later, Governor Slaton, who took the brave decision to
pardon Frank at his peril, wrote in 1954, just a few months before
his death on December 11, 1955, a memorandum since placed in
Georgia's National Archives. Returning at length to the unfolding of the Frank affair, and to Watson's antisemitic campaign,
he references the Dreyfus affair once again and mentions the
false testimony of Esterhazy who, once found out, allowed Dreyfus to be called away from the drilling grounds in France.

> Medals and other testimonials of honor were torn from his uni-
> form and he was sent to Devil's Island where he remained five
> years.
>
> At the end of that time, it was discovered that he was con-
> victed on the testimony of Count Esterhazy, who admitted he
> committed perjury. Thereupon, Dreyfus was granted an uncon-
> ditional pardon and was brought back on the drilling grounds and
> all his honors restored to him. It was solely a matter of justice. I

write the above and a statement of the facts as they came to me and I was compelled to do the same thing and had the only alternative been with me to grant an unconditional, or an absolute pardon, I should have granted an absolute pardon. The effect of this action upon my future career was a matter of no consequence. Had I done otherwise, I should have been haunted the remainder of my life, which would have been very short, with the conviction that I committed a murder.[114]

The fact that Captain Dreyfus's fate is consistently alluded to by so many actors in this tragedy only serves to confirm, much like the reference to Kishinev, the intrusion of a history built of tears all the way into the Deep American South. A history that is, moreover, shared by all actors, be they Jewish or not, partisans or adversaries of Frank. Even today these affairs arouse much passion and, for some, such uncertainty that they still doubt Captain Dreyfus's innocence as well as Leo Frank's! In 2008, the Atlanta William Breman Jewish Heritage and Holocaust Museum organized a remarkable exhibit entitled *Seeking Justice* around the Leo Frank affair by taking into account a local context in which some remain convinced of Frank's guilt.[115] Be that as it may, Dreyfus, after having been pardoned against his will like Frank, was finally found innocent in 1906 by the Court of Appeals, whereas Frank never was, and the uncertainty, the suspicion, remains. To such an extent that in the final months of 2019 a commission was created, comprised of a number of former judges, a former governor born in Marietta, as well as academics, whose goal was to prove Frank's innocence, igniting the anger of Mary Phagan's great-niece, who has loudly protested.[116] Steve Oney, who dedicated his life to the meticulous study of the Frank affair, did not always hide his hesitation, staying more than prudent, allowing doubt to remain. Through the formation of this commission, he hoped to finally have an indisputable answer thanks to the rigorous study of the handwritten notes found next to Mary's body, which Conley admitted to writing.[117] According to him, Mary's murder remains a "mystery,"[118] and he judged that antisemitism played no part in the course of the trial. In a conference given in Savannah on February 17, 2020, he confirmed that "there is no new fact that can change the verdict,"[119] a doubt that echoes the convoluted comments on Dreyfus's innocence still uttered today.[120] At that same time, others considered that this Frank affair was built upon fake news, which led to his condemnation.[121] Film and television also seized upon the Frank affair, reviving his memory even recently, as in *Murder in Harlem* (1936), *They Won't Forget* (1937), *Profiles in Courage*, which celebrates John Slaton's courage, *The Murder of Mary Phagan* (1988), and *The People vs. Leo Frank* (2009), all returning to this tragedy without bringing a definitive answer to the true unfolding of events.[122]

In reality, the Frank affair is radically different from the Dreyfus affair, if only because the innocence of the latter was the only one to be recognized by the Court of Appeals, whereas the former's remains controversial. France's strong state knew how to protect Dreyfus from all physical attacks and admit his innocence, whereas the weak American state and the Georgian state alike turned out to be powerless. The American federal government played no role in the Frank affair, while the French state had a central role in the Dreyfus affair. Faced with this kind of unseen and exceptional antisemitic mobilization in the United States, the federal government did not interfere, despite reiterated pleas by Jewish circles, and Frank was hanged. Conversely, in France, the state was capable of confronting angry mobs. The United States was not living through an antisemitic moment of national scope the way that France was. No mobs of hundreds of thousands of people amassed, as in 1898, throughout the land to cry "Death to the Jews!" without succeeding in killing a single one,[123] whereas this unseen burst of antisemitic populism achieved its aim in the United States. It seized Frank and lynched him. This tradition of lynching, so alive when it comes to the African American population, shows the state's lack of control, the powerlessness of the armed forces, and explains Frank's lynching, an inconceivable event for centuries in France where public power alone can render justice.

And yet strange parallels have come to light between both cases. Dreyfus and Frank exhibited the same behavior. Proud and certain of their rights, they aroused little sympathy. Frank's wife Lucille and Dreyfus's Lucie both showed unparalleled love and dedication. The role played by Marshall—the great nationally renowned New York lawyer who attempted to exert influence over national actors and intervened with the Supreme Court— calls to mind that of Joseph Reinach, the deputy at the center of the French political body who played a major role in the fight to prove Dreyfus's innocence. But the parallels end there: one was a state Jew in France whose legal actions occurred at the heart of public institutions with which he was familiar, whereas Marshall was an American lawyer who attempted to mobilize the civil society of a nation whose state is weak and decentralized. Henceforth, Reinach is an important participant in the battle to exonerate Dreyfus, while Marshall failed at his task. On the other hand, Tom Watson's antisemitic ire shares similarities with Édouard Drumont's vindication, which was much more violent, but directed against the government Jews of a strong state and not against a prominent figure in the American South. These indisputable parallels have not escaped contemporary historians who have worked on the Leo Frank affair.[124]

Two crucial and almost identical moments occurred over the course of the two affairs: Alfred Dreyfus arrived completely innocently to the convocation by the army. To his great astonishment, he was asked to sit and write a strange text he knew nothing about. This unexpected and inexplicable dictation played an essential part in the accusation of treason that would be directed against him. Expert upon expert would examine this dictation. Alphonse Bertillon, the great graphologist, swore that Dreyfus's writing, that of the famous dictation, was the same as the famous note found by the housekeeper of the German Embassy, confirming the treason of a French serviceman. Other experts contradicted this similarity, supposed to be incontestable proof of Dreyfus's treason. Confusion settled in, conspiracies flew. The dictation and its comparison would play an essential role in Dreyfus's conviction. Others would later challenge this similarity. A similar controversy concerning the famous partly unintelligible notes found next to Mary Phagan's body plagued the Frank affair. Again, authorities wondered: who could have written them or have solicited someone else to write them? Who could have dictated these texts whose vocabulary and syntax are so strange? According to one observer, "no white man, of the North or the South, could be capable of writing such notes. A white man cannot imitate them. They are entirely written by negroes." Did they point to the killer? Were they written to conceal him? Seeming to prove Conley's guilt, were they written at Frank's request, under pressure, in exchange for a payment? If Frank ordered them to be written, was it to point the finger at Lee, the night watchman, which might explain the term "night witch?" Might not this expression be more evocative of the Black legend according to which Black children cry at night when night witches fly over them? If nobody wakes them up, they are found the next morning with a rope around their necks, like the little

Mary Phagan, a superstition that Frank could not have known about since he had a "weak knowledge of negroes."[125] Conley denied this by swearing he was unable to write, which Frank contradicted, stating that Conley knew perfectly well how to write, that he has received numerous written requests for money signed with his name.[126] Though Conley was considered stupid according to prevailing prejudices of the time, he would have never written or used the word *negro*. In reality, the dictation to which Conley was subjected recalls the literary tests given to African Americans, but instead of succeeding, he had to fail, use "dis" and "dat," in order to prove an innocence that was reliant on his poor knowledge of correct English. Prosecutor Dorsey, an old Southerner who called Conley "Old negro" according to regional customs, pushed him to fail in order to prove Frank's guilt.[127] The question was: what vocabulary *did* Conley master? Thus, he maintained during his interrogation that he could read "dis" and "dat," but his attorney, William Smith, argued that he never used "dis" and "dat," but rather "this" and "that," which proved his guilt, his manipulation of the found notes, a fact recognized by Conley himself. Another observer stated that a Northerner could not speak "negro," did not know that they used "dis" or "dat," and as such Frank could not have dictated these notes.[128] Another, on the contrary, underscored Frank's great intelligence, as a Jew who easily mastered all languages, as they are all allegedly capable of doing, and believed he was absolutely the author of these notes. Reuben Arnold, one of Frank's attorney's, disagreed: "The man who wrote these notes is the murderer. Prove that that man was there, that he wrote these notes, and you will find the assassin. Conley admits he has written these notes and witnesses admit he was present in the building."[129] Just like the dictation to which Dreyfus subjected himself, Conley's played quite a crucial role in the trial to prove or

disprove his innocence or guilt and, moreover, Frank's innocence
or guilt.

Other similarities are evident, for example, as concerns sexuality: Alfred Dreyfus was accused of having illegitimate relations
with women, and rumors of homosexuality of some of the central characters in this affair were constantly insinuated in court
and police records.[130] Similarly, in his frenzied delusion, Watson
praised Mary Phagan's innocence, this pure young woman
depraved by a Jew, somewhat like how Drumont praised the
innocence and the purity of the blond, allegedly assassinated at
Fourmies under the command of a Jew.[131] Above all, Dreyfus and
Frank were accused of all manner of sexual baseness. They were
ascribed innumerable mistresses and were even accused of homosexuality. The sexual aspect of these cases was undeniable: it
echoed the mythological representation of perverse and sex-
hungry Jews, of strange accusations, Frank having supposedly
participated in unnatural sex practices—sodomy but also cun-
nilingus and sexual acts involving his nose—and of having, from
this perspective, an abnormal body. He was also accused of
having sexual obsessions that led him to spy on young female
factory workers while they changed into their work clothes, of
wanting to seduce them at the expense of the white male workers, and of thus being at the origin of an unacceptable social
disturbance. He was accused of attacking the virtue of the
young women in the city, of being a regular patron of the area's
brothels, of attempting to pimp out some of his female workers
and of reducing them to slave work. Frank was also described in
some testimonies as a homosexual with ambiguous mannerisms.

The ensuing social anxiety could be said to have led the
Atlanta mobs to express their rage against a man who undermined their authority and their control over the virtuous young

women of the city. The arrival of this Jew from the decadent and industrialized North, a foreigner to the rural South, whose customs threatened white supremacy, was cause for great fear. In this imaginary conception of the world, the factory was metamorphosed into a place of debauchery where young female factory workers openly flirted, freeing themselves from the control of their parents, who were deeply attached to social conservatism, and were put in danger by these "dirty Jews" who used their wealth to seduce poor young virtuous girls. This anxiety was also transferred from African Americans to Jews, considered just as perverse and brutal, and who could only be punished by lynching, with complete disregard for the protections of rights and laws. White men thus intended to reconstruct a mythical community where they remained the masters of their home, far from government control. Frank's lynching symbolized, from this perspective, the power of a people who proudly applied their own laws. From then on, "the Frank case could never have incited the passions it did without changes in female behavior and family relations as the context, and without the charged issues of sexuality and power between the sexes and generations as the trigger."[132] And thus the torments and anxieties of Old Europe came pouring out in the United States. The rumors that had haunted centuries of the old continent regarding the sexual perversity of the Jews have come to affect the American continent right at its innocent center, the rural South.

# 3

# FROM THE *JEW DEAL* TO THE STORMING OF THE CAPITOL

When Philip Roth imagined the seizure of power in 1940 by the antisemitic populist Charles Lindbergh in his 2004 novel *The Plot Against America*, he indicated that "the sheer surprise of the Lindbergh nomination had activated an atavistic sense of being undefended that had more to do with Kishinev and the pogroms of 1903."[1] As Lindbergh secures his hold over the country and reigns through terror, one of the novel's protagonists says to his son upon catching him painting the portrait of a pretty peasant whose "physique has titillated him":

> "You never heard of Leo Frank? You never heard of the Jew they lynched in Georgia because of that little factory girl? Stop *drawing* her, damn it! . . . For Christ's sake, put those drawing things away, and don't draw any more girls!" . . . The famous 1913 case of poor Mary Phagan—found dead with a noose around her neck on the floor of the pencil factory basement after going to Frank's office on the day of the murder to collect her pay envelope. . . . At about that time my father, an impressionable boy of twelve who'd only recently left school to help support his family was at work in an East Orange hat factory obtaining a first-class

education there in the commonplace libel that linked him inextricably to the crucifiers of Christ. After Frank's conviction . . . a lynch mob of respectable citizens finished the job by abducting Frank from his jail cell and—much to the satisfaction of my father's co-workers on the factory floor—hanging "the sodomite" from a tree in Marietta, Georgia (Mary Phagan's hometown) as a public warning to other "Jewish libertines" to stay the hell out of the South and away from their women.

To be sure, the Frank case was only a part of the history that fed my father's sense of danger in rural West Virginia on the afternoon of October 15, 1942. It all goes further back than that.[2]

In his uchronia featuring an America that has turned its back on democracy and surrendered to Lindbergh's antisemitic populism,[3] the Leo Frank and Kishinev tragedies have once again found their place. The story opens with Franklin Roosevelt's election and the implementation of the New Deal, which in turn arouses a virulent antisemitism echoing the one that reigned freely during the Frank affair and whose vehemence was comparable to the Kishinev pogrom. Roth imagines that Charles Lindbergh secures the presidency in reaction to the New Deal. A famous aviator-turned-antisemite, Lindbergh puts an end to this dangerous period with an even worse nightmare: the establishment of a Nazi regime in the United States, complete with its police surveillance and its camps. As J. M. Coetzee observes, "that is what the plot of Roth's title is meant to achieve and, at the level of the imaginary, does achieve: to expel Jews from America. *Juden raus.* That is what Philip cannot forget."[4] In this novel, the Jewish hero who is pitted against Lindbergh and who obstinately refuses any compromise while many others rally with him, spontaneously remembers the Frank affair in 1942, as well as the approval of Frank's colleagues, satisfied by his hanging.

This shows the pervasiveness of the memory of the Frank case in the 1940s.

Today, the Trump years have given Roth's novel an unforeseen and worrisome relevance, as though Lindbergh's rise to power had been repeated in real life despite Roth himself, who remained, despite his fable, confident in the resilience of American democracy.[5] As if Philip Roth's warning has suddenly taken on its full impact, meaning that "it can happen" in the United States, that fascism under the push of extreme populism can also reach the shores of the New World.[6] At the end of January 2017, soon after Donald Trump's accession to the White House, Roth opined that "it is easier to comprehend the election of an imaginary President like Charles Lindbergh than an actual President like Donald Trump."[7] The following year, before passing away on May 22, 2018, he compared Trump to the populist and anti-semitic Charles Lindbergh, the hero of his uchronia, by underscoring their shared racism, before adding that, if Lindbergh was a hero, "Trump, by comparison, is a massive fraud, the evil sum of his deficiencies, devoid of everything but the hollow ideology of a megalomaniac."[8]

Starting in September of 2016, even before Donald Trump's victory, many were those who made references to Roth's prescient work to confirm that "this happens in the United States": without a doubt, "Trump and Lindbergh share an isolationist ethos that bleeds into ethno-nationalism," they have in common a "shared xenophobia and explicitly racist rhetoric" that denotes "a resurgence of white nationalism that we'd rather believe remains buried in the past."[9] In 2016, the Lindbergh era is different from Trump's on one essential point: "anti-Semitism had ceased to be a major problem in the United States by 2004. And, though Roth makes anti-Jewish riots in Boston and Detroit seem plausible in 1942, they are unimaginable in 2004, despite the increasing intrusion of Christian symbolism and doctrine into public discourse and policy."[10] This overly optimistic premonition will practically be contradicted a few years later when 60 percent of American Jews claim to have been victims of antisemitic acts or confirm they have heard comments that were hostile to Jews.[11] In the context of the powerful rise of the radical American right, it is not surprising the Leo Frank affair is also often mentioned, appearing on numerous extremist websites, in order to demonstrate, in the past as today, the guilt of the Jews.[12] Forever present in the memory of American Jews, the lynching of Leo Frank reappears, as a leitmotiv, in the work of many observers of contemporary America,[13] as though a cycle of antisemitic hate were becoming more explicit day by day, leading straight from the Leo Frank of the New Deal to Charlottesville and then to Pittsburgh.[14]

The uchronia imagined by Philip Roth calls to mind the one that Sinclair Lewis elaborated in the 1930s in his novel *It Can't Happen Here*,[15] whose relevance has also been reignited with Donald Trump's arrival to power, and which has revived the question of fascism in the United States. Immediately following Trump's rise to power, Sinclair Lewis's novel became a bestseller and sold out on Amazon.[16] Published before 1935, before Hitler's imposition of Nazi order over all of Germany, Sinclair Lewis's novel imagines in a strikingly prescient manner the different stages of the rise to power of a populist leader; a leader who like Hitler takes on the press and the intellectuals, dismisses Congress, and enforces limitless terror through the creation of camps. The novel became progressively relevant during the last years of Trump's presidency, even as the alt-right became increasingly menacing.[17]

In *It Can't Happen Here*, the most violent antisemitism descends upon the Jewish population, accused of all evils and above all of consorting with communists. A member of this new regime, recently appointed secretary of education, addresses himself to a rabbi using the following words: "Why don't you kikes take a tumble to yourselves and get out, beat it, exeunt bearing corpses, and start a real Zion, say in South America?" When the rabbi retorts with "my people have learned to ignore persecution," thus invoking the eternal history of suffering and tears, the minister takes out his revolver and kills him.[18] With the return of the blood libel, the antisemitism from the old continent, as old as time itself and still alive in Russia, seems to reemerge in this idyllic America, in the perpetuation of some of the delusions we saw surrounding the Leo Frank case. And yet, unlike Roth, Lewis's memory does not dive into this truly Jewish history of America: his uchronia, unlike Roth's, does not bring up the Frank affair. If, in *It Can't Happen Here*, some Jews are expedited to concentration camps, they are hardly alone. On the contrary, all opponents—primarily communists and all antiestablishmentarians—are imprisoned and tortured there. Roth's novel is almost entirely focused on the tragic fate of Jews in Lindbergh's America, whereas Lewis's story, despite having been written less than thirty years after Frank's lynching, is only marginally interested in their unique destiny.

The explosion of antisemitism in the 1930s was indeed radically different from the one that characterized the Frank affair. It could also be distinguished from the era of the pogroms as symbolized by Kishinev. Far from Atlanta, faraway from the Deep South, antisemitic mobilizations against the New Deal were occurring in Washington and New York. Jews were not attacked according to libidinal fantasies, delusions around the particular nature of their bodies or their seduction strategies. It was primarily their political domination that was denounced. It was no longer Russia but indeed French society this time that had exported its own conflicts, its ultra-French wars that fed into a revival of far-right thought during the "Jew Deal," when, in the 1930s, the New Deal implemented by Franklin Roosevelt gave the appearance of a new "Jewish Republic" under Jewish control. Antisemitic violence had found favor among certain thinkers of the far right who were directly inspired by Édouard Drumont's work, which vehemently excoriated a now Jewish France, claiming, daily, "France is for the French." Adopting the conspiratorial view of the author of *Jewish France*, many are those who believe they can reveal the omnipotent power of a Jewish state dominating American society. And thus we find, for the first time, transposed onto the American scene, a political anti-semitism that emerged out of the French counterrevolutionary tradition, an antisemitism previously so foreign and unknown to the United States.

This occurred because the New Deal represented a rupture with America's weak-state society, anchored in Protestantism and fairly closed to the Jews. The latter were granted access to politico-administrative functions belatedly and with difficulty. Oscar Solomon Straus was the first and only Jew appointed, again in 1906, to Theodore Roosevelt's Cabinet. The *Washington Post* describes Strauss as an "American Disraeli," an honor that did not go unnoticed by Édouard Drumont, who saw in it the proof of a Jewish stranglehold over Theodore Roosevelt's administration.[19] At the time, the great private Ivy League universities that produced the majority of the ruling class remained hostile to Jews, enforcing entry quotas until the 1960s, excluding them from fraternities, which were crucial to the formation of long-term friendships and the creation of connections necessary for professional careers. Institutional power remained under the control of a WASP culture that rejected Catholics, African

Americans, and Jews. Access to the State Department remained closed to Jews, as was the vast majority of positions in upper civil or military administration. As an example, in the 1930s, a Dreyfus affair would have been unthinkable in the United States given that no Jew had access to the most eminent positions in the army. We would have to wait for the second half of the twentieth century. From then on, if some violent antisemitic eruptions flared up in the country's periphery, such as in Atlanta, in accordance with antiquated prejudices, if certain forms of social exclusions surfaced in private clubs, beaches, and hotels, a purely political antisemitism remained unthinkable given that Jews were almost entirely excluded from the executive functions of a weakly institutionalized state.

Everything changed with the arrival of Franklin Roosevelt, who turned his back on American exceptionalism, abandoned its liberalism, and challenged the autonomy of the federal states in order to attempt to impose, when faced with the ravages of the 1929 crisis, a more powerful federal state, closer to the French model than to American democracy. Through centralization and interventionist measures, Roosevelt sought to profoundly transform society. Influenced by John Maynard Keynes, he implemented an economic policy buttressed by a state that imposed its management onto large firms. From then on, it was necessary to change the nature of the state, to turn away from a weak and liberal state by adopting the kind of measures that were popular in Europe, particularly in France. In order to do this, Roosevelt fabricated strong "pieces of a state," specific institutions charged with applying his economic strategy in industrial and agricultural sectors. The Industrial Economic Act, as well as the Agricultural Adjustment Act, were like a clap of thunder in an American economic life that was dedicated to free trade. Both immediately stirred the opposition of Wall Street, which had at its disposal important means of influence to be heard in Washington.

Just as in France, this privileged role allotted to the state, or at least to fragments of a strong state, implied the admittance of new elites at the heart of politico-administrative structures: previously excluded, some Jews were now, for the first time, among the appointees. Included among the most famous were Henry Morgenthau Jr., appointed by Roosevelt in 1934 as treasury secretary, a crucial position that he would occupy for a long time during these years of deep economic crises and of vigorous state interventionism, during which time he became responsible for fiscal policies, aid to the unemployed, and monetary reforms. Jerome Frank was appointed at the head of the Agricultural Adjustment Administration, and David Lilienthal became the head of the Tennessee Valley Authority, two strong "fragments of State" with essential functions in these years of rampant unemployment and deep social crisis.[20] As for Felix Frankfurter, a Harvard professor, he represented Roosevelt's *éminence grise*, given how close he was to the president. He could be considered a "tutor for the new Administration," since his proximity to Roosevelt allowed him to influence the appointment of senior officials. In January 1936, according to *Fortune* magazine, Frankfurter is

> the most influential single individual in General Johnson's United States. Mr. Frankurter has "insinuated" his "boys" into "obscure but key positions in every vital department" of the present Administration and is presumably therefore boring at the Constitution of the United States and the American plan of government from within. . . . M. Frankfurter's relation to the appointment of bright young men to fill Washington jobs remains today about what it has been for twenty-odd years.[21]

Frankurter could be seen as a state Jew *à la française*, passionate, as he said himself, about state service: in 1937, in a letter to
Roosevelt, he wrote, that "no aspect of public affairs are more
my business than the improvement of public service as a permanent career open to the nation's most competent." Attracted to
serving a state that would truly ensure the leadership of the
nation, Frankfurter incarnated those mad statesmen who, as in
France, suddenly reach the top of the state thanks to nothing
other than their meritocratic competence, strangers though they
may be to the WASP world and to the Protestant economic elite.
The New Deal allowed, for the first time in American history, a
purely meritocratic access to the state, favorable to the rapid
ascension of outsiders. Louis Brandeis, appointed in 1916 to the
Supreme Court, deeply hostile to management, also actively
assisted President Roosevelt. One must, he always claimed,
exclude the business world from government affairs, something
widely performed in a country whose state is strong but that is
unthinkable in a society whose state is weak and occupied by
external elites. The enthusiasm of American Jews was immense,
and Roosevelt's world fulfilled their expectations: in this way, it
was said at the time that Jews had *dray weltn—di velt, yene velt,
un Roosevelt* (they have three worlds: this world, the future world,
and Roosevelt).[22]

It was not long before the "cabal" denounced by *Fortune* magazine reverberated. Some front-line Jews were particularly targeted, among whom Felix Frankfurter was considered to be the
strong man at the heart of a welfare state that was contrary to
the libertarian and liberal traditions of the United States. It was
against this *Jew Deal* that emerged—as in France, from the
Dreyfus affair to the presidency of Leon Blum—a political antisemitism that denounced the role of Jews at the heart of the

state and the birth of a "Jewish Republic."[23] As it was observed in a report written in 1941, "the more Jews in political positions, the more convincing will the anti-Semitic propaganda appear—the more probably will Jews be used as scapegoats for whatever difficulties the country encounters."[24] As though to confirm this prescient judgment, antisemitic leagues began to form: the White Shirts, the Brown Shirts, the German Nazi Party. Nearly 120 antisemitic organizations emerged, all parading their flags, their banners, their uniforms, according to their Hitlerian model. Demonstrations broke out across the United States. Galvanized mobs performed the Nazi salute after having listened to the inflammatory speeches by Father Coughlin (Charles Edward Coughlin) on the radio, speeches that brought together millions of listeners mesmerized by his vitriolic denunciations of Jewish power. Giant crowds cheered him on in New York. According to Father Coughlin, "the Jew should retire from the field of politics and government. He has no more business in that sphere than has a pig in a china shop."[25] For Franklin Thompson, once rid of its disguise, the New Deal is nothing other than a Ju-Deal. "The present Administration in Washington is predominantly Jewish. . . . Frankfurter may be colloquially termed the lawyer of the Ju-Deal."[26] The populist governor of Louisiana, Huey Long, imposed martial law in his state and ran as Hitler's candidate. For his part, Robert Edmondson spoke out against this "Roosevelt's New Deal, under the influence of powerful Jews holding strategic governmental positions," and one of his followers opined that "Jews and Niggers run France today . . . America will have no Leon Blum."[27] Similarly, William Pelley, the leader of the Silver Shirts, declared: "We know that the various administrative boards would be packed with Jews, all of which leads to the logical conclusion that this entire scheme is one leading up to the wholesale inoculation of Gentiles with vaccine syphilitic germs."[28] For him, Roosevelt was "the first Jewish Kosher president at the head of a great Kosher Administration."[29] While Henry Ford disseminated over seven hundred thousand copies of *The Protocols of the Elders of Zion*, many were those who compared Roosevelt to Leon Blum, the head of a popular front seen as a messianic Jew imposing his foreign values on a Christian society, and wished for Lindbergh to be president.[30] In his tale, Roth imagines that Lindbergh's election is followed by the imprisonment of Felix Frankfurter, Louis Brandeis, New York's mayor Fiorello La Guardia, as well as all the Jews in Roosevelt's entourage, while synagogues everywhere are burned down and antisemitic riots lead to the murder of some hundred Jews.[31]

The legacy of these American Nazis would not be lost. Following the Second World War and the defeat of Nazism, it was not long before other extremists inherited the torch. It is in Atlanta in 1958, site of the Frank affair in a different context, that these extremists gave free reign to their violent antisemitism. And thus an anti-Jewish hate had taken root. It was far from the traditional biases that cost Frank his life, but it gave life to a far right eager to attack governmental power supposedly held by the Jews, a radical right in alignment with the European model that shattered American exceptionalism. Édouard Drumont's imported delusions were followed by Hitler's. Starting in 1946, a new Nazi organization was created in Atlanta, the Columbians. In their brown shirts, two hundred members of this militia marched in rhythm through the streets of the city, repeating the Nazi salute and distributing antisemitic tracts.[32]

Symbolically, the 1958 attack against Atlanta's synagogue, in the same South that saw the Leo Frank affair, marks this deep mutation in the nation's antisemitism, and it leads directly to Charlottesville and to the Pittsburgh massacre. On October 12, 1958, fifty packs of dynamite were left at the entrance of Atlanta's oldest synagogue, the Hebrew Benevolent Congregation. Immediately, the memory of Leo Frank impressed itself upon the Jewish population of the city, who feared a new explosion of antisemitism, though it was condemned by the people and town councilmen.[33] This time, it was new rabbi Jacob Rothschild's close proximity to the Black civil rights movement—which had been fighting against segregation following the *Brown v. Board of Education* Supreme Court decision (1954)—that provoked the antisemitic mobilization. The ruling had given rise to mass opposition on the part of Southern whites, particular those in Atlanta, pointing to a Jewish conspiracy led by the Supreme Court. An anti-Jewish Christian party was created and distributed pamphlets in which could be read: "The Jews have destroyed racial segregation. . . . All major Jew organizations are against segregation. . . . Don't let the white race die."[34] Other extremist organizations were in turn created to protest. Hitler was lauded as a "Whiteman [who] once meted out justice to the Jews." The Shoah was denounced as a "GIANT PROPAGANDA HOAX." Leo Frank's lynching was celebrated by burning crosses on hilltops, and the "chosen and circumcised elite" were targeted.[35] This was the justification for the attack against the synagogue, which followed four other attacks on synagogues that same year. It appears that, while Atlanta Jews during Frank's lifetime kept a low profile and sought to integrate, Rabbi Rothschild's activism in support of African Americans was shocking to some of the city's inhabitants. Jews saw in it the aftershocks carried by the Leo Frank affair.[36] The federal state sent out seventy-five police officers to find the culprits. Five people were arrested, members of far-right parties or of the Knights of the White Camelia.[37]

At the time of his arrest, Wallace Allen—presumed to be behind the attack—was found in possession of a letter addressed to him by George Lincoln Rockwell, the Nazi leader. "We are prepared to roast the Jews alive," it said, in order to "free America from Jewish domination."[38] Rockwell, Allen's muse, illustrates this shift. He was a great admirer of Hitler's. *Mein Kampf* was his bible, and he was also a staunch reader of *The Protocols of the Elders of Zion*. Rockwell was a Nazi fanatic determined to impose Aryan power in the United States by rejecting both Blacks and Jews from a profoundly Christian society. Familiar with the South, where he had long lived (in Atlanta, for example), he hated the African American minority as much as the presence of Jews. He rose to the rank of the "most notorious anti-Semite since Hitler,"[39] close to the Ku Klux Klan, which denied the existence of the Shoah and which, three years later, would march with other militants wearing Nazi uniforms through many cities of the United States. Rockwell gave innumerable conferences in universities in which he lauded the Hitlerian system. He founded the American Nazi Party in 1959, a group responsible over many years for countless demonstrations and counterdemonstrations of varying degrees of violence. His program was explicit: as a "Nazi at heart," he believed in the "separation of the races as a means of survival for the White Race. To preserve the White Race of people and Western civilization and counter against Jewish Communism," because "national socialism is the only form of government that can save the world."[40] A few years after the liberation of Auschwitz, in the Deep South of the United States, antisemitism repeated the refrain of European extremist movements in the name of white supremacy by establishing links with the prejudices of a Christianity that was hostile to Jews. A candidate for governor in Virginia, Rockwell incarnated this move to antisemitic white supremacy, now in the name of Nazism, whose legacy can still be felt in the twenty-first century. At all of his meetings, he donned a brown uniform, boots, a swastika, and used the Roman salute with his troops, equipped with Nazi banners. His ultimate goal was to "separate African-Americans from the Whites and gas the Communist Jews."[41] This explosion of a nationalism that celebrated the merits of the white race marked the forceful return of a racialized vision advocated, as early as 1916, by Madison Grant in his famous *The Passing of the Great Race,* which extols the purity of Nordic features and in 1924 gave rise to the political restriction of non-white emigration. A work celebrated by Adolf Hitler himself, who considered it to be his "bible."[42] This book, which influenced both Presidents Warren Harding and Calvin Coolidge in the 1920s, has found today a strong audience among extremist militants who deplore a "white genocide" and accuse Jews of manipulating white workers.[43]

The Atlanta attack carried out in the name of this ideology "created a national sensation [for] it looks like the work of organized conspirators" whose allegiance to the far right was unmistakable.[44] Atlanta Jews wonder: "Does this mean a return to the era of Leo Frank?" The *Forward,* the great newspaper published in both Yiddish and English editions, featured a long string of articles on the attack, pondering the best response to this internationally condemned assault.[45] Members of the Klan from various states attended the trial, which concluded without any culprit being sentenced. Ralph McGill, the "conscience of the South," who received the Pulitzer Prize in 1959 for his articles dedicated to this attack and to the actions of the Ku Klux Klan, denounced this "harvest" of hate produced by "hate pamphlets, who shrieked that Roosevelt was a Jew; who denounce the Supreme Court as being Communist and controlled by Jewish influences."[46] As though to prove the truth of this thesis, posters were put up around Atlanta representing a python named Rabbin encircling the Capitol.[47] The bombing was both preceded and followed by eight other attacks on synagogues in 1957 and 1958, primarily in the South, in Tennessee, Alabama, Georgia, and Mississippi. On November 11, 1957, eleven packs of dynamite were found at the Beth-El Synagogue in Charlotte. Other attacks were carried out, the most serious one being in Miami where, on March 16, 1958, a bomb was set off at the Bet-El Synagogue, while another exploded the same day at a Nashville synagogue where a phone call threatened to "kill in cold blood" all Jews.[48] The South had become a stage for attacks against synagogues, from Nashville to Jacksonville, Miami to Gastonia. Meanwhile Florida was covered in graffiti: "Jews must be expelled from Florida."[49]

We are indeed witnessing the birth of a new kind of antisemitism, different from the one that led to the execution of Frank. This time, following the *Jew Deal*, and akin to nineteenth-century France or 1930s Germany, the Jews were accused of controlling the highest institutions of the United States, of having turned this nation into an unacceptable "Jewish Republic." In 1977, Joseph Paul Franklin, like Wallace Allen, undertook his murderous journey in the name of his loyalty to Nazi ideology. He did not hide his radical ideas. Born in Alabama, he was an outspoken supporter of white superiority who still dreamed of the long-gone Confederacy and proclaimed loud and proud his admiration for Hitler. He embarked upon a long spree of murders during which he assassinated twenty-two people, among whom were many African Americans. These murders symbolize the move from lynchings to mass shootings.[50] Far from the South, these murders took place in the center of the United States. Over the course of his murderous rampage, Franklin attacked several synagogues, including one in Chattanooga, Tennessee, before attacking another in St. Louis, the Shaare Zedek Synagogue, during a bar mitzvah.[51] In this major city, he fired on the participants of the religious service, killing one

Gerald Gordon and critically wounding many others. The first killing since the Leo Frank affair thus occured at a remove from Georgia, a symbol of the transformation of antisemitism now increasingly receptive to the ideologies that have come out of Europe, such as Nazism.

Franklin belonged, like Allen, to the far-right white supremacist movement. In his view, Jews were the enemies of the white race. His real name was James Clayton Vaughn, but he chose to change it to Paul (Goebbels's first name) Franklin (Benjamin Franklin's patronym), as though he who symbolizes America could be allied with the masters of Nazism. As a member of both the Ku Klux Klan and the American Nazi Party, Franklin had worshiped *Mein Kampf* and been a follower of Adolf Hitler since his youth. A true believer in conspiracy theories, he denounced a cabal that allowed Jews to dominate the world, particularly in Washington. Like Allen, he was a follower of Rockwell, the American Nazi leader, admirer of Hitler, who in that same year founded a white supremacist organization that sought to deport African Americans and execute Jews. Seduced by his ideas, Franklin then took a step back from them. Upon Franklin's return to Atlanta, he joined the National States Rights Party, led by J. B. Stoner, another extremist group that combined the ideology of the Klan with that of Nazism in the name of a more fanatic antisemitism. "The only thing I find wrong with Hitler," Stoner told his followers, "[is] that he didn't exterminate all those six million Jews he's credited with."[52] After multiple journeys, a lengthy return to his childhood in Alabama, where he joined the United Klan of America, endless wanderings from place to place, and following multiple trials from the Missouri Supreme Court to the Supreme Court of the United States, Franklin the neo-Nazi was executed in 2013.[53]

On January 1, 1981, in Denver, Alan Harrison Berg, a liberal Jewish radio host, was gunned down by one of the members of a dangerous white supremacist organization, The Order, a Christian antisemitic offshoot of the Aryan Nation. Some of its heavily armed killers were previously members of the Ku Klux Klan. In 1984, Robert Pires, a member of The Order, traveled to Coeur d'Alene in Idaho and bombed a priest he mistook for a rabbi.[54] A third Nazi antisemitic deadly attack was carried out in April of 1986. As he was peacefully returning from the Kollel Beis Yitzchok in Pittsburgh, Neal Rosenblum, an Orthodox Jew wearing his traditional garb and having arrived that same day from Toronto to celebrate Passover, was accosted by Steven Tielsch, who displayed swastika tattoos on his forehead and leg. Without a word, the latter shot Rosenblum five times. Rosenblum, mortally wounded, crumbled. The following day, Tielsch said to a police officer, "I just wanted to kill Jews."[55]

A litany of antisemitic murders motivated by a supremacist hatred of Jews henceforth haunts the core of American society. It is inscribed in a proliferation of terrorist acts stirred up by organizations that belong to the general movement of the alt-right, inheritors of small fascistic groups from the 1930s whose influence was such that they encouraged "lone wolves" to act.[56] Even more spectacular was the Oklahoma bombing on April 19, 1995, a blind attack that was aimed at no one in particular. It was instead the federal government that was targeted in order to protest, following the reasoning of the radical right, the power it exercises over its citizens. Equipped with *The Turner Diaries*, the extremely violent antisemitic bible of the American alt-right that imagines the destruction of Washington and the arrest and internment of Jews and Blacks, Timothy McVeigh, a former member of the Ku Klux Klan often seen wearing a White Power

T-shirt, parked a truck carrying over two tons of various explosive devices in front of a federal building in Oklahoma City, killing 168 people and wounding many hundreds more.[57] Arrested along with his accomplices, he was sentenced to death and executed. His example would nourish the alt-right's feats of arms and inspire its actions for a long time in order to fight, in particular, against Barack Obama's interventionist state.

*The Turner Diaries* influenced McVeigh and a number of militant extremists. They inspired many antisemite attacks such as, in 2001, the plan to bomb the Holocaust Museum in Washington, organized by the Aryan Unity. The terrifying antisemitic uchronia published in 1978 also fed into anti-Latino hate and became, at the end of the twentieth century, the bible of the white supremacy movement. It was written by William Pierce, whose pseudonym was Andrew Macdonald, and who left the white National Socialist Party to form another equally radical movement. In his uchronia, the Jews incite a Black revolution that will be squashed by white supremacists who manage to destroy New York and Israel. Pierce envisions how, soon, in 1991, the white race will finally overcome Jewish domination. In the words of one of the soldiers of the movement, "one must not distinguish between a good and a bad Jew," as the Jewish "race" is the principal peril of the white "race." Pierce adds: "Your day is coming, Jews, your day is coming."

The sheer violence exuding from this work is head-spinning. It exposes the radical project of a conquest of power in the United States, to destroy the system of white slavery put in place by the Jews: "We are in a war to the death with the Jew." The mysterious group The Order, analogous to the Klan in its rituals, recruits its members through dramatic ceremonies, over the course of which they swear absolute obedience to the grand master: "Now our life truly belongs only to the Order." Clandestine and disciplined units are created to patrol the territory, obeying the most extreme orders without question, with the goal of liberating the white population: "We are already slaves. We have allowed a diabolically clever, alien minority to put chains on our souls and our minds. . . . The corruption of our people by the Jewish-liberal-democratic-egalitarian plague which afflicts us is more clearly manifested in our soft-mindedness. . . . Liberalism is an essentially feminine, submissive world view. . . . There is no way a society based on Aryan values and on Aryan outlook can evolve peacefully from a society which has succumbed to Jewish spiritual corruption." Day after day, Pierce minutely describes the military strategy set up to destroy the system commanded by Jews and Israel, whose all-powerful ambassador coordinates the repression of whites. The Capitol, FBI headquarters, the Pentagon, major newspapers, and ministries are bombed, burned, and hundreds of thousands of people die. Nuclear bombs are dropped on major cities, and entire regions are seized, such as California, over which a new order is imposed. Originally from Oregon, Idaho, Montana, or Wyoming, these neo-Nazis draw the borders of an Aryan State, a new nation. Missiles are sent against Tel Aviv, Moscow, and Leningrad, inciting the survivors to murder any Jews that are left. "Within 24 hours after we hit Tel Aviv and half a dozen other Israeli targets last month, hundreds of thousands of Arabs were swarming across the borders of occupied Palestine. . . . Within a week the throat of the last Jew survivor in the last kibbutz and in the last smoking ruin in Tel Aviv had been cut." In the world, the hunt against "Yids" is without pity, because "this is "a war to the death with the Jew." Millions of African Americans and Jews are deported to camps, and hundreds of thousands of people are hanged for having helped the Jews or for sharing their values, thus betraying the white race. And this time, unlike in Egypt, Persia, Rome, Spain, Russia, and Germany, when Jews "emerged triumphant from the ruins," despite their desire for vengeance, the principal centers of Judaism have been permanently destroyed: "by hitting New York and Israel, we have completely knocked out two of world Jewry's principal nerve centers." Despite the desperate counterattack by the Jews and their collaborators who manage to temporarily seize Pittsburgh and kill all of the white men of the city, the organization's control spreads throughout the country and the world, sterilizing entire territories in order to establish the domination of the white race.[58]

The alt-right that has been inspired for generations by *The Turner Diaries* also targets, with tenfold violence, African American and Latinos. On July 17, 2015, Dylann Roof, a white supremacist brandishing the Confederate flag, murdered eight African Americans as well as their pastor during collective prayer at the Emanuel African Methodist Episcopal Church in Charleston, the oldest church of this faith in the Deep South, witness to so many lynchings.[59] Terrorist attacks also targeted Latino-Americans in the name of a rejection of original immigration from Latin America. The most tragic occurred in August 2019 in El Paso, where white supremacist Patrick Crusius opened fire and killed twenty-three people in the name of the Great Replacement conspiracy theory, elaborated by Renaud Camus and imported to the United States.[60] But their limitless admiration for Hitler and Nazism leads them to point to Jews, year after year, as their preferred target. An FBI report confirmed that between 1969 and 2018, "Jews have been the target of the largest number of hate crimes directed against a religious group."[61]

Accordingly, the hostility of white supremacists against Jews in the United States greatly prevails over the antisemitic animosity of many Blacks and Muslims. It is true that there are numerous conflicts between Jews and Blacks, such as in 1991 in Crown Heights where, following a car accident provoked by religious Jews, a young Black boy died. Riots broke out and, out of vengeance, twenty or so African Americans attacked a young Australian Jew, Yankel Rosenbaum, who was just a tourist. He was mortally stabbed. Other extreme violent antisemitic acts transpired in the name of Islamist demands. In March 1977, members of the Nation of Islam attempted to seize a building of the B'nai B'rith. Attacks of this nature were also carried out on March 1, 1994, when Jewish students were wounded on the Brooklyn Bridge, one of whom, Ari Halberstam, mortally. Other attacks happened on October 8, 2000, in the Riverdale neighborhood of the Bronx, the night before Yom Kippur, and in Syracuse, New York, on October 13, 2000. In May of 2002, John Allen Muhammad attacked a synagogue in Washington. Another attack took place in Seattle on July 28, 2006 at the Seattle Jewish Federation, where Naveed Afzal Haq shot four Jewish women, one of whom, Pamela Waechter, died. May 2009 saw two failed attacks against synagogues committed by the members of Islamist organizations. In June of 2009, an Islamist opened fire on the houses of two rabbis. Another targeted a synagogue in Chicago on October 29, 2010. On April 29, 2016, a member of the Islamic State planned to attack a synagogue in Florida before being arrested.

Nonetheless, the reality is that attacks against synagogues were most often carried out, as in Atlanta in 1958 or St. Louis in 1977, by members of the far right. Between 1994 and 1999, thirty synagogues and Jewish institutions were attacked by these extremist militants. Among them, after St. Louis, it was in Oregon, in California, and then again in Pittsburgh, that additional antisemitic acts were committed by white supremacists. In March 1994, two skinheads attacked a synagogue in Eugene, Oregon.[62] In their homes, the police found supremacist literature and Nazi flags and shirts. Put on trial and found guilty, they were sentenced to ten to twenty years in prison. California, another state that is central to American modernity and far from the Deep South, was hit multiple times. In June 1999, two members of the white supremacist group Aryan Nation, who denounce the "international Jewish Media," set fire to three synagogues in Sacramento. They were also planning attacks against Jewish community leaders, whose addresses they had found, and were sentenced to twenty to thirty years in prison.[63] On July 2, two white supremacists shot six worshippers who, on the Sabbath, were returning home from their synagogue in an Orthodox neighborhood of Chicago. On August 10, 1999, a Jewish child-care center in Los Angeles was attacked at gunpoint. The shooter, Buford Furrow, was arrested; in his home the police found far-right supremacist propaganda preaching "the race war in the United States."[64] Later, California was again hit. In December of 2001, another white supremacist attempted to burn down a synagogue in Reno. In 2002, again in Eugene, Temple Beth Israel found itself the target of three supremacist skinheads who threw stones marked with swastikas against Jews in mid-prayer. They were sentenced to many years of prison. On each of these occasions, the neo-Nazis belonged to an extremist group called Volksfront. Back in Pittsburgh, on April 28, 2000, Richard Baumhammers, another white supremacist, murdered his Jewish neighbor and burned down her house. He then moved on to various synagogues on which he opened fire, executing an Indian immigrant as well as the owner of a Chinese restaurant. Before embarking on his spree, he had visited a far-right pro-Aryan-domination website as well as the *Stormfront* website. He had also downloaded documents from the Nazi National Alliance.[65] Arrested, he was eventually sentenced and executed.

In August of 2005, Sean Gillespie, a skinhead "Corporal" of the Nazi group Aryan Nation, donning a swastika shirt, bombed Temple B'nai Israel in Oklahoma. In a video posted just before his attack, he proudly takes responsibility for the attack in the name of "white power" and signs it "Jewslayer 88," the well-known code of worldwide Nazi extremism in reference to Hitler.[66] This growing power of far-right extremism in the 2000s was boosted by a conspiracist rhetoric that availed itself of anything and everything. White supremacist and Nazi organizations found inspiration in *The Protocols of the Elders of Zion* and denounced the power of the ZOG (Zionist Occupational Government), meaning of Washington under the control of Jews, masters of manipulation when it comes to ensuring their domination. The destruction of the World Trade Center on September 11, 2001 was likewise used as fodder for an explosion of denunciations of the power of the Jews, masters of this machination from which they allegedly escaped by warning their coreligionists who worked there. If, on the far left, there were traces of similar accusations aimed at President Bush and Dick Cheney, said to have organized the attack to justify their own enforcement of "law and order," they were for the most part bereft of any explicit antisemitic connotations.[67] Fueled by Arab websites, this rumor reinforced the paranoid vision of the far right in which it had become wholeheartedly invested. According to this mindset, the attack on the Twin Towers was a plot from Israel in order to push the United States to attack the Arab world out of vengeance.[68]

Conspiracy theories were additionally fueled by Barack Obama's inauguration on January 20, 2009. It would profoundly shake up the political scene in America and have unintended consequences. The shock created by the access of a man of color to the position of head of state at the heart of these extremist white movements is indescribable. An explosion of anti-Black hate and a deluge of antisemitic propaganda followed almost immediately. Obama symbolizes the alliance between African Americans and Jews in the eyes of the alt-right, an alliance that reinforces Jewish domination in American government and their reign over the white race. What followed, the election of Donald Trump, the demonstration in Charlottesville, and the Pittsburgh massacre, can be understood as the brutal reaction of a population pushed to its boiling point by the neo-Nazi propaganda disseminated by the Klan, but also by so many other extremist organizations whose prejudices have been widely spread through society by a media raised on these delusions.

When Obama also decided to commit himself to implementing a welfare state that would take care of all of its citizens regardless of their situation, when he established Obamacare, emphasizing the role of the state in the American economy, many were those who pointed out, as was the case under the New Deal, the presence of numerous Jewish advisers at the heart of his political entourage. Since the start of his first presidential campaign, his campaign staff had included many Jews, such as Dan Shapiro.[69] In September of 2008, when Senator Obama was preparing his candidacy, it was supported by nine hundred rabbis. Obama attended their conference, quoted the *Pirke Avot*,[70] discussed the meaning of the shofar that would be heard in a few days in every synagogue,[71] displayed precise knowledge of Jewish culture,[72] and peppered his speeches with references to the biblical Exodus.[73] After his presidential victory, a number of Obama's closest collaborators walked the halls of the West Wing: David Axelrod, first adviser to the president, or Rahm Emanuel, his chief of staff, both loyal to him since Chicago. These positions at the heart of governmental power have become legendary thanks to the series *The West Wing*. The Jewish presence in Washington continued to be prominent when, following Axelrod and Emanuel, Obama called upon more Orthodox Jews such as Jacob Lew, who scrupulously observed the Sabbath and became Obama's chief of staff in 2012.[74]

Obama often referenced the history of Jewish experience. He wanted "his daughters to know the Haggadah, the story at the center of Passover"; he celebrated the Passover Seder, for the first time in the White House, surrounded by his family and friends and wearing a kippah.[75] *New York* magazine published a portrait of Obama with a kippah on the front page, titled "The First Jewish President,"[76] a title that he would claim for himself in May 2015 during his visit at the Adas Israel Synagogue in Washington. He declared himself "flattered to be considered a member of the tribe" and emphasized that he was the "most Jewish of any that have sat in the Oval Office," especially given that he had held seven seders at the White House.[77] In January 2016, he declared that in the face of antisemitism "we are all Jews."[78]

The ascent of an African American as head of the state turned the political scene upside down, opening the door to a radicalized far right. The Obama Deal replaced the Jew Deal, and "Roosevelt, the first Jewish president" logically became "Obama the first Jewish president," a phrase that he himself boasted about, almost in provocation. In reaction, posters were disseminated all over the United States showing a Star of David covering the face of Obama, who "takes his orders from Rothschild." Venomous antisemitic caricatures quickly emerged showing Obama controlled by Jewish money. Another caption read: "Rothschild's Choice: Barack Obama and the Hidden Cabal Behind the Plot to Murder America." The presence of "Talmudists of Wall Street" in Washington was denounced, just like during Roosevelt's era, and it was claimed that "all of Obama's money comes from Jews." Franklin Delano Obama incarnates the new face of the "Jewish Republic": in this perspective, "Barack Obama is the first American Jewish President. Mazel tov!" Just as during the time dominated by the delusions of Édouard Drumont, who saw Jews everywhere in the personnel of the Third Republic should their last name not sound entirely French, interminable lists of supposed Jews to target were created. Whether in the shadows or in the light of day, they were henceforth accused of controlling Washington.[79] Pamphlets made the rounds, like *The Jew in Yellow*, in which could be read words like "the presence of the Jews in the close circle around Obama isn't good for the Jews in this era that calls to mind the Weimar Republic during which Walther Rathenau was assassinated."[80] In reality, despite its many Jewish friends, Obama's policies regarding Israel have often been harsh, his criticism of Israeli settlements severe and unkind, especially given that his closest collaborators Axelrod, Emanuel, and even Dennis Ross, shared these views, creating a rising tension with a number of Jewish organizations that complained of Obama's abandonment, leading disappointed American Jews from joy to tears.[81]

Tea Party militants and armed militias were in full recruit mode; the Ku Klux Klan was mobilizing; skinheads, neo-Nazis, and other believers in white supremacy have declared war, stirring deep worry among security services who feared the direst consequences from these outbursts of violence. According to an official report from one intelligence agency, "Anti-Semitic extremists attribute [the loss of jobs] to a deliberate conspiracy conducted by a cabal of Jewish 'financial elites.' These 'accusatory' tactics are employed to draw new recruits into rightwing extremist groups and further radicalize those already subscribing to extremist beliefs . . . Many rightwing extremists are antagonistic toward the new presidential administration."[82] In the name of "America, a Christian nation," the Tea Party disseminated a satanic view of Jews, denied the Shoah, accused Rothschild of dominating the United States, spread racist propaganda in favor of white domination, and forged ties with supremacists and national organizations that were hostile to Obama and organizing into armed militias.[83] Obama's victory was shocking to the Deep South, which opposed any kind of intervention by the federal government in support of minorities, African Americans, women, or immigrants, who were accused of benefiting from special privileges, of not "respecting the rules" of upward mobility, the way that average whites must—whites who saw themselves as a "foreign minority in their own country," who were denied every advantage and despised. They felt betrayed, excluded from the nation. They saw their Christian values, their social life, the culture they inherited from their attachment to the Confederacy, their honor, repudiated. Henceforth, "it's particularly in the South that this turn towards the right occurs," symbolized by the Tea Party.[84]

From Roosevelt to Obama, the same reasoning provoked a populist and antisemitic crisis in identity politics.[85] The Anti-Defamation League asserted that 7,034 antisemitic incidents of varying degrees of seriousness occurred during the years Obama was president.[86] One of the most serious took place at the Holocaust Museum in Washington on June 10, 2009, when James von Brunn, a revisionist white supremacist, killed a museum security guard.

This Nazi antisemitic fury continued to increase until it led to the Pittsburgh massacre, unimaginable in Tocqueville's United States. The American pluralist and liberal dream of a "nation of nations" brutally collapsed right in the middle of the Obama years. On April 12, 2014, on the eve of Passover, Frazier Glenn Miller Jr, a member of The Order, with cries of "Heil Hitler," attacked the Overland Park Jewish Community Center followed by Shalom Village, a Jewish retirement home, two institutions located in Overland Park, Kansas. Resolved to "exterminate the Jews,"[87] he wounded numerous people, and killed three, two of whom were members of a Methodist church, and one Catholic woman. The police discovered a copy of *Mein Kampf* in his home and a red shirt with a swastika. Miller turned out to be a member of the Ku Klux Klan, the leader of the White Patriot Party, which he founded in North Carolina, and of a Nazi organization, the National Socialist Party of America. His act symbolizes a rupture between the Leo Frank era and the birth of a European type of antisemitism. Miller was a Southern man, an admirer of the struggle of the Confederacy. He organized parades set to the music of Dixie, started a magazine called the *White Carolinian*, was a fierce defender of the Ku Klux Klan of which he had been a leader, was even in contact with people from Marietta where Frank was hanged, participated in marches in innumerable cities in North Carolina, brandishing the emblems of the Confederacy, wearing Klan clothes, and, in the name of "White Power," called for the "unification of the White Southern Nation." Close to David Duke, the Klan leader who also belonged to the Nazi Party elected in Louisiana in 1989, Miller incarnates this transition between Southern xenophobia to political antisemitism in the wake of the Brown Shirts of the 1930s with, this time, a brutal move to action. Arrested once and imprisoned, he writes in his memoirs:

> You were born in bondage to the Jews. . . . And so the Jews have turned us over to the One World Government. . . . Not one of the 535 members of the U.S. Congress, nor the President and

vice-president, nor anyone else working within the federal government for that matter, would be there if he or she had been opposed by the Jews. . . . Six million Jews did not die during WWII. This whole fabrication was invented by the Jews to gain sympathy. . . . Their goal is to Weaken the White man. Divide and conquer. . . . The Jews intend to exterminate the White Aryan Race from the face of the earth. . . . Hitler said it. Henry Ford said it. Martin Luther said it. Mussolini said it. George Lincoln Rockwell said it. And, I believe it, because it is true. . . . In many ways, I would try to emulate Hitler's methods of attracting members and supporters. In the years to come, for example, I placed great emphasis on staging marches and rallies. It had been successful with Hitler, and I felt it would be successful with me. . . . You're alone in a closet of your home. There's a large bright red button on the wall. You can push that button, and presto, all Negroes, all Jews, and all other colored people are instantly removed from the North American continent and returned to their native countries.

He closes his memoirs with the following: "He who fights the Jew fights the devil. . . . Pass the ammunition, Sieg Heil, and Heil Hitler! . . . I'll see you in Valhalla."[88]

In 2014, before targeting the Overland Park Jewish Community Center and Shalom Village, he issued a "declaration of war": "May the blood of our enemies flood the streets, rivers and fields of the nation, in Holy vengeance and justice. . . . The Jews are our main and most formidable enemies, brothers and sisters. They are truly the children of Satan."[89] For Miller, "the white man has become the most cowardly being on earth. . . . Make no mistake about it, the Jews intend to exterminate the White Aryan Race from the face of the earth. . . . They have no other choice. They must exterminate us to insure that future Aryan men do not come for their throats seeking to settle accounts. . . . The U.S. government and the establishment media are our enemies because they are controlled by Jews. It's as simple as that. So never forget it."[90] Miller does not hide his profound admiration for Joseph Paul Franklin, the St. Louis synagogue shooter, "the bravest of heroes, the best white nationalist white hero to be born in the United States." It is in his honor that he chose Franklin's birthday to attack the Overland Park Jewish Community Center, with cries of "Heil Hitler." When arrested, he asked the police officer, "How many fucking Jews have I killed?" and then later, from prison, for an interview in the newspaper *Star*, declared: "Thanks to my action, Jews will now feel less safe. . . . My conscience told me to kill Jews. My biggest fear was to die without having killed Jews. The white race is dying because of a genocide caused by the Jews." During his trial, he continuously repeated the Roman salute and yelled "Heil Hitler!" Condemned to the death penalty, he yelled again, "Death to Jews!" He died in prison before he could be executed.[91]

Three years later, the election of Donald Trump fit perfectly into a context likely to reactivate all of the anxieties about social categories that could be hostile to liberalism. Anxieties that were further upset by the cultural reforms that affect family values, for instance, and anxieties that were affected by the economic consequences of globalization. The fear on the part of the "forgotten whites," their resentment, became polarized by Hillary Clinton's candidacy, which to them symbolized this liberal America that is open to minorities but ignores their helplessness. Trump himself even tweeted a far-right image representing Hillary Clinton, "the most corrupt of candidates," whose face is placed in the center of a Star of David. In a 2011 interview, Trump identified with the demands of the Tea Party: "I think," he said, "the people of the Tea Party like me, because I represent a lot of the ingredients of the Tea Party."[92] As a possible member of the extremist John Birch Society, Trump fully adheres to its extremist values and had attracted, even before his election, the favors of the conspiracist alt-right, neo-Nazis, Patriots, and the Ku Klux Klan. On the white nationalist website VDare, in July 2015, one could read: "We are all Donald Trump now."[93] He received the explicit approval of David Duke, ex-grand master of the Klan, who laughs at "Jewish *chutzpah* [that] knows no bounds."[94] Throughout Trump's presidential campaign, one could hear "Trump: realizing the goals of the whites" or "Jew lies matter" or "The Holocaust is a joke." For Andrew Anglin, a white supremacist leader, "we support Trump because he is the savior of the White race, sent by God to free us from the shackles of the Jew occupation and establish a 1000-year Reich."[95] Trump's speeches are interspersed with antisemitic allusions. In the final speech of his presidential campaign, he denounced a global power robbing his country of its wealth, as the faces of three easily recognizable Jews scrolled by, including that of George Soros, shedding doubt on Jews' loyalty to their nation. Without fully endorsing the explicit antisemitic rhetoric of the alt-right, Trump adhered to the globalist view that puts the blame on the Jews. He also targeted East Coast liberal elites, commonly identified as Jewish, and sought to galvanize the American population in abandoned rural regions or large cities left impoverished by deindustrialization.

Soon after Donald Trump's victory, on November 21, 2016, radical neo-Nazi militants descended on Washington to celebrate on the steps of government buildings. Richard Spencer, the head of the National Policy Institute, yelled "Heil Trump, heil our people, heil victory," while some in the crowd did the Nazi salute, others later repeating the same Hitlerian salute.[96] Interviewed after the demonstration, Spencer shared his belief that Jews are omnipotent in the establishment, and white people are divested of their power.[97] Fringe groups, explicitly influenced by Nazism and ready to act, proliferated, including the Atomwaffen Division, an armed extremist movement acknowledging its debt to Hitler and declaring itself a revolutionary national-socialist organization whose favorite motto is "Gas the Kikes!" Its members train all around the country and have been implicated in many assassinations, including, in January 2018, that of a Jew and homosexual, Blaze Bernstein.[98] For the CEO of the Anti-Defamation League, Jonathan Greenblatt, "anti-Jewish public and political discourse in America is worse than at any point since the 1930s."[99] Returning to the similarities with Lewis's uchronia, Sarah Churchwell believes that

> American fascist energies today are different from 1930s European fascism, but that doesn't mean they're not fascist, it means they're not European and it's not the 1930s. They remain organized around classic fascist tropes of nostalgic regeneration, fantasies of racial purity, celebration of an authentic folk and nullification of others, scapegoating groups for economic instability or inequality, rejecting the legitimacy of political opponents, the demonization of critics, attacks on a free press, and claims that the will of the people justifies violent imposition of military force. Vestiges of interwar fascism have been dredged up, dressed up, and repurposed for modern times. Colored shirts might not sell anymore, but colored hats are doing great. . . . In the end, it matters very little whether Trump is a fascist in his heart if he's fascist in his actions.[100]

The conclusion of the *Haaretz* correspondent in Washington, ending his long study on the growing influence of antisemitic white supremacists since Donald Trump's election, is final and irrevocable: "The election of Donald Trump has shattered the Jewish idyll, all across the board. Although one must give the president-elect the benefit of the doubt that he is not an anti-Semite himself, he has frequently promoted disparaging Jewish stereotypes in his personal statements. . . . And under his wings, America has seen an unprecedented outburst of blunt and naked hatred of Jews, which has only gotten worse since his election."[101]

The years 2016 and 2017 saw innumerable marches by uniform-wearing alt-right groups, accompanied by members of the Klan in their white hoods, cropping up from Portland to Seattle, Washington, Boston, and even New Orleans,[102] as though proof of the efficiency of a strategy founded on Southern values.[103] Trump had just been inaugurated as president on January 20, 2017, and suddenly came the shock of Charlottesville. On August 11 and 12, an unimaginable resurgence of the American far right, which has openly taken the torch passed on by the 1930s, came out of the shadows for all to see. In this same region of the Deep South, still devoted to the Confederacy and to the Klan, hundreds of far-right militants united to protest the removal of the statue of Robert E. Lee, the Southern hero who led the Confederate States Army during the Civil War.

The demonstration was attended by all extremist trends inspired by Rockwell's program, with their banners: National Socialist movement neo-Nazis, negationists, Vanguard America, the Traditionalist Worker Party, the White Knights of the Confederate Ku Klux Klan, parading with their leader, David Duke, the skinheads of Crew 38 and of the Blood and Honor Social Club, the neo-Confederates of the League of the South and of Identity Dixie, members of Christian Identity, and other groups like the Proud Boys. Many of them openly used the fascist salute and extoled a "sacred racial war," denouncing the Shoah, while the *Daily Stormer* was handed out, designed according to its Hitlerian model to reject the Jewish hold over America. In the first months of 2016, its website received over five hundred thousand views.

The aim of these radical groups is to "unify the right" and make their voices heard in an America that has become, in their eyes, too liberal, multicultural, tolerant, and that threatens, by legitimizing minorities, the white majority at the heart of the nation's creation, giving rise to a true "cultural genocide."[104] Hundreds of supremacists flip the motto put forward by antiracist demonstrators, "Black Lives Matter," into "White Lives Matter," accompanied by these words addressed to their Black fellow citizens: "You will not replace us." During their torchlight parades, according to Nazi tradition, they brandish swastika flags and yell, as in the 1930s, "Blood and Soil," before shouting themselves hoarse with "Jews will not replace us!" Armed men crowd around the Beth Israel Synagogue, where members of the congregation hurry to remove Torah scrolls and hide them.

Upon seeing images of the Charlottesville demonstration, David Nirenberg, a specialist in the long history of antisemitism, revealed that "books and ideas that I had treated as very marginal in our society are not as marginal as I might have hoped."[105] The memory of the Leo Frank affair immediately resurfaced in this intermingling of antisemitism and anti-Black racism, like parallel hatreds that feed on one another.[106] To this effect, "antiSemitism forms the theoretical core of White nationalism,"[107] but this time "hate, bias and racism have been empowered and taken from the margins into the mainstream."[108] Henceforth, with the election of Trump and the vertiginous rise of the alt-right, "Pandora's box and Hydra of racism" are wide open.[109] This particularly impacts the Southern states that see themselves in Trump.

In numerous meetings held in the South, such as in Louisiana, citizens who did not necessarily subscribe to the Ku Klux Klan and did not always condone the violence in Charlottesville, were "ecstatic" that Trump was rehabilitating the Christian nation, the Confederacy, and opposing immigrants and affirmative action, thus reintegrating them—at least they believed—into this nation in which they felt they had become strangers.[110]

Events in Charlottesville turned violent when antiracist counterdemonstrators, often partisans of Black Lives Matter, protested the presence and slogans of alt-right demonstrators. Blows were exchanged, and many were wounded. Tragedy arose when James Fields, a member of the far-right who founded, in 1970, the white National Socialist Party—a successor to Rockwell's American Nazi Party—charged the crowd in his car, knocking down and killing Heather Heyer, an antiracist demonstrator, and also wounding a dozen people, many of whom were left in critical condition. According to the Southern Poverty Law Center, this was "the largest [rally] by the radical right in a decade."[111] Soon after, James Field would be sentenced to life in prison. Other radical demonstrators were also sentenced to prison, such as the leader of the Maryland chapter of the Ku Klux Klan, who had fired his gun, Richard Preston, and other supremacist leaders.

The country was gripped by strong emotions as people realized the vitality of the far-right, hateful against minorities whom it accuses of monopolizing power. Renaud Camus's theory of the Great Replacement had crossed the Atlantic, giving these radical movements their watchwords. In France, it is both Arabs and Jews who threaten to allegedly "replace" the Gauls one by one; in the United States, it is the African Americans and their Jewish friends, both of whom are foreigners to the blood and soil of the founding fathers, who are the preferred targets. Imported from France, Camus's ideas influenced the leaders of the American alt-right. Journalist Thomas Chatterton Williams painted an intimate portrait of Camus in his medieval castle in Plieux, Dordogne. He noticed that in Camus's view, Emmanuel Macron, a high official turned banker who had worked at the French branch of the Rothschild bank, is an incarnation of the "forces of replacement" that the "Davos-cracy" has established in order to impose its conception of the world, inhospitable to the rooting of nations.[112] As Williams states, not without irony:

> Yes, the French first gave us post-structuralism and, today, we have "replacism, . . ." We are naturally talking about completely different things. It was previously the American left that had its eyes riveted on Paris; now it's the far right that spreads ideas that appeared in France throughout the United States. . . . Now that in the United States, the right has become radicalized and that part of it considers the conservative movement with scorn, it has found in the French tradition certain concepts that are useful to it, a very sophisticated racist and anti-Semitic current of thought.[113]

This new manifestation of political antisemitism has given rise to the renewal of an extremist movement that now draws from the contemporary French ideology of the "Great Replacement" what it needs to nourish its mobilization. The Conservative Republican current was quickly overwhelmed by conspiracy theories for which Donald Trump had become the spokesperson, to such a degree that following the Charlottesville events, the latter stated mawkishly:

> You had some very bad people in that group, but you also had people that were very fine people, on both sides. You had people in that group. . . . There were people in that rally—and I looked

the night before—if you look, there were people protesting very quietly the taking down of the statue of Robert E. Lee. I'm sure in that group there were some bad ones. The following day it looked like they had some rough, bad people—neo-Nazis, white nationalists, whatever you want to call them. But you had a lot of people in that group that were there to innocently protest, and very legally protest.[114]

Approved by the leaders of the Ku Klux Klan, this judgment provoked indignation among many political figures, including that of a Democratic Jewish senator who tweeted that "as a Jew, and as an American, as a human being, I cannot find the words to express my disgust and my disappointment. This is not my president."[115] For his part, Bernie Sanders, then future Jewish Democratic candidate to the presidency, tweeted: "You are embarrassing our country and the millions of Americans who have fought and died to defeat Nazism."[116] In the same vein, Philip Roth compared the rise of Trump to power to a new populist conspiracy against America to the tune of Charles Lindbergh's motto: "America first."[117]

From this point on, as during the era of the New Deal, each attempt to reinforce the state undertaken in the name of social justice has provoked an ensuing violent racist and antisemitic reaction analogous to the one elicited by the rise to power of Leon Blum in France.[118] The myth of the Jewish Republic is thus transposed onto the American political scene, with its corollary, the emergence of a political antisemitism that has generated violent mobilizations like the one in Charlottesville. Antisemitic incidents followed one another in a frenzied rhythm throughout the year 2017, to the point that one of the national leaders of Jewish organizations finally declared, "People will begin to think that they are not safe in the United States."[119] The year 2017 was thus a turning point: antisemitic hate had literally exploded.[120] The Anti-Defamation League assessed that 2,017 antisemitic acts occurred during 2019, "the highest level of anti-Semitism since 1979," and even higher than in 1977, which counted 1,986 antisemitic incidents.[121]

A little over a year later, the direct consequences of Charlottesville inevitably came crashing down as many supremacist militants were arrested all around the country during the planning stages of various attacks. Some, such as Patrick Little, traveled to California in 2018 to lead an antisemitic campaign against Dianne Feinstein, the Jewish Democratic senator, by initiating a popular campaign whose motto was "Name the Jew."

The worst, which would belie Philip Roth's optimistic vision, quickly ensued.[122] On the morning of Saturday, October 27, 2018, a Shabbat service had begun at the Tree of Life–Or L'Simcha Congregation, in the Squirrel Hill neighborhood of Pittsburgh. Built in 1953, this immense liberal synagogue located in the middle of the densest Jewish population in the United States, faithful in respect to gender equality, could welcome up to 1,250 people. The service began at around 9 a.m. and brought together three distinct congregations in and around the same building: Tree of Life, New Light in the basement, while members of Dor Hadash waited at the building's entrance to join a study session dedicated to the Talmud.

At 9:50 a.m., a bearded white man suddenly entered the building, headed for the basement, and for twenty long minutes, armed with a Colt AR-15 semiautomatic and three Glock 357 SIGs, deadly weapons, opened continuous fire, shooting Rabbi Jeffrey Myers and the synagogue president, Melvin Wax. At 9:57, the man left the basement, using the stairs to enter the sanctuary where Tree of Life was holding its service, screaming "all Jews must die!" and coldly executed seven other worshippers. At

9:59, the police had already arrived on the premises. There followed an exchange of fire between law enforcement and the killer, who managed to hide in the building. At 10:30 a.m., special armed forces gained entry to the building, wounding the madman, who nevertheless managed to hide on the third floor after seriously wounding two police officers. At 11:08 a.m., the shooter surrendered after having confessed to police officers that he wished death to all Jews responsible for the genocide of his people.

In a few hours, the long history of American Jews had just turned into a nightmare: eleven worshippers assassinated, many more wounded. The "Pittsburgh pogrom that took place 80 years after the Night of the Kristalnacht" marks a turning point.[123] It is an unheard-of event in the history of American society. Robert Gregory Bowers, a forty-six-year-old truck driver living in Baldwin, Pennsylvania, had just delivered the fatal blow to the American dream. Before beginning his attack, he recorded a manifesto on the antisemitic American website Gab.com. "I wanted all Jews to die," he declared while being treated for his wounds. Invoking the specter of white Americans facing "genocide," he singled out HIAS, a Jewish American refugee-support group, and accused it of bringing "invaders in that kill our people."[124] The anti-Latino rhetoric that dominated Donald Trump's discourse to such a degree that he dreamed up a wall to separate the United States from Mexico fed off of a deadly fantasy: that Jews have allegedly helped immigrants not for humanitarian reasons but in order to establish their domination over the white nation.

Bowers was a regular of the far right who hurled "Heil Hitlers," was close to neo-Nazis and white supremacists, and assiduously visited revisionist conspiracy websites. He had formed close bonds with British neo-Nazis and claimed loud and clear that "Jews are the children of Satan." He even criticized Donald Trump for being in favor of a globalism that favors Jews even though they facilitate the illegal entry of immigrants coming in from the south. He exclaimed, "I can't sit by and watch my people get slaughtered," echoing the words of the Great Replacement. Bowers used his site to lambaste George Soros's pernicious influence. He did not hide that he was a member of the League of the South or that he was in Charlottesville with the thousands of neo-Nazis who proudly invaded the city. Though opposed to Trump's pro-Israel stance, denouncing his daughter's marriage to a Jew, "Bowers does identify with some of Trump's goals and rhetoric, because Trump has inspired the racist far right to a degree surpassing any modern American president."[125]

For many, Bowers "has the look of a lonely crackpot, but . . . on the contrary, he is a vanguard representative of the largest and most protean mass movement of modern history, which is the movement to exterminate the Jews. The movement got started in a primitive version in 1881 in Russia. . . . He is a brother of the Russian village bigots of the 1880s . . . a brother of these people, too, Ukrainian Whites and German Nazis alike." He symbolizes the "American version" of the belief in a Jewish genocidal threat that threatens the identity of nations.[126] Accordingly, the Pittsburgh massacre is a continuation of the Ukrainian pogroms, transposing to the United States the same hatred that motivated the Nazis and bringing forth for the first time at the heart of the American nation the most brutal form of antisemitism, thus revealing the underground strength of the alt-right.

Indicted, on October 31, by a federal grand jury, of 44 counts of hate crimes, obstruction of free exercise of religious freedom, and ethnic intimidation, Bowers would incur 535 years of prison.[127] In an America practically paralyzed by the large-scale shooting sprees in schools, restaurants, malls, and even military residences, by so many massacres that overwhelm public opinion, the Pittsburgh attack nevertheless marked an undeniable tipping point. For the first time since the birth of the "nation of nations," the Jews were the deliberate victims of a large-scale attack. In this America that has not known the pogroms that punctuated Europe's long history, the entire nation was in a state of bewilderment. According to the reasoning in his declarations following the Charlottesville demonstration, Donald Trump stated that nothing would have happened if the synagogue members had been armed in order to defend themselves, inciting the ire of the local population. Over two thousand people, including a considerable number of the members of the bruised and battered synagogue, protested his visit to Pittsburgh; seventy thousand people signed a petition demanding that before going to the synagogue he speak out against "white nationalism."

Emotions ran high. Crowds made up of people with diverse religious beliefs assembled in various parts of the city. Some recited the Kaddish; others lit candles; American flags were lowered at half-mast in front of public buildings, while in New York City, the Empire State Building was purposefully left in the dark; in Paris, the Eiffel Tower also went dark in homage to the victims. Tel Aviv's City Hall donned the colors of the American flag, and in Jerusalem images of the American and Israeli flags were projected onto the Wailing Wall. Pope Francis led a religious ceremony at Saint Peter's Square, imploring God to "help us to put out the hotbeds of hate that flare up in our societies." In Pittsburgh, the astonishment is all the greater since this deadly attack has reanimated the memory of the murder of rabbinical student Neal Rosenblum in the same city on April 17, 1986. Arrested in 2000, Steven Tielsch was sentenced to fifteen years of prison. He was freed in October 2017, only one year before the new Pittsburgh massacre. Between 1986 and 2018, the most brutal form of antisemitism struck the same city twice.

Hatred has continued to erupt a little more with each year. It has been fueled by Donald Trump, who declared in August of 2019 that "if [Jews] want to vote Democrat, [they] are being very disloyal to Jewish people and very disloyal to Israel," implying that their loyalty to Israel should force them to vote for him. He added that Jews who vote for this party "either a total lack of knowledge or great disloyalty."[128] This is the theme of dual loyalty that reemerges to explicitly challenge the integration of Jews into the American nation by echoing a traditional accusation that has been used for centuries and has justified so many antisemitic mobilizations. It practically means restating the accusation of a Jewish Republic, circulated in the United States by far-right groups, according to which Jewish loyalty would be to the Jewish people rather than to the American republic. On December 7, 2019, Donald Trump told the crowd at a rally in Florida: "A lot of you are in the real estate business, because I know you very well. You're brutal killers. Not nice people at all. But you have to vote for me; you have no choice. You're not going to vote for Pocahontas, I can tell you that. You're not going to vote for the wealth tax. . . . Even if you don't like me; some of you don't. Some of you don't like me at all, actually. And you're going to be my biggest supporters, because you'll be out of business in about 15 minutes, if they get in."[129] If Donald Trump, following the Pittsburgh attack, denounced the "poison of anti-Semitism," if he "promises to combat anti-Semitism" and signs on December 11, 2019, an executive order against "anti-Semitic hate" while strangely declaring that "my administration will never tolerate the suppression, persecution, or silencing of Jews,"[130] his ambiguous discourse shows his ideological closeness to the tenets of the alt-right.

The nomination of Steve Bannon, cofounder of Breitbart News, which he himself considers to be a "platform for the alt-right," to the role of chief executive officer for Trump's first presidential campaign, and his subsequent accession to the White House as chief strategist and senior counselor to the president, and finally the challenge to his nomination by the National Security Council, all emphasized the grip that the far right held at the top of the state. Bannon explicitly wished to "deconstruc[t] the administrative State" and call into question the dominance of a state that was supposedly at the service of a global capitalism that goes against the interests of the people.[131] Though Bannon was dismissed in August of 2016 under pressure of Congress and other advisers to the president, his presence symbolized the influence of white supremacists. It aroused the worry of Jewish circles who thought Bannon, despite his support of Israel, "is bad for the Jews,"[132] especially since a large number of texts published by Breitbart News are openly accompanied by antisemitic comments, one of which even closes with a "Heil Hitler."[133] Bannon's access to the White House was enthusiastically welcomed by David Duke, as well as by many supremacist movements such as American Renaissance, the American Nazi Party, and Occidental Dissent; Bannon also received the support of populist European far-right leaders such as the Front National, and when he met Marine Le Pen he told her: "Let them call you racists, let them call you xenophobes, let them call you nativists, wear it as a badge of honor."[134] Hostile to Muslims, whom it constantly accuses of also wanting to "replace" the Christian American nation, Breitbart News does not hide its exacerbated antisemitism.[135]

In this tense context of a nationalist thrust hostile to minorities, a brand-new threat reignited the flame of antisemitism. On

April 27, 2019, John Timothy Earnest attacked the Chabad synagogue in Poway, located near San Diego, at gun point, on a day of Shabbat that also coincided with Passover. One woman was killed, and three people, including the rabbi, were wounded. The killer, a Presbyterian parishioner, is a Christian who also made references to the actions of Robert Bowers in Pittsburgh. He was also inspired by a Nazi novel, *The Turner Diaries*, that has influenced so many white extremists, including Timothy McVeigh, who placed a bomb in Oklahoma, killing 168 people. Similarly, in a video posted before the Poway attack, Earnest also invoked the actions of Brenton Tarrant, a white supremacist who attacked the Christchurch Mosque in New Zealand a month prior, leading to the death of 50 Muslims. Arrested, he said: "I want to defend our nation against the Jewish people who wants to destroy all white people." He was sentenced to life in prison.[136]

In November of 2019, one year after the Pittsburgh tragedy, undercover FBI agents prevented an attack on another Jewish house of worship, Temple Emanuel in Pueblo, Colorado, by a white supremacist, an antisemite and member of a Nazi organization, just as he was ready to act. Richard Holzer is an adherent of holy race war. His home was full of Nazi material and insignia. During his attempted attack on the Reform temple, he carried a copy of *Mein Kampf.* He justified his act by declaring: "I wish the Holocaust really did happen. They need to die."[137] One month later, in December 2019, a kosher deli in an ultra-Orthodox neighborhood in New Jersey was attacked at gunpoint by two individuals who would ultimately die in their confrontation with the police; a police officer was killed, as were three people, including the owner and a yeshiva student; more were wounded.[138] Violent antisemitic acts took place throughout 2019, particularly in New York and especially in Brooklyn. Many Orthodox Jews were wounded during a Hanukkah celebration by another adherent of Nazism and of Hitler's ideas, while "Heil Hitlers" and "Gas the Jews" were scrawled on the walls of Columbia University.[139]

In this atmosphere of both latent and explicit violence, the coronavirus gave way across the world to a new conspiracy theory that accused the Jews of causing the virus; antimasking demonstrations included signs showing a rat wearing a Star of David underneath the slogan "The real plague."[140] The alt-right, as well as other conservative movements, took advantage of this pretext. The Tea Party was once again front and center. Its militants began to protest against any violation of their freedoms, such as mask mandates and confinements imposed by East Coast elites, accused of wanting to muzzle the protests not only of rural America but of all Americans who feel abandoned and fear the supposed expertise of elites who want to destroy their paradise. Standing in solidarity with various reactionary movements, Jenny Beth Martin, one of the founders of the Tea Party, played an important role in this populist thrust.[141] The Jews found themselves accused of controlling the Chinese laboratories that created the coronavirus in order to destroy Christian civilization.[142] According to the Anti-Defamation League, the virus allowed conspiracy theorists to "advance their antisemitic theories that Jews are responsible for creating the virus, are spreading it to increase their control over a decimated population, or they are profiting off it."[143] A supremacist sheriff in Milwaukee even claimed that, thanks to the virus, George Soros could better establish his world domination.[144] Boldly maintaining the most outlandish comparisons, the leader of a white militia in Idaho denounced the passivity of the Jews during the Shoah and promised that white Americans would know, unlike them, how to fight against a confinement that aims to annihilate them.[145] And thus the coronavirus was integrated into the long list of accusations that have circulated through the mists of time, from the myth of the blood libel to the poisoning of wells or the dissemination of the plague of which the Jews are accused in the United States.[146] This last incrimination, which smells a lot like a return to the Middle Ages,[147] is the perfect setting for a rapid increase in antisemitic threats and violence.[148] To such a degree that "the current popular writing about American Jews in the era of the pandemic (and Trump) feels eerily like *Leidensgeschichte* (the history of suffering), but without the *Gelehrtengeschichte* (the history of learning) that was equally a hallmark of much nineteenth-century Jewish historiography."[149]

Even if the population in its entirety does not share these antisemitic prejudices, the American Anti-Defamation League showed that attacks have increased by 30 percent in 2016 and 2017, and by 57 percent between 2017 and 2018. In an explosive report published May 12, 2020, it counted 2,117 antisemitic acts in the first six months of 2020 alone.[150] Similarly, in May of 2020, the Counter Extremism Project estimated that 199 groups—either Nazi-inspired or influenced by antisemitic white supremacist ideology—are active in the United States.[151] Between California, New York, and Pittsburgh, the true target is a United States that has embraced globalization, associated with modernity and Jewish domination in the minds of those in the radical right, and not the Deep South of Leo Frank. And Pittsburgh, far from Atlanta and the South, at the heart of this modern Pennsylvania, a symbol of cultural and technological revitalization after having known the tragedy of deindustrialization, continues to be a den for radical white supremacists who are solidly implanted at the heart of American society. It is a firmly patrolled city and territory. "In just the past several weeks, a white supremacist group held a march down a main boulevard there. About

100 people attended a white supremacist music festival in the area. A vocal white supremacist who had posted a call online to murder local Jews was released from prison. And flyers with white nationalist slogans have papered the city."[152] The trauma is such that a number of Pittsburgh Jews took their children out of schools, and attendance at synagogues has brutally declined. Everywhere, on every part of the territory, considerable efforts are made to protect Jewish institutions.[153]

What will happen post-2021, after Donald Trump's campaign, which has explicitly called for the mobilization of far-right organizations like the Proud Boys, ordering them to "stand back and stand by?"[154] Will the crusade of the white supremacists magically disappear by the end of the Trump years? There is certainly room for doubt given that, on several occasions, Donald Trump, reusing the same rhetoric before his riled crowds, has called Joe Biden a "a servant of the globalists, lobbyists, wealthy donors and Washington vultures who got rich bleeding America dry."[155] Will this antisemitic mobilization experience an upswing with the arrival of Joe Biden, who intends to restore the role of an interventionist state and who is surrounded, like Barack Obama, by Jewish figures such as Janet Yellen, treasury secretary, Merrick Garland as attorney general, Antony Blinken as secretary of state, Alejandro Mayorkas as secretary of homeland security, Avril Haines as director of national intelligence, Ron Klain as chief of staff, and David Cohen as director of the CIA?[156] Even more noticeable, it is certainly the first time in American history that so many of them are part of the Cabinet rather than being limited to the president's entourage. On their own, "they are enough to constitute a minyan . . . whether 'it's good for the Jews' remains to be seen."[157] This access to the Cabinet, shared with other people from various minority groups, is occurring at the same time as the number of Jewish judges on the Supreme

Court is decreasing. If, in the Obama years, three Jewish judges sat on the court without there being any Protestants, things have profoundly changed after the death of Ruth Bader Ginsburg and the nomination of conservative judges during the Trump years.

As a final nose thumbing, the fate of Biden's presidency played out in Georgia during that week of January 2021 when two crucial Senate seats threatened to tip the majority of the Senate and grant more latitude to the new president. For the first time, an African American, Raphael Warnock, born in Savannah, in the Deep South whose long history with slavery is connected to the memory of the Confederacy, campaigned at the same time as Trump and managed to win one of the two senate seats. In his speeches, he recalled and condemned the bombing of the Atlanta synagogue in 1958 as well as the Pittsburgh massacre. His opponent was a Republican candidate who explicitly defended white supremacy. Some members of her entourage were accused of being close to the Ku Klux Klan and of being conspiracy theorists. Her success confirmed the deep shifts revealed by the election of an African American representative for South Carolina in 2018 and by the words of the white mayor of New Orleans condemning white supremacy.[158] The other Democratic candidate for these senatorial races in Georgia, in a final irony at this historical moment, happened to be a young Jewish candidate, Jon Ossoff, born in Atlanta. In a letter addressed to the Jewish community in this city so often close to the narrative, he spontaneously evoked the history of his family of "Ashkenazi immigrants who fled pogroms at the turn of the 20th century." He continued: "I am running against a virulent and unrepentant anti-Semite, Sen. David Perdue, who lengthened my nose in attack ads and refused to apologize for it despite the demands of the American Jewish Committee." Finally, he emphasized that his opponent "has supported the growth of right-wing extremism,

which is a threat to Jews in America."[159] Married to a Jewish doctor, his success sounds, at least symbolically, like the end of the
Frank affair, like a deep transformation of this South where so
many newcomers have come, far from any form of racism, thanks
to the birth of a new "Southern nation" that has succeeded in
slowly moving away from the lost causes of the Confederacy, as
is seemingly indicated by the support given to Obama in 2008
by three Confederate states and five Southern states.[160]

Nonetheless, nothing is written in stone. The myth of the
Jewish Republic emerged in the United States in the 1930s with
Franklin Roosevelt, and then again in 2000 with Barack Obama.
Will it be rejuvenated with its procession of antisemitic move-
ments, each more deadly than the last, nourished by the recent
nominations to Biden's Cabinet, a president who "dreams of
Franklin Roosevelt" and whose "audacious program is modeled
on what Roosevelt did when he rose to power in 1922?"[161]

Does the putsch attempt on January 6, 2021, at the Capitol,
intended to prevent the definitive nomination of Joe Biden to the
presidency of the United States, announce this new extremist
mobilization? During this violent attack at the Capitol, one militant wore a shirt on which could be read "Camp Auschwitz,"
"Work sets you free"; on signs, "Save the children," which evokes
the children who have supposedly been taken by the proponents
of globalism, headed by George Soros. Also present: the neo-
Nazis of the NSC-131 (Nationalist Social Club, 131st Division),
the Oath Keepers, and the Proud Boys, some of whom wore
T-shirts with the letters "6MWE," meaning "6 Million Wasn't
Enough," a continuation of the radical extremist group The
Order.[162] This organization is comprised of many thousands of
members and has been responsible for numerous violent acts
denounced by the FBI.[163] Other demonstrators brandished Cru-
sader crosses, while one individual resembling an Orthodox

priest held up a sign that read: "Exclude court judges, Senators, and American Presidents who are nothing but deadly circumcisers and perverts." A true "Christian insurrection" was at play here with its giant crosses and its supplicants kneeling in prayer, while others blew a shofar to topple, under the banner of Jesus, the walls of the Capitol, like Joshua and the walls of Jericho before them.[164]

Some of the members of the mob brandished the Confederate flag inside the Capitol under the portraits of the founding fathers.[165] They hailed from that Deep South with such a dark reactionary, racist, and antisemitic past, a past with which it had nonetheless just parted. Other demonstrators flew the Betsy Ross flag, the first iteration of the American flag with thirteen stars displayed in a circle. Others openly exhibited various signs of the extreme right, of QAnon conspiracy theorists, as well as gallows with nooses (brought to threaten Mike Pence and perhaps Nancy Pelosi) hanging from them to evoke the lynching of Blacks and Jews, as described in *The Turner Diaries* whose Nazi imaginary has already inspired so many deadly attacks against synagogues.[166] Unused bombs and weapons were found inside the building.[167] The reasoning was similar to that of the Charlottesville events, but disorganized. Like rioters crawling out from the dregs of society rather than like organized militants, it is the state itself they threaten now. More worrisome, they act, as the FBI will condemn, thanks to the complicity of the police, which has been infiltrated by these white supremacists set on destroying an abhorred state.[168]

That same day, antisemitic tracts were handed out on the streets of New York, announcing a Jewish war against whites, and two days later a Confederate flag was planted on the facade of the

Museum of Jewish Heritage of New York, which commemorates the Shoah. From Atlanta to Washington and New York, the Confederate flag resurges from the depths of history as a symbol of the alt-right's ambition to contest white people's feelings of exclusion by extending their hold over the city that symbolizes the Jewish presence in the United States.[169] The fate of American democracy seems for a moment to be tipping toward the worst outcome, given how incapable the state seems to be to contain this armed mob. For many dramatic hours, the ideas behind Charlottesville, here pushed to their paroxysm, threatened to destroy the symbols of American democracy and to annihilate its exceptionalism, despite the multiplicity of semi-independent institutions.[170]

Its failure conferred another dimension to this quasi-coup performed by far-right supremacist fringe groups with Southern ideals. It seemed to close a chapter in American history opened by the lynching of Leo Frank: with the election of Jon Ossoff, born in Atlanta, who swore on the Jewish Bible that used to belong to Rabbi Rothschild, who officiated during the tragedy at the Atlanta synagogue, "the South buries its Jewish past." "An inextricable link" between "Frank's lynching and the election of Ossoff is constituted, between the past and the future of Jewish life in the South," a Jewish community that has taken root in Marietta, the cursed location of Frank's lynching.[171] From one century to another, is it a history of tears that has come to a close in the South, while a violent antisemitic mobilization on the part of far-right supremacists takes hold at the very heart of the great cities in Northern states, from New York to California, including Pennsylvania where, in November of 2020, the Republican candidate for governor, Doug Mastriano, a spokesperson for the antisemitic radical right who participated in the January 6 insurrection, circulated an image in which he claimed abortions are worse than the Shoah? And still it maintains part of its influence in rural Georgia, as is shown by the election of Marjorie Taylor Greene to the House of Representatives, a Republican who is also a fierce adept of antisemitic ideas and of QAnon conspiracy theories inspired by *The Protocols of the Elders of Zion*.

# CONCLUSION

## Kishinev *à l'américaine*—the End of Hope?

History has been known to experience unforeseen twists. It just so happens that the oldest synagogue in Pittsburgh, the place that will forever symbolize the most extreme antisemitic violence at the heart of the United States, a kind of American pogrom, was built in 1905 by survivors of Kishinev. This city, cursed in Jewish memory, already haunted the memories of Atlanta Jews when Leo Frank was lynched. There it took root even more solidly after the recent Pittsburgh attack, comparable in its impact on the Jewish population to the "city of slaughter" that Kishinev has continued to represent in Jewish memory. Kishinev became a turning point in Jewish history, one that led Jews to flee to New York, "the promised city."[1] In May of 2018, Avishai Margalit still wondered why "this pogrom receive[d] world-wide attention and acquire[d] a symbolic status in the modern Jewish life as the exemplary pogrom."[2] He believed that, similarly to how Picasso's *Guernica* repudiates the Nazi bombardments over the city, how Franz Werfel's book *The Forty Days of Musa Dagh* speaks out against the massacre of Armenians, or how Yevgeny Yevtushenko's poem "Babi Yar" condemns the 1941 massacre of Jews in Kiev, Kishinev has found its place at the heart of Jewish memory through Bialik's poem "In the City of Slaughter." It singlehandedly incarnates all pogroms and, through Bialik's poem, becomes their "archetype."[3] If "In the City of Slaughter" has ingrained itself deep into the conscience of American Jews, across generations, to the point that they continuously reference it, it is also because Bialik's famous poem raises the question of Jewish distress in the face of violence, fear, and the call to self-defense that have now come to affect Jewish Americans.[4]

Aside from Hayim Nahman Bialik and Philip Roth, it is also "in response" to Kishinev and to Kiev that Shalom Aleichem published his pogrom letters (1905–1906) shortly after his arrival to the United States. In this imagined correspondence between Jacob, who emigrated to the United States, and Yisroel, who remained in Russia, the references to Kishinev and to pogroms are constant.[5] Similarly, Abraham Cahan, born in 1860 near Vilna, emigrated to the United States in 1882. In 1917, he published his famous fictional autobiography, *The Rise of David Levinsky*, in which he evokes the violence of the Kishinev, Odessa, and Kiev pogroms.[6] During the same period, Lamed Shapiro left Russia for the United States where in 1919 he published *The Jewish Government and Other Stories*, short stories written in reaction to the Kishinev pogroms and to Zhytomyr, whose extreme bestiality he describes.[7] In 1942, Saul Bellow published "Katz and Cohen," a short story about two Jews who emigrate to the United States, set in 1922. During the course of a conversation, Cohen confides to Katz that he was in Kishinev during the pogrom.[8] In 1966, Bernard Malamud publishes *The Fixer*, a work that often references the Russian pogroms. It fictionalizes the 1911 tragedy of Menahem Mendel Beilis, who in Kiev was accused of having committed ritual murder against a young boy whom he stabbed repeatedly in order to collect his blood to make matzoh for Passover. Gru-beshov, the prosecutor who has been persecuting him for almost two years, threatens Yacov Bok (the protagonist repre-senting Beiliss) with a "bloodbath . . . that will outdo the ferocity of the so-called Kishinev massacres" if he does not confess to the crime.[9]

Kishinev is also on Ira Stigman's mother's mind when he emi-grates to the United States, in Henry Roth's autobiography pub-lished in 1994, at a period when the United States was already experiencing an abundance of antisemitic violence. "Who in all the world is more benighted than the Russian *mujik?* Who doesn't remember their pogroms, the Kishinev pogroms, in 1903? Pogroms led by seminary students, especially on Easter— Kishinev when I was still a maid."[10] Kishinev reappears in Ira's writing, aka Henry Roth's, in his vehement attack against James Joyce, once sanctified, now vilified for "bringing to an end the self-imposed exile" by being mad at Leopold Bloom who remem-bers nothing: "Of the Kishinev pogrom the year before, noth-ing, of Dreyfus, nothing." He has "no recall of Friday candles, no recall of *matzahs*. . . . no *cheder*, no *davening*, no Yom Kippur, no Purim. . . . Not a brass candlestick, not a *dreidel*, a *challah* on Fri-day night, the agony of 1942, the expulsion? No."[11] American Jews find themselves also "at the mercy of a rude stream."[12] Kishinev is an obsession to a number of authors who, stricken, remember this pogrom: while it is not the deadliest, it terrorizes through its evo-cation of a past that is nevertheless receding.[13]

Does the romance of American exceptionalism, sanctified by Salo Baron as by the majority of historians of American Juda-ism, find itself irreversibly belied by Pittsburgh, by this Ameri-can version of Kishinev, even if the frenzied muzhiks are replaced by lone neo-Nazis? Was this exile, which has become an excep-tion and a protective home, a lure all along? Does this succession of antisemitic attacks led by white supremacists invalidate the peaceful vision of an integration so perfect that it managed to "whitewash" the Jews?[14] With Pittsburgh, have American Jews joined the long list of victims of massacres both denounced and celebrated by the tenants of a lachrymose view of history? Has their current and future history also become a history of tears? As Matthew Friedman, a professor of American history, observes with emotion:

> We have been saying Kaddish all week for eleven people murdered in the sanctuary of the Tree of Life synagogue in Pittsburgh. We have said it in our schuls, standing in the autumnal chill at candlelight vigils, contemplatively in the solitude of our homes. We have said these words before, for the dead of Babi Yar, Kishinev, Würzburg, Mainz, York, and so many places of horror over two millennia. But this time feels different. Kishinev was in 1903. Babi Yar was in 1941. This was Pittsburgh, in the United States of America, in the 21st century. We told ourselves that it wouldn't happen again. . . . But that's a lie, and we know it. Antisemitism is the background static of our daily lives, a persistent and unremitting noise that we have chosen to ignore, or choose to live with. . . . We were shocked by the massacre in Pittsburgh, but I doubt that many of us were surprised. This was a pogrom, and we have seen those many, many times before. It feels like all of the rhetoric, the politics of division, and the mobilization of an explicitly Christian national identity have been leading to this exact point. . . . Robert Bowers did not *need* a direct order from Donald Trump or the Republican Party to inspire his rampage in Pittsburgh. It was enough for him to know that his antisemitism was legitimate, that his national community was under threat of invasion from the outside, and that this invasion was sponsored by *others* within his community's borders, and that is what Trump's

America gave him. . . . And in the America of Robert Bowers and many, many more like him, the only good Jews are dead Jews. This will happen again.[15]

Kishinev haunted the memory of Atlanta Jews during the lynching of Leo Frank, which occurred only a few years after the Russian pogrom. Again, it is to Kishinev, as we mentioned, that Philip Roth makes reference during the candidacy of the fascist Lindbergh to the 1940 presidential elections. The "sheer surprise of his nomination" had awoken an "atavistic sense of being undefended that had more to do with Kishinev and the pogroms of 1903."[16] Its memory returned forcefully during the Pittsburgh pogrom. The white supremacist Robert Bowers joined the ranks of "the posterity of Kishinev murderers."[17] Bialik's "In the City of Slaughter" even inspires the reasoning that connects the two cities.[18] Henceforth, between Kishinev, Pittsburgh, and Paris, bloodbaths the world over punctuate the history of modern Jews who cannot escape a lachrymose vision of their history. The Pittsburgh massacre executed in the name of Nazi racial theories singlehandedly nullified Baron's irenicism, his faith in a "nation of nations." Despite its exceptionalism, this American home also turns out to be bathed in tears. Pittsburgh shook the peace of mind of American Jews who had always been so proud to evoke George Washington's fabulous letter to the members of the Newport synagogue. All of a sudden,

the problem with the deep-seated faith Jews have maintained in America is that it has propped up a broader vision of American exceptionalism and occluded the damages of exceptionalist thinking. As a description of American Jewish life, exceptionalism has brushed under the rug the exclusion and discrimination Jews have faced. Worse, it has stood in the way of an honest reckoning with the violent possibilities that have long simmered under the surface of its claims. The Pittsburgh shooting, on top of the more open expressions of anti-Semitism in the past few years, makes that brutally clear. For American Jews, that reckoning will be painful. It will challenge the very basis of our acceptance in this country and make us ask whether the opportunities and privileges we gained came not because America held particular promise for Jews, but rather because it withheld that promise in so many ways to so many other people. Should we ever have believed in American exceptionalism, even just for Jews, when all around us was evidence of the limitations and ravages of that exceptionalism?[19]

Is it not now advisable to "return to a lachrymose conception" as "an essential tool to understand the Jewish past?"[20] The most tragic past has not allowed itself to be forgotten. Far from Europe, it shapes consciousnesses, releases fears. Kishinev is its symbol, given that, beyond the Russian pogroms—those from the nineteenth century as those during the interwar period—the Crusades rarely make a resurgence in the most enviable environments in Jewish history. The period of the Crusades surfaces only episodically in Jewish memory, in this country of abundance where the Second Amendment is like a talisman that keeps fears at bay. It does not seem, in contrast to what Arno Mayer claims, that across the Atlantic the memory of the pogroms implemented by the pilgrims who went to liberate Jerusalem from Turkish hold during the first Crusade, that the memory of "the attack on the Jews set a disastrous precedent, depositing a fatal poison in the European psyche and imagination,"[21] of which the Shoah would be the ultimate consequence. But in Georgia, as in California or Mississippi, Worms or Mainz mean very little.[22] Across American society, in Atlanta, Charlottesville, or Oklahoma City, the

Crusades barely emerge from the depths of time and do not haunt the imagination of its Jewish communities.

All the more since Jewish emigrants left the old continent and its tragedies ages ago. The great waves of emigration occurred in the nineteenth and at the start of the twentieth centuries, first from Germany between 1820 and 1840 following the "Hep-Hep" riots in Wurzburg that spread throughout the country. Later, at the turn of the century, it is from the Russian Empire that Jews leave en masse for the United States. Leo Frank's lynching occurs immediately following the great wave of Russian pogroms, while the Pittsburgh massacre happens a full century after the frantic flight of the Jews leaving behind them the violence but also the misery of Eastern Europe. The grandparents of American Jews confronted with the Pittsburgh tragedy are those who rejected the Europe of the pogroms, of Kishinev, which has remained deeply anchored in their memory; this was not the case for German Jews from the first wave of immigration.[23] Perhaps the Russian Jews at the turn of the twentieth century still remembered the distant Crusades that unfolded far from their own geographical space? Truth be told, it was more likely the massacres organized by the Cossack Chmielnicki, mentioned by Baron, that populated their nightmares and then came to life with Kishinev and the era of the pogroms. Far from any teleological conception of history, the massacres during the Crusades are no longer at the heart of the American Jewish collective consciousness, whereas they remain largely present in the psyche of European Jews.

The persistence of this distant past has faded away on the new continent. Its contemporary resonance can no longer be taken for granted within a society bereft of any early history. Moreover, American Jews are not facing the same accusations. The

Christian antisemitism that considered them the murderers of Jesus Christ concerns them even less. The religious messianism that overtook the Crusaders does not have an equivalent in a society where militants for a Christian renewal support Jerusalem: no holy war threatens the Jews. And *kiddush Hashem*, the collective suicide to sanctify the name of God in extreme circumstances, hardly registers in the lives of peaceful suburban Jews, mostly untouched by any form of martyrology, and whose souls nobody tries to save through conversion. The Rhineland massacres, or those of Blois in 1171, are bathed in a highly charged mystical atmosphere that evoke distant biblical episodes or the collective suicide of Masada more than the prosaic realities of America's society of abundance.[24] The minds of Atlanta or of Pittsburgh Jews of today are crossed by no tragic notion of redemption. If American Jews seem not to remember these massacres that nevertheless marked a shift in Jewish history, it is that their lives are unfolding within the pluralist context of a society that they consider to be their permanent home, a home where no danger should threaten them. The period of the Crusades is a universe that is foreign to them. The violence to which they are confronted is empty of any apocalyptic religious foundation, which previously required a forced conversion. While the crowds that lynched Leo Frank may have evoked the hordes of fanatical peasants from the Crusades, their violence was not rooted in messianic beliefs. And contemporary murders are carried out by lone wolves who claim to defend an Aryan nation; the Church has nothing to do with it. In the context of twentieth-century America, the motivations of Crusaders belong to a bygone era, although the greed that motivated many peasants could be linked to myths surrounding the economic power of the Jews,[25] ideas shared by so many contemporary murderers of the far right.

The situation is similar for the most atrocious episode of modern Jewish history before the Shoah. The systematic slaughters carried out by Cossacks in the seventeenth century, frequently allied to the Tartars, do not haunt American Jews, who seem unaware of their abuses when they lived through Frank's lynching or through the multiple slaughters of recent years. Like the Crusades, these pogroms, unrivaled in scope and in savagery, have disappeared from their imaginary. In Atlanta, just like in Pittsburgh, but also in Oklahoma City, in Pueblo, or in Brooklyn, Kishinev is spontaneously brought up. The imperative to remember does not reach further back than that. The very name of Chmielnicki, which terrified generations of European Jews, seems to have gotten lost in the United States. No one thinks of the Crusaders, and even less of the cruel Cossack leader who was so feared by their European ancestors. From 1648 to 1649, these slaughters, whose extent far surpassed the atrocities of the Crusades, these pogroms that led to one hundred thousand deaths and the elimination of one-third of the Jewish population of Ukraine, a part of which were sold as slaves in Istanbul, these pogroms whose bestiality almost foreshadow the Shoah itself as they were recounted in various chronicles (including that of Nathan Hanover),[26] also date back to a period that wildly predated the birth of the United States and the arrival of Jewish emigrants. These horrors do not enter into the psyche of American Jews any more than the Crusades do. They are instead focalized on the Kishinev moment, still alive in a memory transmitted from one generation to the next at the heart of families who emigrated from these regions.

Sheltered within peaceful communities shaped by a liberal Judaism that was barely concerned with messianisms, by millenarianisms, or by conflicts surrounding orthodoxy, American Jews link the unexpected violence they experience neither to the

Crusades nor to the Ukrainian pogroms, nor even, on the other side of history, to the Shoah, which remains the absolute catastrophe, which confirms a lachrymose conception of history that is the purview of the old country. These events remain foreign to the United States, who have lynchings and attacks, small beans compared to the Shoah. True, in 2013, for example, 73 percent of American Jews believe that remembering the Shoah is an essential component of their personal condition.[27] True, the vital role that the Shoah plays in the lives of American Jews is undeniable and remains "central to it," even while it has known some shifts over time.[28] True, American Jews have dedicated an endless number of ceremonies and museums to the extermination camps, honoring the victims of Auschwitz, keeping alive their memory, and revering the heroes of the Warsaw Ghetto, as well as the Righteous Among the Nations. They have internalized the Shoah such that it has taken a central place at the heart of a proper civil religion. A proposition was even made to celebrate, as in Israel, the Day of the Shoah, with a day of rest.[29] Nevertheless, despite the shock provoked by commercial films such as *Holocaust* or *Schindler's List*, despite the fears aroused by the Yom Kippur War and the risks of total annihilation facing Israel, the Shoah remains so unique that it seems to belong to a European history made of tears from which most American Jews have moved away, to which they do not belong, and that does not trigger their fear when they are in turn faced with radical antisemitic violence, in Pittsburgh, for example. If Kishinev or Captain Dreyfus are often mentioned in the available testimonies of individuals faced with extreme antisemitic acts, neither seems to evoke, in one way or another, the Shoah. It is as though, by virtue of its exceptional dimension, it could not be compared to any other tragic event, as though through its inconceivability, it escapes any historical analysis. As though, finally, following the example of so many Jewish historians of the diaspora who study Jewish life throughout time, and who avoid the Shoah as though it were separated from normal Jewish history by a "wall,"[30] the only possible reference for American Jews to the murders they endure could be Kishinev and the era of the pogroms. "Jewish suffering" can be identified, before the Shoah but likely after as well, with this pogrom elevated to the status of absolute distress.[31]

In Europe, on the contrary, as David Nirenberg observed, the memory of the Crusades comes flooding back with the appearance of the Russian pogroms and those at the turn of the twentieth century, to ingrain itself into Jewish consciousness, along with the Shoah, and establish in the minds of many European commentators a kind of continuity between the twelfth century and Auschwitz.[32] It justifies, for Yitzhak Baer, the tragic and lachrymose conception of Jewish history, against which Salo Baron rises up from the summit of his Chair at Columbia University. Far from the United States, Baer celebrates the martyrs of the Crusades. In his view, this tragic moment foreshadows the catastrophes that await the Jews during the years of the rise of Nazism. This is a similitude bereft of meaning for Baron, as for American Jews who fully subscribe to Roosevelt's New Deal, in which they see nothing ominous. In the prolongation of the first decades of the twentieth century, anti-Jewish violence would incessantly repeat a cyclical pattern, each time signaling the reemergence of the issue of suicide, from the Crusades to the Shoah. The "trauma" of the Crusades permanently shaped the collective memory of European Jews, whereas the period of the pogroms forced an identification between the Shoah and the long martyrology of centuries past.[33] This remembrance pushes Baer to radically reject exile at the very moment when Salo Baron is theorizing its potential in the New World. The memory of the Crusades that culminates with the Shoah—that Baer seems to anticipate in 1936—would thus impose itself as proof of the impossibility of the diaspora, justifying this lachrymose conception of the history of exile that Baron is opposing in the United States.[34]

The profound pessimism founded on an absolutely lachrymose view of history that demonstrates, in Baer's view, the soundness and urgency of the Zionist project, leaves Salo Baron—despite his Zionist sympathies—completely cold. It is because, in the second half of the twentieth century, he is theorizing the collective consciousness of American Jews who are almost immune to the tears that flow abundantly on the old continent. Is it the case today, when antisemitic hate is knocking on their door, when 35 percent of American Jews claim to have been confronted with violent acts in the past five years? For Gary Rosenblatt, "In all those years, I never encountered such a level of palpable fear, anger, and vulnerability among American Jews as I do today, with attacks—verbal, physical, and, in two tragic cases, fatal— coming from the far left and the far right of our own society, and from attackers whose only common denominator is hatred of Jews. We had believed that such worries were relegated to our brothers and sisters in Europe, with its centuries of ugly history of Jew hatred and pogroms, culminating in the Holocaust. Now the attacks are *the* main topic of discussion among an American Jewish community shaken to its core."[35] While commemorating the second anniversary of Pittsburgh, one survivor of the event exclaimed, "I always thought our government would protect us, I don't think that anymore!" To protect themselves from any further large-scale attacks in 2021, and avoid the charge of passivity or cowardice levied by Bialik after Kishinev, a number of American Jews have decided to arm themselves. Meanwhile, the number of supporters of a far-right movement symbolized by

QAnon continues to rise dangerously, constituting over 15 percent of the American population.[36]

Faced with these fears, subjective though they may be, is American happiness a thing of the past? All the more since the recent political visibility of American Jews—who henceforth ignore the advice of Stefan Zweig and also Salo Baron, both of whom urged American Jews to immerse themselves in their own local communities—makes of them perfect targets of antisemitic campaigns? Since their proximity to the leaders of the Democratic Party, from Barack Obama to Joe Biden, has given new life to the myth of the Jewish Republic, decried from Drumont to Hitler? Since the racist Trumpian crowds risk permanently threatening democracy?[37] Since the attachment, though hedged and increasingly reserved, of American Jews to the state of Israel has also brought the resurgence of that other myth of the double allegiance, the idea of a Jewish conspiracy destined to incite the American government to lead wars against its own interests?[38]

And what if the foundation of America was coming to its end? If the tears came to flow in the New World? What would become of the diasporist dream glimpsed by Salo Baron, far from the Old Country where Jews have become practically invisible, reduced to a tiny minority? They number 1,300,000 on the European continent these days, whereas the Jewish population was estimated at near 10,000,000 on the eve of the Second World War. They are mostly found in Western Europe: about 400,000–500,000 in France; 300,000 in Germany; in Russia, only 160,000 Jews are left. Together, they make up only 9 percent of the world's Jewish population. In 2020, there are not more Jews in Europe than there were in the year 1,000. In that distant past, as today, they represented only 0.5 percent of Europe's entire population.[39] The Europe of today is almost *judenrein*.[40] The tears have indeed flowed so abundantly, the suffering there was so horrendous, so interminable, that the diasporist project is practically reduced to the *goldene medine*. But the latter has itself been shaken, as the fear not of a Russian or Ukrainian pogrom but of a deadly attack by the supremacist far right becomes a starker reality with every passing day, casting doubt over the long-term viability of this American home.

In the end, does not a lachrymose conception of history find its raison d'être through this challenge to American exceptionalism, the only place left where one could escape violent antisemitic movements? Salo Baron would turn in his grave. Such an iconoclastic interrogation overturning his American dream would be unbearable to him. What stupidity, he would say, to compare Pittsburgh to Kishinev! Yet does not America, so dear to Tocqueville, nevertheless join, much to Baron's displeasure, a long cohort of persecutions, even when these cannot be comparable to the pogroms or even less to the Shoah? Does it not from now on, against all expectations, subscribe to a lachrymose conception of history that it alone thought it could escape? The American home, the golden land, does it not reveal itself to be, despite the flamboyant destiny of American Jews, despite their exceptional integration, a utopia that has annihilated the logic of diasporists, a utopia already brutalized by the tragedies and expulsions of modern and contemporary history?

The future seems to be in danger for both "homes" that gather,[41] at present, the vast majority of diasporic Judaism. At the heart of the American home, the always increasing visibility of the Jews and the progressive transformation of some into state Jews—while a populist mobilization infused by radical alt-right currents is in full swing—does not bode well. By leaving the periphery to gain access to the center, they stoke this hatred and, despite their increasing detachment from the Jewish state, which does not prevent the flames of violent antisemitism, such as the ones provoked on American soil by the clashes between Hamas and Israel,[42] their membership in the nation of nations is weakened. The French home experiences other challenges that dampen many hopes and that also reanimate worries when faced with the rapid increase of antisemitic acts over the turn of the twenty-first century, acts inventoried each year by the Commission nationale consultative des droits de l'Homme (National Consultative Commission on Human Rights). Equally concerning is the glaring lack of public reaction after the assassination of Jewish children in Toulouse—those of Ilan Halimi, Sarah Halimi, and Mireille Knoll. These violent attacks have sown fear, and forced a number of children to leave public schools as their parents hasten to find new homes in less hostile neighborhoods. Since Vichy, the trust in a protective state has been eroded, and the royal alliance of the past is flickering, all the more as the state loses some of its strength and legitimacy with each passing day. Instead of moving toward the state, as they do in the American home in order to achieve their integration while distancing themselves from Israel, a number of French Jews seem to move away from it. Sensitive to the zeitgeist, they withdraw into their communities and turn their hopes, as though by substitution, to the Jewish state as an imagined home.

True, the United States, with France—the "two homes"—continues to be the solid foundation for a pleasant place to live, for liberal and pluralist societies where every day new vibrant forms of sociability are imagined, where harmonious relationships are forged with neighbors, where the most diverse forms of creativity can blossom, and where, despite recurring threats—the recent explosion of antisemitic acts, from Toulouse to Pittsburgh—the certainty of a happy life remains, justifiably, deeply rooted generation after generation. Does not this hope for a good life nevertheless reveal a new illusion on both sides of the Atlantic? This, just when identity politics are in full bloom, when ethnic solidarities are taking root, turning their backs on universalism? This at a time when religious anathemas are springing up everywhere, and when an authoritarian civilization that rejects the Enlightenment is looming on the horizon? This at a time when intolerant populist mobilizations are on the rise and when the imagined protection of the state is receding slowly, as is the idea of a communal citizenship that draws its foundation from a shared public space?

Salo Baron would no longer recognize the American model he so often lauded. He would have sunk into pessimism, would have glimpsed with sadness a new and improbable vale of tears. At the dawn of the twenty-first century, his loyal student Yosef Hayim Yerushalmi is also alarmed and has become an echo of Baronian nostalgia for a Middle Ages that alone managed to escape the terrors of modern tyranny. Nevertheless careful to try and discern some signs of hope in today's life, he did not hide his hopelessness, his fear of seeing "his people" once again threatened in their very existence. He knew that "we cannot explore the history of Jewish hope without at the same time exploring the history of Jewish despair," that a number of "fallen" Jews in their "loneliness" have given up out of "a genuine despair in a Jewish future." From then on, he traced the successive lineage of a "geography of hope" fluctuating between Spain and Poland, Lithuania and Germany.[43] Currently, this diasporist geography of hope seems henceforth to be limited, despite all these causes for worry, despite these tears and this hopelessness, to these two lone homes. Despite the bad winds that, every day, or almost, sweep across them?

# NOTES

## PREFACE TO THE AMERICAN EDITION

1. John Higham, *Strangers in the Land: Patterns of American Nativism, 1860–1925* (New Brunswick, N.J.: Rutgers University Press, 2002), 52 and 90–91.

2. Naomi Cohen, *Jews in Christian America* (New York: Oxford University Press, 1992); Philip Hamburger, *Separation of Church and State* (Cambridge, Mass.: Harvard University Press, 2004); Noah Feldman, *Divided by God: America's Church-State Problem—and What We Should Do About It* (New York: Farrar, Straus and Giroux, 2005); John Fea, *Was America Founded as a Christian Nation?* (Louisville, Ky.: Westminster John Knox, 2011). Geoffrey Stone, "The Second Awakening: A Christian Nation?" *Georgia State University Law Review* 26 (2009–2010).

3. See Morton Borden, *Jews, Turks, and Infidels* (Chapel Hill: University of North Carolina Press, 1984); as well as Jonathan Sarna, *When General Grant Expelled the Jews* (New York: Schocken, 2012).

4. Robert Rockaway and Arnon Gutfeld, "Demonic Images of the Jews in the Nineteenth-Century United States," *American Jewish History* 89, no. 4 (December 2001): 355–81.

5. Quoted by Higham in *Strangers in the Land*, 93. The caricatures of Irish Catholics are racist in nature, representing turned-up noses and monkeylike traits. They are often seen as "white negroes" and are excluded from leadership positions in upscale clubs. John and Robert Kennedy's

father was himself rejected from the Cohasset Country Club. When it came to applying for jobs, the answer was often "No Irish need apply." As Catholics, they were seen as potential traitors.

6. Neil Baldwin, *Henry Ford and the Jews: The Mass Production of Hate* (New York: Public Affairs, 2001).

7. See Henry Feingold, *A Time for Searching: Entering the Mainstream* (Baltimore: John Hopkins University Press, 1995), 2.

8. Pierre Birnbaum, *Les deux maisons: Essai sur la citoyenneté des Juifs en France et aux Etats-Unis* (Paris: Gallimard, 2012).

9. The foremost book on antisemitic behavior continues to be Michael Dobkowski's *The Tarnished Dream* (Westport, Conn.: Greenwood, 1979).

10. See Leonard Dinnerstein, "The Funeral of Rabbi Jacob Joseph," in *Anti-Semitism in American History*, ed. David Gerber (Urbana: University of Illinois Press, 1986).

11. David Gerber, "Anti-Semitism and Jewish-Gentile Relations in American Historiography and the American Past," in *Anti-Semitism in American History*, 16–17.

12. Jonathan Sarna, "Anti-Semitism in American History," *Commentary* 71 (March 1981): 47.

13. Hasia Diner, *A Time of Gathering: The Second Migration, 1820–1880* (Baltimore: John Hopkins University Press, 1992), 169.

14. Diner, 198.

## INTRODUCTION

1. Alexis de Tocqueville, Gerald E Bevan and Isaac Kramnick, *Democracy in America: And Two Essays on America* (London: Penguin, 2003), 563 and 266.

2. National Archives, https://founders.archives.gov/documents/Washington/05-06-02-0135.

3. Thomas Jefferson to Mordecai Manuel Noah, dated May 28, 1818, in *New Era Illustrated Magazine* (1904): 490.

4. "ADDRESS BY EX-PRESIDENT GROVER CLEVELAND." *Publications of the American Jewish Historical Society*, no. 14 (1906): 11–17.

5. John Higham, *Send These to Me* (Baltimore: Johns Hopkins University Press, 1984), 95.

6. Dennis Wrong, "The Rise and Decline of Anti-Semitism in America," in *The Ghetto and Beyond*, ed. Peter Rose (New York: Random House, 1969), 326.

7. Irving Howe, *World of Our Fathers: The Journey of the East European Jews to America and the Life They Found and Made* (New York: Harcourt, 1976), 128.

8. Albert Hirschman, *Shifting Involvements: Private Interest and Public Action* (Princeton, N.J.: Princeton University Press, 1982).

9. Sombart Werner and C. T. Husband, *Why Is There No Socialism in the United States?*, rev. ed. (White Plains, N.Y.: Vintage, 1976).

10. Will Herberg, *Protestant, Catholic, Jew: An Essay on American Religious Sociology* (New York: Doubleday, 1960), 189–90. See Robert Seltzer and Norman Cohen, eds., *The Americanization of the Jews* (New York: New York University Press, 1995).

11. Yuri Slekine, *The Jewish Century* (Princeton, N.J.: Princeton University Press, 2004), 323.

12. I would like to thank François Azouvi, Jean Baumgarten, Judith Lamberger-Birnbaum, and Michael Stanislawski for agreeing to read this manuscript attentively and making numerous pertinent observations to make it more coherent. As always, my gratitude toward Éric Vigne is without limits. Bless him for having waited for this manuscript, which we imagined together many years ago.

## I. SALO BARON, THE GOLDEN LAND, AND THE REFUSAL OF A LACHRYMOSE HISTORY

1. See Robert Liberles, *Salo Wittmayer Baron, Architect of Jewish History* (New York: New York University Press, 1995), chapter 1. Rebecca Kobrin, ed., *Salo Baron: The Past and Future of Jewish Studies in America* (New York: Columbia University Press, 2022).

2. A school for Jewish children in which they learn to read religious texts in Hebrew.

3. For Natan Sznaider, "It could even be claimed that Baron finished what Dubnow had begun." *Jewish Memory and the Cosmopolitan Order* (Cambridge: Polity, 2011), 72.

4. Salo W. Baron, "Ghetto and Emancipation: Shall We Revise the Traditional View?," *Menorah Journal* 14 (June 1928): 514–26.

5. Quoted by Michael Brenner, *Prophets of the Past: Interpreters of Jewish History* (Princeton, N.J.: Princeton University Press, 2010), 122.

6. Joseph Ha-Kohen, *La Vallée des pleurs: Chronique des souffrances d'Israël depuis sa dispersion jusqu'à nos jours* (Paris, 1881), ix–x (my translation).

7. Salo Baron, "Heinrich Graetz, 1817–1891," in Salo Baron, *History and Jewish Historians* (Philadelphia: Jewish Publication Society of America, 1964), 267 and 274.

8. Isaiah Berlin, "Benjamin Disraeli, Karl Marx and the Search of Identity," *Jewish Historical Society of England* 22 (1968–1969): 1.

9. Baron, "Ghetto and Emancipation," 50–51.

10. Baron, 58. In the first half of the seventeenth century, Bogdan Chmielnicki led the revolt of the Cossacks and the Ukrainians against Polish authorities, during which time the worst pogroms happened: it is estimated that over one hundred thousand Jews were massacred. The Human, or Ouman, pogrom took place in 1768; the Ukrainian and Cossack rebels massacred between twenty and thirty thousand Jews.

11. Baron, "Ghetto and Emancipation," 58–59.

12. Baron, 57.

13. Baron, "Heinrich Graetz," 267.

14. Baron, "Ghetto and Emancipation," 52.

15. Baron, 55.

16. Baron, 51.

17. Baron, 50.

18. Baron, 50.

19. Salo Wittmayer Baron, *A Social and Religious History of the Jews*, vol. 9: *Late Middle Ages and Era of European Expansion, 1200–1650* (New York: Columbia University Press, 1965), 9:3–4.

20. Arthur Hertzberg, *The French Enlightenment and the Jews* (New York: Columbia University Press, 1968).

21. Erik Marc Greenberg, "A Prophet and His People: Israel Zangwill and His American Public, 1892–1926 and Beyond" (PhD diss. University of California, Los Angeles, 2012), 68.

22. Horace Kallen, "A Meaning of Americanism," in Horace Kallen, *Culture and Democracy in the United States* (New Brunswick, N.J.: Transaction, 1989), 50–56. See William Toll, "Horace Kallen: Pluralism and American Jewish Identity," *American Jewish History* 85, no. 1 (March 1997): 57–74.

23. Salo Baron, "Is America Ready for Ethnic Minority Rights?," *Jewish Social Studies* (Summer-Autumn 1984): 196. It seems that Baron never mentions Horace Kallen's name in his books and articles.

24. Greenberg, "A Prophet and His People," 83, 125.

25. See Mordecai Kaplan, *Judaism as a Civilization: Toward a Reconstruction of American Jewish Life* (New York: Macmillan, 1934), 284. See Pierre Birnbaum, "The Missing Link: The State in Mordecai Kaplan's Vision of Jewish History," *Jewish Social Studies* 12 (Winter 2006): 64–72.

26. See, for example, Salo Baron, *Steeled by Adversity* (Philadelphia: Jewish Publication Society of America, 1971), 667.

27. Michael Walzer, *On Toleration* (New Haven: Yale University Press, 1997), 83. See Pierre Birnbaum, *Géographie de l'espoir: L'exil, les Lumières et la désassimilation* (Paris: Gallimard, 2004), 308 ff.

28. Michael Walzer, *What It Means to Be an American* (New York: Marsilio, 1992).

29. On the links between Dubnow and Kaplan, see Robert Seltzer, "From Graetz to Dubnov: The Impact of East European Milieu on the Writing of Jewish History," in *The Legacy of Jewish Migration: 1881 and Its Impact*, ed. David Berger (New York: Columbia University Press, 1983). From the same author, see "Graetz, Dubnov, Baron," in the *Jewish Book Annual* 48 (1990–1991).

30. Simon Dubnow, "Diaspora," in *Encyclopedia of the Social Sciences* (New York: Macmillan, 1935), 5:126–30.

31. A *kehillah* is Jewish congregation, an autonomous community led by a counsel of prominent Jews acknowledged and protected by the king.

32. Robert Liberles nevertheless considers that Kallen, like Kaplan, fears the assimilationist consequences of the community as Baron imagined it (*Salo Wittmayer Baron*, 320). He also believes that Kaplan, unlike Baron, wished for more control over the local lives of communities (264).

33. Baron, "Ghetto and Emancipation," 53.

34. Baron, 54.

35. Baron, 62.

36. Baron, 63.

37. Baron, 63.

38. See Robert Liberles, "Salo Baron and Jewish Studies," *Judaism* 45, no. 3 (Summer 1996): 340. However, in certain studies, such as *The Russian*

*Jews Under the Tsar and the Soviets* (New York: Macmillan, 1964), Baron paradoxically lingers to write at length about the suffering that Jews endured, in opposition to his general theory.

39. Salo Wittmayer Baron, *A Social and Religious History of the Jews*, vol. 2: *Christian Era: The First Five Centuries* (New York: Columbia University Press, 1952), 2:40.

40. Quoted by David Engel, "Crisis and Lachrymosity: On Salo Baron, Neobaronianism, and the Study of Modern European Jewish History," *Jewish History* 3/4 (2006): 248. See also Isaac Barzilay, "Yishaq Baer and Salo W. Baron: Two Contemporary Interpreters of Jewish History," *Proceedings of the American Academy for Jewish Research* 60 (1994): 21. On the contrary, Bonfil recognizes the protective nature of the ghetto and emphasizes the Jews' belonging in the city, as well as their creativity. Roberto Bonfil, *Jewish Life in Renaissance Italy* (Berkeley: University of California Press, 1994). On this debate, see David Ruderman, "The Cultural Significance of the Ghetto in Jewish History," in *From Ghetto to Emancipation*, ed. David Myers and William Rowe (Scranton: University of Scranton Press, 1977).

41. David Engel, *Historians on the Jews and the Holocaust* (Stanford: Stanford University Press, 2010), 83.

42. Adam Teller, "Revisiting Baron's 'Lachrymose Conception:' The Meanings of Violence in Jewish History," *AJS Review* 2 (November 2014): 431–39. Teller adds that "when pre-modern Jews thought about themselves and their place in the world, they did so not in liberal, but in lachrymose terms. And if those were the terms in which they understood their own 'normality,' then when we try to do the same, we should not dismiss them, but take them very firmly into account" (439). Similarly, Elsa Marmursztejn notes that Salo Baron overlooks the massacres of 1096 and hides "incidences of suicides and infanticides" (my translation) in *A Social and Religious History of the Jews*. See Elsa Marmursztejn, "La Raison dans l'histoire de la persécution. Observations sur l'historiographie des relations entre juifs et chrétiens sous l'angle des baptêmes forces," *Annales* 1 (2012): 29.

43. The royal alliance was theorized by Salomon Ibn Verga in his 1550 (untranslated) book *Shevet Yehuda* ("Scepter of Judah"). According to him, during the Middle Ages, the king committed to protect Jews from

the mobs, from neighbors, and from antisemitic violence by confer-
ring upon them a unique status in exchange for their loyalty and financial contributions. Ibn Verga did acknowledge that the king could not
always control antisemitic acts, and that this alliance was more legend
than reality. Nonetheless, he constructed a model of the relationship
between the Jews and the state that has remained a key element of Jewish political history, including in modernity. Admittedly, the Shoah,
with the decisive role that the state played in it, is a scathing repudia-
tion of this model.

44. See Yosef Hayim Yerushalmi and Éric Vigne, *Serviteurs des rois et non
serviteurs des serviteurs: Sur quelques asspects de l'histoire politique des juifs*
(Paris: Allia, 2011); Maurice Kriegel, "L'Alliance royale, le mythe et le
mythe du mythe," *Critique* 632–33 (January–February 2000): 14–30;
Loïs Dobin, "Yosef Yerushalmi, the Royal Alliance, and Jewish Political Theory," *Jewish History* 28, no. 1; and Pierre Birnbaum, "Prier pour
l'État," in *Les Juifs, l'Alliance royale et la démocratie* (Paris: Calmann-
Lévy, 2005).

45. Baron, *A Social and Religious History of the Jews*, vol. 2: *Christian Era*,
2:26.

46. Baron, "Ghetto and Emancipation," 53.

47. Salo Baron, "New Approaches to Jewish Emancipation," *Diogenes* 29
(1960): 57.

48. David Sorkin finds that Baron does not pay enough attention to the
extreme diversities in situations by pointing out, for example, the very
different situations in the cities of Holland alone. David Sorkin, "Salo
Baron on Emancipation," *AJS Review* 2 (November 2014): 428.

49. Baron, "New Approaches to Jewish Emancipation," 65.

50. Baron, 68.

51. Liberles, *Salo Wittmayer Baron*, 276 and 281.

52. Engel, *Historians of the Jews and the Holocaust*, 49–50. Engel writes that
"Baron displayed little conviction that the Holocaust demanded a new
approach to writing the history of the Jews" (50). For more on this
point, see "A Conversation about Salo Baron Between Robert Liberles and Steven Zipperstein," *Jewish Social Studies* 3 (Spring 1995): 76.

53. The Nizkor Project, the Trial of Adolf Eichmann, 13th session, parts
5 to 7, 36. https://www.nizkor.org.

54. The Nizkor Project, 12th session, parts 5 to 7, 16.

55. The Nizkor Project, 12th session, parts 5 to 7, 16. On Baron's testimony at Eichmann's trial, see Annette Wieviorka, *Eichmann, de la traque au procès* (Brussels: André Versailles, 2011); as well as Claude Klein, *Le cas Eichmann: Vu de Jérusalem* (Paris: Gallimard, 2012), 92 ff.

56. Salo Baron, "Newer Emphasis in Jewish History," *Jewish Social Studies* 4 (October 1963): 240.

57. Baron, 240. In this article—a true turning point in his thinking—Baron writes on page 242 that "it is to be hoped that this newer emphasis on politics, economics and military affairs, however justifiable on objective as well as psychological grounds, will not totally displace the understanding for the *Leidens—und Gelertengeschichte* [lachrymose conception of history and knowledge] which had so completely dominated Jewish historical writing of the nineteenth and twentieth centuries," repudiating anew his attachment to the socioeconomic dimension of Jewish history. In evoking this text, Elsa Marmursztejn considers that "it appears less like a correction than like an appendix added to 'Ghetto and Emancipation,'" (my translation) in her "La Construction d'un passé meilleur: Salo Wittmayer Baron et la condition des Juifs d'Europe avant l'Émancipation," *Penser/rêver* (Spring 2011): 119. This text, as well as the testimony at Eichmann's trial, indeed constitutes perhaps more of an appendix. Baron confirms that emancipation was tragic, but he extends this new interpretation, born of the Shoah, to the Middle Ages, whose relatively peaceful situation for Jewish life he praised. On this shift, see Arthur Hertzberg, "Salo Baron and the Writing of Modern Jewish History," in *Writing a Modern Jewish History. Essays in Honor of Salo Baron*, ed. Barbara Kirshenblatt-Gimblett (New York: Jewish Museum, 2006), 21–22.

58. Salo Baron, "Changing Patterns of Antisemitism: A Survey," *Jewish Social Studies* 38, no. 1 (Winter 1976): 16. Baron often cites these striking words by Clermont-Tonnerre as an example of state assimilation that Jews encounter under the grip of the nation-state. See also his "Civil Versus Political Emancipation," in *Studies in Jewish Religious and Intellectual History, Presented to Alexander Altman*, ed. Siegfried Stein and Raphael Loewe (Tuscaloosa: University of Alabama Press, 1977), 34.

59. Salo Baron, "The Jewish Question in the Nineteenth Century," *Journal of Modern History* 10 (March 1938): 59.

60. Baron, *The Russian Jews Under the Tsar and the Soviets*, xxii.

61. Engel, "Crisis and Lachrymosity," 250.

62. This is in reference to the biblical verse, "We came to the land to which you sent us. It flows with milk and honey" (Deuteronomy 13:27).

63. Baron, "Newer Emphasis in Jewish History," 96.

64. Hasia Diner, "Salo Baron: An American," in *The Enduring Legacy of Salo W. Baron*, ed. Hava Tirosh-Samuelson and Edward Dabrowa (Kracow: Jagiellonian University Press, 2017), 252.

65. Salo Baron, "American Jewish History: Problems and Methods," in Baron, *Steeled by Adversity*, 32.

66. Salo Baron, "The Emancipation Movement and American Jewry," in Baron, *Steeled by Adversity*, 105.

67. Gil Rubin, "Hannah Arendt and Salo Baron—an Intellectual Friendship," *Naharaim* 9, nos. 1–2 (2015): 79.

68. Hannah Arendt, *On Revolution* (New York: Penguin, 1977), 168.

69. Arendt, 165. See Francis Moreault, "Hannah Arendt, la modernité et les Etats-Unis," *Politique et Sociétés* 18, no. 3 (1999): 121–44.

70. Arendt, *On Revolution*, 195.

71. Marc Melissa, "La Révolution américaine en tant que non modèle dans On Revolution," in *Hannah Arendt, la Révolution et les droits de l'homme*, ed. Yannick Bosc and Emmanuel Faye (Paris: Kimé, 2019).

72. Arendt, *On Revolution*, 205.

73. Hannah Arendt, "From the Dreyfus Affair to France Today," *Jewish Social Studies* 4, no. 3 (1942): 195–240.

74. Klein, *Le cas Eichmann*.

75. Hannah Arendt, *The Jewish Writings*, ed. Jerome Kohn and Ron Feldman (New York: Schocken, 2007), 303.

76. Natan Sznaider, "Hannah Arendt: Jews and Cosmopolitism," *Socio* 4 (2015): 39.

77. Baron, "American Jewish History," 32.

78. Oscar Handlin, "New Paths in American Jewish History," *Commentary* 7 (April 1949): 392.

79. Salo Baron, "Can American Jewry Be Culturally Creative?" in Baron, *Steeled by Adversity*, 549–551. In this same work, see also Salo Baron,

"Cultural Pluralism of American Jewry," 503–5. For more on this question, see Beth Wenger, "Salo Baron and the Vitality of American Jewish Life," in *The Enduring Legacy of Salo W. Baron*, 263–65.

80. Debra Dash Moore, "Review of Salo Wittmayer Baron: Architect of Jewish History, by Robert Liberles," *AJS Review* 22, no. 1 (1997): 149.

81. Baron, "American Jewish History," 32. See Liberles, *Salo Wittmayer Baron*, 318.

82. Salo Baron, "United States: 1880–1914," in Baron, *Steeled by Adversity*, 325.

83. Salo Baron, "American and Jewish Destiny," in Baron, *Steeled by Adversity*, 24.

84. Louis Wirth, *Le Ghetto* (Grenoble: Presses universitaires de Grenoble, 2006).

85. Louis Wirth, review of Salo Baron, "The Jewish Community: Its History and Structure to the American Revolution," *Historia Judaica* 6 (1944): 86. See Birnbaum, *Géographie de l'espoir*, 154–55.

86. Greenberg, "A Prophet and His People," 92.

87. Yitzhak Baer, *Galut* (Paris: Calmann-Lévy, 2000), 199.

88. Anke Hilbrenner, "Civil Rights and Multiculturalism: Simon Dubnov's Concept of Diaspora Nationalism," *Osteuropa* 58, nos. 8/10 (2008): 115.

89. Liberles, *Salo Wittmayer Baron*, 160 ff.

90. Marsha Rozenblit, "A Zionist Who Spoke Hebrew: Salo Baron in Vienna," in *The Enduring Legacy of Salo W. Baron*, 109.

91. Salo Wittmayer Baron, *A Social and Religious History of the Jews*, vol. 1: *To the Beginning of the Christian Era* (New York: Columbia University Press, 1952), 1:16. See David Engel's observations, "Salo Baron and Poland," in *The Enduring Legacy of Salo W. Baron*, 193.

92. Ismar Schorsch, "The Lachrymose Conception of Jewish History," in *From Text to Context* (Hanover, Mass.: Brandeis University Press, 1994), 383.

93. Baron, *A Social and Religious History of the Jews*, vol. 2: *Christian Era*, 2:433.

94. Eric Goldstein, "The Reluctant Evaluator: Salo Baron as an Historian of American Jews," in *The Enduring Legacy of Salo W. Baron*, 276 ff.

95. On the influence of his insertion within American society and his conception of community, see Elisheva Carlebach, "Between Universal

and Particular: Baron's Jewish Community in Light of Recent Research," *AJS Review* 2 (November 2014): 420.

96. Quoted by Goldstein, "The Reluctant Evaluator," 284.

97. Baron, "Can American Jewry Be Culturally Creative?" 549.

98. Baron, "Cultural Pluralism of American Jewry," 504.

99. Salo Baron, "American Jewish Scholarship and World Jewry," in *Steeled by Adversity*, 533.

100. Baron, "Can American Jewry Be Culturally Creative?" 547.

101. Goldstein, "The Reluctant Evaluator," 295.

102. See Brenner, *Prophets of the Past*, 122.

103. Todd Endelman, for example, rejects this optimistic view. See *The Jews of Georgian England, 1714–1830: Tradition and Change in a Liberal Society* (Philadelphia: Jewish Publication Society of America, 1979).

104. Baer, *Galut*, 94.

105. Baer, 198–99.

106. Baer, 66 and 67.

107. Baer, 125–26.

108. Barzilay, "Yishaq Baer and Salo W. Baron," 20, 38, 45. On the relationship between Baron and Baer, see Eleazar Gutwirth, "Mourning, Melancholy and Hexis: Towards a Context for Fritz Yshaq Baer," *European Journal of Jewish Studies* 9 (2015). There are in this article many very cordial letters exchanged between the two. See also Yitzak Conforti, "State or Diaspora: Jewish History as a Form of National Belonging," *Studies in Ethnicity and Nationalism* 15, no. 2 (2015): 234 ff.

109. Baer, *Galut*, 126.

110. Schorsch, "The Lachrymose Conception of Jewish History," 385.

111. Michael Walzer and Alexandra Riebe, *The Politics of Exile in the Hebrew Bible* (Tübingen: Mohr Siebeck, 2001), 10.

112. Yosef Hayim Yerushalmi never mentions Baron's name in his preface. Only in a footnote does he evoke his rejection of "a lachrymose story of history" as well as his "globally positive" judgment of the Middle Ages. Yosef Hayim Yerushalmi, preface to Baer, *Galut*, 46–47.

113. Yosef Hayim Yerushalmi, *From Spanish Court to Italian Ghetto: Isaac Caordoso, a Study in Seventeenth-Century Marranism and Jewish Apologetics* (Seattle: University of Washington Press 1981).

114. Yerushalmi, preface to Baer, *Galut*, 46–47 (my translation).

115. Yerushalmi, 56.

116. Yosef Hayim Yerushalmi, *Transmettre l'histoire juive: Entretiens avec Sylvie Anne Goldberg* (Paris: Albin Michel, 2012), 40 (my translation).

117. David Biale, *Power and Powerlessness in Jewish History* (New York: Schocken, 1986).

118. Yerushalmi, *From Spanish Court to Italian Ghetto*, xi.

119. See Yosef Hayim Yerushalmi, "Servants of Kings and not Servants of the Servants," in *The Faith of the Fallen Jews: Yosef Hayim Yerushalmi and the Writing of Jewish History*, ed. David Myers and Alexander Kaye (Waltham, Mass.: Brandeis University Press, 2014).

120. Pierre Birnbaum, *Les Fous de la République: Histoire des Juifs d'État de Gambetta à Vichy* (Paris: Fayard, 1992).

121. Stefan Zweig, *L'Esprit européen en exil* (Paris: Bartillat, 2020), 275–82 (my translation).

## 2. THE LEO FRANK AFFAIR

1. Jonathan Sarna, "Anti-Semitism and American History," *Commentary* (March 1981): 47. Sarna also writes: "Anti-Semitism is more foreign to American ideals than to European ones" (46).

2. Albert Lindemann, *The Jew Accused* (Cambridge: Cambridge University Press, 1993), 196.

3. Dennis Wrong, "The Rise and Decline of Anti-Semitism in America," in *The Ghetto and Beyond*, ed. Peter Rose (New York: Random House, 1969), 326.

4. See *Lynching in America*, Report from the Equal Justice Initiative of 2017. See also, James Allen et al., *Without Sanctuary: Lynching Photography in America* (Santa Fe: Twin Palms, 2000); as well as Clifford Kuhn, "Lynching," in *The Leo Frank Case Reconsidered*, ed. James Leavey (Atlanta: William Breman Heritage Museum, 2008), 12.

5. For an overview of this question, see David Gerber, ed., *Anti-Semitism in American History* (Chicago: University of Illinois Press, 1986).

6. Edward H. Judge, *Easter in Kishinev: Anatomy of a Pogrom* (New York: New York University Press, 1992).

7. "The influences which have called us together to-night grew out of our recognition of the promptings of Christian civilization and our dutiful devotion to the best and deepest of our National characteristics. . . .

Every American humane sentiment has been shocked by a late attack on the Jews in Russia—an attack murderous, atrocious, and in every way revolting. As members of the family of mankind and as citizens of a free nation we are here to give voice to the feeling that should stir every true man and every American worthy of the name. There is something intensely horrible in the wholesale murder of unoffending, defenseless men, women, and children, who have been tacitly or expressly assured of safety under the protection of a professedly civilized government. Such things give rise to a distressing fear that even the enlightenment of the twentieth century has neither destroyed nor subdued the barbarity of human nature, nor wholly redeemed the civilized world from 'man's inhumanity to man.'" Quoted in Philip Ernest Schoenberg, "The American Reaction to the Kishinev Pogrom of 1903," *American Jewish History Quarterly* 63, no. 3 (March 1974): 270.

8. Steven Zipperstein, *Pogrom: Kishinev and the Tilt of History* (New York: Norton, 2018).

9. Yael Zerubavel, *Recovered Roots: Collective Memory and the Making of Israeli National Tradition* (Chicago: University of Chicago Press, 1995).

10. Quoted in Erik Marc Greenberg, "A Prophet and His People: Israel Zangwill and His American Public, 1892–1926 and Beyond" (PhD diss. University of California, Los Angeles, 2012), 53.

11. Edna Nahshon, ed., *From the Ghetto to the Melting Pot* (Detroit: Wayne State University Press, 2006).

12. Albert Lindemann, *Esau's Tears* (Cambridge: Cambridge University Press, 2009), 297. Monty Noam Penkower, "The Kishinev Pogrom of 1903: A Turning Point in Jewish History," *Modern Judaism* 24, no. 3 (October 2004): 198–99.

13. Chaim Nachman Bialik and Steven Jacobs, "In the City of Slaughter," in *Shirot Bialik: A New and Annotated Translation of Chaim Nachman Bialik's Epic Poems* (Columbus: Alpha, 1987), 126–130.

14. Zipperstein, *Pogrom*, 11 and 103.

15. Max Nordau, one of the theorists of political Zionism, was a thinker at the turn of the twentieth century wishing for the emergence of "muscle Jews" to battle against the degeneration of society.

16. Stanislawski does a sophisticated reading of this translation that erases the biblical aspects of the poem. Michael Stanislawski, *Zionism and*

the *Fin-de-Siècle Cosmopolitanism and Nationalism from Nordau to Jabotinsky* (Berkeley: University of California Press, 2001), 191–195.

17. Jeffrey Gurock, *American Jewish History: East European Jews in America, 1880–1920; Immigration and Adaptation* (New York: Routledge, 1998).

18. Irving Howe, *World of Our Fathers: The Journey of the East European Jews to America and the Life They Found and Made* (New York: Harcourt, 1976), 132.

19. Gerald Sorin, *A Time for Building: The Third Migration, 1880–1920* (Baltimore: Johns Hopkins University Press, 1992), 207.

20. Ben Gidley, "The Ghost of Kishinev and the East End: Responses to a Pogrom in the Jewish London of 1903," in *The Jew in Late Edwardian Culture*, ed. Etan Bar-Yosef and Nadia Valman (London: Palgrave Macmillan, 2009).

21. Zipperstein, *Pogrom*, 204.

22. Quoted in Cyrus Adler, ed., *The Voice of America on Kishineff* (Phildelphia: Jewish Publication Society of America, 1904), 123.

23. Quoted in Adler, 242.

24. Hasia Diner, *The Jews of the United States* (Berkeley: University of California Press, 2004), 184.

25. Zipperstein, *Pogrom*, 11.

26. Zipperstein, 10–11.

27. In Odessa, Jewish victims were numbered at 800 dead and 5,000 wounded; in Kiev, 100 Jews were executed and 406 wounded. Shlomo Lambrozo, "The Pogroms of 1903–1906," in *Pogroms: Antijewish Violence in Modern Russian History*, ed. John Klier and Shlomo Lambrozo (Cambridge: Cambridge University Press, 1992), 212 and 231. See also Gerald Surh, "Russia's 1905 Era Pogroms Reexamined," *Canadian-American Slavic Studies* 44, no. 3 (2010): 253–95.

28. Roni Masel, "Arming Jews Hasn't Saved Us in the Past: Why Would It Now," *+972 Magazine*, October 31, 2018.

29. Howard Rabinowitz, "Nativism, Bigotry and Anti-Semitism in the South," in *Dixie Diaspora: An Anthology of Southern Jewish History*, ed. Mark Bauman (Tuscaloosa: University of Alabama Press, 2006), 271.

30. Bertram Korn, "Jews and Negro Slavery in the Old South," *Jewish Historical Society* 50, no. 3 (March 1961): 151–201.

31. See David Goldfield, "A Sense of Place: Jews, Blacks, and White Gentiles in the American South," *Southern Culture* 3, no. 1 (Spring 1997): 58–79; as well as Marcie Cohen Ferris and Mark Greenberg, eds., *Jewish Roots in Southern Soil: A New History* (Hanover, N.H.: University Press of New England, 2006).

32. Arnold Shankman, *Ambivalent Friends: Afro-Americans View the Immigrant* (Westport, Conn.: Greenwood, 1982). Leonard Dinnerstein, "The Origins of Black Anti-Semitism," *American Jewish Archives* 38 (November 1986): 118–20.

33. Goldfield, "A Sense of Place," 70.

34. Robert Rosen, *The Jewish Confederates* (Columbia: University of Carolina Press, 2000), 115–21.

35. A translation of the halakhic principle *dina di malkhuta dina.*

36. Rosen, 149. See also Jonathan Sarna, *When Grant Expelled the Jews* (New York: Schocken, 2012).

37. Bertram Korn, *American Jewry and the Civil War* (Philadelphia: Jewish Publication Society, 2001), 193.

38. Korn, 210–13.

39. Morton Borden, *Jews, Turks, and Infidels* (Chapel Hill: University of North Carolina Press, 1984), 50.

40. Borden, 113.

41. Leonard Dinnerstein, *The Leo Frank Case* (New York: Columbia University Press, 1968), 67 ff. See also Hasia Diner, *In the Almost Promised Land: American Jews and Blacks, 1915–1935* (Baltimore: Johns Hopkins University Press, 1977), 14 ff.

42. Paul Berger, "Midnight in Tennessee—the Untold Story of the First Jewish Lynching in America," *Forward*, December 20, 2014.

43. Lee Shaï Weissbach, "East European Immigrants and the Image of Jews in the Small-Town South," *American Jewish History* 85, no. 3 (September 1997): 231–62. Gary Zola, "Why Study Southern Jewish History?" *Southern Jewish History* 1 (1998): 1–21.

44. Steven Hertzberg, *Strangers Within the Gate City: The Jews of Atlanta, 1845–1915* (Philadelphia: Jewish Publication of America, 1978). See also Nathan Kaganoff and Melvin Urofsky, eds., *Turn to the South: Essays on Southern Jewry* (Charlottesville: University of Virginia Press, 1979).

45. Quoted in Steven Hertzberg, "The Jewish Community of Atlanta: From the End of the Civil War Until the Eve of the Frank Case," *American Jewish Historical Quarterly* 62, no. 3 (September 1972): 251.

46. Hertzberg, 260–61.

47. John Higham, *Strangers in the Land: Patterns of American Nativism, 1860–1925* (New Brunswick: Rutgers University Press, 1983), 184 ff.

48. The original texts are quoted by Leonard Dinnerstein in *The Leo Frank Case*; 3, or by Harry Golden, *A Little Girl Is Dead* (Cleveland: Avon, 1965), 201–2. "He said he wood love me and land down play like night witch did it but that long tall black negro did by his slef." "Mam that negro hire doun here did this I went to make water and he push me doun that hole a long tall negro black that hoo it was long sleam tall negro I write while play with me."

49. Lindemann, *The Jew Accused*, 240.

50. Steve Oney, *And the Dead Shall Rise: The Murder of Mary Phagan and the Lynching of Leo Frank* (New York: Pantheon, 2003), 60.

51. David Zucchino, *Wilmington's Lie: The Murderous Coup of 1898 and the Rise of White Supremacy* (New York: Atlantic Monthly Press, 2020). See also David Blight, "Uncovering the Tuth About the 1898 massacre of Black Voters in Wilmington, North Carolina," *New York Review of Books*, November 19, 2020.

52. *Cleveland Gazette*, May 23, 1903.

53. Quoted in Zipperstein, *Pogrom*, 187 and 194.

54. Diner, *In the Almost Promised Land*, 3.

55. "The Trial of Leo Frank for the Murder of Mary Phagan, Atlanta, Georgia, 1913," in John D. Lawson, *American State Trials: A Collection of the Important and Interesting Criminal Trials Which Have Taken Place in the United States from the Beginning of Our Government to the Present Day* (St. Louis: Thomas Law, 1914–36), 10:215.

56. 10:203.

57. 10:203–4.

58. 10:243–45.

59. Quoted in Oney, *And the Dead Shall Rise*, 167.

60. Mary Phagan, *The Murder of Little Mary Phagan* (Far Hills, N.J.: New Horizon, 1987), 95.

61. Quoted in Oney, *And the Dead Shall Rise*, 247 ff.

62. Quoted in Oney, 221.

63. "The Trial of Leo Frank for the Murder of Mary Phagan," 10:237.

64. 10:295.

65. 10:277.

66. 10:264.

67. See also Jeffrey Melnick, *Black-Jewish Relations on Trial: Leo Frank and Jim Conley in the New South* (Jackson: University Press of Mississippi, 2000), 40 ff and 65.

68. Eugène Lévy, "Is the Jew a White Man? Press Reactions to the Leo Frank Case, 1913–1915," *Phylon* 35, no. 2 (2d qtr., 1974): 214 ff.

69. "The Trial of Leo Frank for the Murder of Mary Phagan," 10:303.

70. 10:398.

71. 10:409.

72. Egal Feldman, *The Dreyfus Affair and the American Conscience, 1895–1906* (Detroit: Wayne State University Press, 1981), 74.

73. Quoted in Oney, *And the Dead Shall Rise*, 347–48.

74. Feldman, *The Dreyfus Affair and the American Conscience*, 70.

75. On the intervention of prominent New York Jews, see Leonard Dinnerstein, "Leo Frank and the American Jewish Community," *American Jewish Archive Journal* 20, no. 2 (November 1968): 107–26.

76. See Oney, *And the Dead Shall Rise*, 366–74.

77. Lindemann, *Esau's Tears*, 384.

78. Dinnerstein, *The Leo Frank Case*, 95.

79. Tom Watson, "The Leo Frank Case," *Watson's Magazine* 20, no. 2 (January 1915): 143. See also Tom Watson, "Full Review of the Leo Frank Case," *Watson's Magazine* 20, no. 5 (March 1915): 276.

80. Watson, "Leo Frank Case," 158.

81. Watson, 160.

82. *Justia.com US Supreme Court Center, Frank v. Mangum*, 237 U.S. 309 (1915): 345.

83. *Justia.com US Supreme Court Center, Frank v. Mangum*, 350.

84. Oney, *And the Dead Shall Rise*, 480.

85. Quoted in Dinnerstein, *The Leo Frank Case*, 126.

86. Quote in Oney, *And the Dead Shall Rise*, 506.

87. Quoted in Sally Steinberg-Brent, "The Leo Frank Murder Case," in *Jews on Trial*, ed. Robert Garber (Jersey City, N.J.: Ktav, 2005), 130.

88. Quoted in Oney, *And the Dead Shall Rise,* 508.

89. Quoted in Dinnerstein, *The Leo Frank Case,* 131.

90. Tom Watson, "The Rich Jews Indict a State!" *Watson's Magazine* 21, no. 6 (October 1915): 140.

91. Other lynchings of African Americans take place at Marietta, including one, not too much earlier, in 1910. See Clifford Kuhn, "Lynching," 12.

92. Dinnersteirn, *The Leo Frank Case,* 145.

93. Oney, *And the Dead Shall Rise,* 578.

94. Diner, *In the Almost Promised Land,* 97.

95. Quoted in Golden, *A Little Girl Is Dead,* 220, note 2.

96. See Steve Oney, "The People v. Leo Frank," *Atlanta Magazine,* September 24, 2013.

97. Jacob Bogage, "Leo Frank Was Lynched for a Murder That He Didn't Commit: Now Neo-Nazis Are Trying to Rewrite History," *Washington Post,* May 22, 2017.

98. Michael Rosenbaum, "Remembering the Lynching of Leo Frank 100 Years Later," *Hill,* August 20, 2015; *GW Today,* "The Case of Leo Frank," October 28, 2015; Ingrid Anderson, "Pittsburgh Synagogue Shooting," *Conversation,* October 29, 2018.

99. According to Albert Lindemann, "Atlanta was not Kishinev or Kiev." Albert Lindemann, *The Jew Accused: Three Anti-Semitic Affairs (Dreyfus, Beilis, Frank), 1894–1915* (Cambridge: Cambridge University Press, 1991), 252.

100. Quoted in Melnick, *Black-Jewish Relations on Trial,* 120.

101. Quoted in Lévy, "Is the Jew a White Man?" 220.

102. See also Robert Seitz Frey and Nancy Thompson, *The Silent and the Damned: The Murder of Mary Phagan and the Lynching of Leo Frank* (New York: Cooper Square, 1988), 56.

103. Melnick, *Black-Jewish Relations on Trial,* 3.

104. See Jean-Denis Bredin, *L'Affaire* (Paris: Fayard, 1993); Pierre Birnbaum, *L'Affaire Dreyfus, la République en péril* (Paris: Gallimard, 1994); Philippe Oriol, *L'Histoire de l'Affaire Dreyfus* (Paris: Les Belles Lettres, 2014).

105. Quoted in Oney, *And the Dead Shall Rise,* 446.

106. Tom Watson, "The Official Record in the Case of Leo Frank, a Jew Pervert," in *Watson's Magazine* 21, no. 5 (September 1915): 295–96.

107. Bernard Lazare, *L'antisémitisme, son histoire et ses causes* (Paris: Choulley, 1894). Tom Watson, "The Rich Indict a State: The Whole South Traduced in the Matter of Leo Frank," *Watson's Magazine* 21, no. 6 (October 15, 1915): 305 ff.

108. "Trial of Leo Frank," 266. Kuperminc clearly exposes the unfolding of the trial, quotes a significant number of statements, and underscores these references to the Dreyfus affair. Victor Kuperminc, *L'Affaire Leo Frank: Dreyfus en Amérique* (Paris: L'Harmattan, 2008).

109. Dinnerstein, *The Leo Frank Case*, chapter 3.

110. Dinnerstein, 74.

111. See Charles Reznikoff, ed., *Louis Marshall, Champion of Liberty* (Philadelphia: Jewish Publication Society, 1957).

112. Quoted in Eric Freedman, "Leo Frank Lives: Untangling the Historical Roots of Meaningful Federal Habeas Corpus Review of State Convictions," *Alabama Law Review* 51 (Summer 2000): 1498.

113. Quoted in Oney, *And the Dead Shall Rise*, 578.

114. Stephen Goldfard, "The Slaton Memorandum: A Governor Looks Back at His Decision to Commute the Death Sentence of Leo Frank," *American Jewish History* 88, no. 3 (2000): 338.

115. Natasha Barnes. See her review of the exhibit in the *Journal of American History* 96, no. 3 (December 2009): 792–96. According to Barnes, "though the exhibit's title suggests otherwise, 'Seeking Justice' did not try to answer the question of Frank's guilt or innocence," 794.

116. *Atlanta Journal-Constitution*, May 7, 2019. See also Rosenbaum, "Remembering the Lynching of Leo Frank 100 Years Later."

117. Steve Oney, "Did Leo Frank Kill Mary Phagan? 106 Years Later, We Might Finally Find Out for Sure," *Atlanta Magazine*, May 31, 2019. In July, *Atlanta Magazine* accused Oney of having "falsified" documents and of being an "activist for Frank's cause."

118. Quoted in Brett Jennifer, "After More Than 100 Years, Will Leo Frank Be Exonerated?," *T.C.A. Regional News*, August 22, 2019.

119. *The Phagan Family Newsletter*, no. 5.

120. Jean Doise, *Un Secret bien gardé: Histoire militaire de l'Affaire Dreyfus* (Paris: Seuil, 1994).

121. Ingrid Anderson, "What the Leo Frank Case Tells Us About the Dangers of Fake News," *Conversation*, April 24, 2017.

122. Matthew Bernstein, "The Leo Frank Case on Film and TV," in Jane Leavey, *Seeking Justice: The Leo Frank Case Revisited* (Atlanta: William Breman Jewish Heritage Museum, 2008), 19–22.

123. Pierre Birnbaum, *Le Moment antisémite: Un tour de la France en 1898* (Paris: Fayard, 1998).

124. Thus, Harry Golden writes: "In many respects Leo Frank in America paralleled the agony of Alfred Dreyfus in France. The anti-Semitic Tom Watson who whipped up a lynch mob with his editorials in his *Jeffersonian*, was a blood brother of editor Edouard Drumont, of Paris, who slandered the Jews in his journal *La Libre Parole*. In August of 1915, the parallel came to an end. A lynch mob hanged Frank. Dreyfus was finally exonerated and free from Devil's Island." This author even reached out to Bertillon, the expert who examined Mary Phagan's fingerprints, evoking Bertillon's crucial role in the Dreyfus affair. *A Little Girl Is Dead*, 14 and 65). Albert Lindemann, on his part, considers that Governor Slaton is comparable to Georges Picquart; by neglecting the latter's antisemitism, he establishes a parallel between Watson and Drumont as well as Marshall and Mathieu Dreyfus (*The Jew Accused*, 260, 266 and 268).

125. Jeffrey Melnick, "'The Night Witch Did It': Villainy and Narrative in the Leo Frank Case," *American Literary History* 12, nos. 1/2 (Summer 2000): 122.

126. Trial minutes, "The Trial of Leo Frank for the Murder of Mary Phagan," *American State Trials*, 10:236.

127. Melnick, "'The Night Witch Did It,'" 120.

128. Melnick, 119.

129. Trial minutes, 10:278.

130. Pierre Gervais, Pauline Peretz, and Pierre Stutin, *Le Dossier secret de l'Affaire Dreyfus* (Paris: Alma, 2012).

131. Édouard Drumont, *Le secret de Fourmies* (Paris: Albert Savines, 1892). See Pierre Birnbaum and Mazal Holocaust Collection, *The Jews of the Republic: A Political History of State Jews in France from Gambetta to Vichy* (Stanford: Stanford University Press, 1994), chapter 11.

132. Nancy MacLean, "The Leo Frank Case Reconsidered: Gender and Sexual Politics in the Making of Reactionary Politics," *Journal of American History* 78, no. 3 (December 1991): 947. See also Kristoff Kerl, "The

Pure and the Sodomite: Masculinity, Sexuality, and Anti-Semitism in the Leo Frank Case," *Gender Forum*, no. 32 (2011): 32.

## 3. FROM THE *JEW DEAL* TO THE STORMING OF THE CAPITOL

1. Philip Roth, *The Plot Against America* (New York: Random House, 2004), 18.
2. Roth, 359 ff.
3. Philip Roth believes that Orwell "imagined a dystopia, I imagined a uchronia." Philip Roth, "The Story Behind the Plot Against America," *New York Times*, September 19, 2004.
4. J. M. Coetzee, "What Philip Knew," *New York Review of Books*, November 18, 2004.
5. See Judith Thurman, "Philip Roth E-Mails on Trump," *New Yorker*, January 30, 2017; Mark Bresnan, "America First: Reading *The Plot Against America* in the Age of Trump," *Los Angeles Review of Books*, September 11, 2016; also Brett Ashley Kaplan, "Grotesquery to the Surface: 'The Leo Frank Case' and Philip Roth's *The Plot Against America* Revisited in Trump's Alt-Right America," *Studies in American Jewish Literature* 39, no. 1 (2020): 44–72. The article by Kaplan, a scholar of Roth's novel, is based on her precise understanding of this work. She also links the Frank affair and the atmosphere during the Trump years. I thank her for sending me her article.
6. See Roth, "The Story Behind *The Plot Against America*"; and Ezra Klein, "Philip Roth's 2004 Warning About Demagogues Is More Relevant Than Ever: Philip Roth, Donald Trump, and *The Plot Against America*," *Vox*, May 28, 2018.
7. Thurman, "Philip Roth E-Mails on Trump."
8. Charles McGrath, "No Longer Writing, Philip Roth Still Has Plenty to Say," *New York Times*, January 16, 2018.
9. Bresnan, "America First."
10. Steven Kellman, "It Is Happening Here," *Philip Roth Studies* 4, no. 2 (Autumn 2008): 119.
11. Yonat Shimron, "Poll: American Jews Report Increasing Incidents of Anti-Semitism, Mostly Online," Religion News Service, March 31, 2021.

12. See also "Leo Frank Was Lynched for a Murder He Didn't Commit: Now Neo-Nazis Are Trying to Rewrite History," *Washington Post*, May 22, 2017.

13. See, for example, Alissa Wise, "I Am a Rabbi and I Am Done with Trump Using My People to Cover for His Racism," *Newsweek*, July 23, 2019. The author remarks on how "real murderous anti-Semitism is allowed to fester in the United States to a degree not seen since the Leo Frank lynching."

14. Dahleen Glanton, "Neo-Nazis, Anti-Semitism and the Cycle of Hatred in America," *Chicago Tribune*, August 28, 2017.

15. See Martin Jacobi, "Rhetoric and Fascism in Jack London's *The Iron Heel*, Sinclair Lewis's *It Can't Happen Here*, and Philip Roth's *The Plot Against America*," *Philip Roth Studies* 6, no.1 (Spring 2010): 85–102.

16. Ellen Strenski, "*It Can't Happen Here*, or Has It? Sinclair Lewis Fascist America," *Terrorism and Political Violence* 29 (2017): 425–36.

17. See Beverly Gage, "Reading the Classic Novel That Predicted Trump," *New York Times Book Review*, November 17, 2017.

18. Sinclair Lewis, *It Can't Happen Here* (New York: Signet Classics, 1970).

19. Quoted in Naomi W. Cohen, *A Dual Heritage: The Public Career of Oscar S. Straus*, (Philadelphia: Jewish Publication Society of America, 1969), 150.

20. See Theda Skocpol and Kenneth Finegold, "Economic Intervention and the Early New Deal," *Political Science Quarterly* 97 (Summer 1982): 255–78.

21. "Felix Frankurter," *Fortune* (January 1936): 63, 87.

22. Quoted in Henry Feingold, "Equality to Liberty: From the Changing Political Culture of American Jews," in *The Americanization of the Jews*, ed. Robert Seltzer (New York: New York University Press, 1995), 107.

23. Pierre Birnbaum, *Un Mythe politique: "La République juive." De Léon Blum à Pierre Mendes France* (Paris: Fayard, 1988).

24. Donald Strong, *Organized Anti-Semitism in America* (Washington, D.C.: American Council on Public Affairs, 1941), 179. See Myron Scholnick, *The New Deal and Anti-Semitism in America* (New York: Garland, 1990). See Nelson L. Dawson, *Louis D. Brandeis, Felix Frankfurter, and the New Deal* (Hamden, Conn.: Archon, 1980), 40; Peter H. Irons, *The New Deal Lawyers* (Princeton, N.J.: Princeton

University Press, 1982), 20–21; Melvin I. Urofsky, *Louis D. Brandeis: A Life* (New York: Schocken, 2009), 691.

25. Quoted in Charles Tull, *Father Coughlin and the New Deal* (Syracuse: Syracuse University Press, 1965), 229.

26. Franklin Thompson, *America's Ju-Deal* (New York: Woodhaven Community Press, 1935), 31–33.

27. Dov Fisch, "The Libel Trial of Robert Edward Edmondson: 1936–1938," *American Jewish History* 71, no. 1 (September 1981): 93.

28. See Strong, *Organized Anti-Semitism in America*, 160.

29. Wiliam Pelley, *New Dealers in Office* (n.d., n.p.), 3.

30. Regarding these antisemitic organizations, see Pierre Birnbaum, *Les deux maisons: Essai sur la citoyenneté des Juifs en France et aux Etats-Unis* (Paris: Gallimard, 2012), chapter 4.

31. Roth, *The Plot Against America*, chapter 7.

32. Melissa Fay Greene, *The Temple Bombing* (Reading: Addison Wesley, 1996), 33.

33. Janice Rothschild Blumberg, "The Bomb That Healed: A Personal Memoir of the Bombing of the Temple in Atlanta, 1958," *American Jewish History* 73, no. 1 (September 1983): 36.

34. Greene, *The Temple Bombing*, 159.

35. Greene, 152 ff. It seems that, from 1931 to 1981, crosses are burned in these regions in memory of Frank's lynching.

36. Eric Goldstein, one of the most eminent specialists on this question in the American South, is insistent about the "aftershocks of the Leo Frank Affair" over the attitudes of Jews in 1958 who continue to fear violence. See "Temple Bombing, 50 Years Ago in Atlanta," WABE 90.1, FM.

37. See Edward Hatfield, "Temple Bombing," *New Georgia Encyclopedia*, January 6, 2007. Greene, *The Temple Bombing*.

38. Quoted in Herman Obermayer, *American Nazi Party in Arlington, Virginia, 1958–1984* (Cambridge, Mass.: Harvard University Press, 1997), 174, https://www.google.com/books/edition/American_Nazi_Party _in_Arlington_Virgini/thQuAgAAQBAJ?hl=en&gbpv=1.

39. William Schmaltz, *Hate: George Lincoln Rockwell and the American Nazi Party* (Sterling, Va.: Brassey, 1999), 33.

40. Schmaltz, 112.

41. Schmaltz, 187.
42. James Q. Whitman, *Hitler's American Model: The United States and the Making of Nazi Race Law* (Princeton, N.J.: Princeton University Press, 2017).
43. For more on this renewal of Grant's ideas during the Trump era, see Adam Serwer, "White Nationalism's Deep American Roots," *Atlantic*, April 2019.
44. Nichols Lemann, "The Temple Bombing," *New York Review of Books*, September 19, 1996.
45. Boris Smolar, "60 Years Ago It Was a Bombing in an Atlanta Synagogue," *Forward*, October 30, 2018.
46. Ralph McGill, "A Church, A School," *Atlanta Constitution*, October 13, 1958.
47. Arnold Shankman, "A Temple Is Bombed—Atlanta 1958," *American Jewish Archives* 23, no. 2 (November 1971): 127.
48. The most precise study of this attack on the synagogue of Atlanta is that of Shankman, "A Temple Is Bombed."
49. Hasia Diner, *The Jews of the United States* (Berkeley: University of California Press, 2004), 272 ff.
50. David Green, "From Lynchings to Mass Shootings: The History of Deadly Attacks on Jews in America," *Haaretz*, October 20, 2018.
51. See Jeremy Kohler, "Up Next for Execution," *St Louis Post-Dispatch*, November 17, 2013. See also Jack Rosewood and Dwayne Walker, *Joseph Paul Franklin: The True Story of the Racist Killer* (Wiq Media, 2016).
52. The most complete book on Franklin and his Nazi inspiration is Mel Ayton's *Dark Soul of the South: The Life and Crimes of Racist Killer Joseph Paul Franklin* (Washington, D.C.: Potomac, 2011).
53. Franklin v. State. Paul Vitello, "White Supremacist Convicted of Several Murders Is Put to Death in Missouri," *New York Times*, November 20, 2013.
54. *Jewish Telegraphic Agency*, October 8, 1986.
55. Antonia Noori Farzan, "Before Synagogue Mass Shooting, a 1986 Murder Shook Pittsburgh's Jewish Community," *Washington Post*, October 29, 2018.
56. Christopher Hewitt, *Political Violence and Terrorism in Modern America: A Chronology* (Westport, Conn.: Praeger, 2005).

57. For more on the bombing: Stuart Wright, *Patriots, Politics and the Okla-homa City Bombing* (Cambridge: Cambridge University Press, 2007); Douglas O. Linder, *The Oklahoma City Bombing and The Trial of Timo-thy McVeigh* (Kansas City: University of Missouri, 2006); Lou Michel and Dan Herbeck, *American Terrorist: Timothy McVeigh and the Okla-homa City Bombing* (New York: Harper, 2001).

58. Andrew Macdonald, *The Turner Diaries* (Tennessee: National Alliance, 2017), 33, 42, 111, 118, 130, 189, 191, 198, 208. The extreme violence that emanates out of this reactionary dystopia is reminiscent of, on the other side of the political scene, another dystopia, that of Jack London, *The Iron Heel*, published in 1908. In this work, an equally radical terror is this time in the service of the bourgeoisie who, with its iron heel, mer-cilessly crushes the rebelling working class. For a comparative analy-sis of Roth's uchronia and the profoundly opposite dystopias of Lewis, London, and Pierce, see Pierre Birnbaum, "Impossible aux États-Unis? Uchronies et dystopies à l'américaine," *Critique* 889–90 (June 2021): 611–22.

59. Matt Ford and Adam Chandler, "Hate Crime: A Mass Killing at an Historic Church," *Atlantic*, June 19, 2015. "On Facebook, Dylann Roof, Charleston Suspect, Wears Symbols of White Supremacists," *New York Times*, June 18, 2015. See also Michael Schmidt, "Charleston Suspect Was in Touch with Supremacists," *New York Times*, July 3, 2015. "Hard-core White Supremacists Elevate Dylann Roof to Cult Hero Status," Anti-Defamation League, August 17, 2019.

60. John Eligon, "The El Paso Screed and the Racist Doctrine Behind It," *New York Times*, August 7, 2019. In this context, the *New York Times* published an article that exposes the ethnicist vision of Renaud Camus, "What Is the Great Replacement?," August 6, 2019. See particularly Michael Hayden, "White Nationalists Praise El Paso Attack and Mock the Dead," Southern Poverty Law Center, August 4, 2019.

61. Yehudit Barsky, "Terrorist Incidents and Attacks Against Jews and Israelis in the United States, 1969–2016," *Community Security Service* (2016): 3.

62. "Two Skinheads Held in Attack on Synagogue," *Seattle Times*, March 23, 1994.

63. *Los Angeles Times*, June 19, 1999; *Washington Post*, June 19, 1999; *Sacra-mento Bee*, June 18, 2014.

64. *Washington Post*, August 12, 1999. Furrow was sentenced to life in prison.

65. Anti-Defamation League, May 2012.

66. Anti-Defamation League, April 2004.

67. Chip Berlet, *Toxic to Democracy: Conspiracy Theories, Demonization, and Scapegoating* (Summerville, S.C.: Political Research Associates, 2009).

68. Linda Grant, "The Hate That Will not Die," *Guardian*, December 18th, 2001. See Jérémy Stahl, "11-Septembre: Et la théorie du complot devint la 'vérité,'" *Slate*, September 12, 2011.

69. "Who's Backing Barack?," *Haaretz*, August 25, 2008.

70. Ethics or Chapters of the Fathers, part of the Mishnah, a collection of commentaries on the Torah.

71. Ram's horn officiants blow to announce the New Year, on Rosh Hashanah and Yom Kippur.

72. Samuel Gordon, "Obama and the Jews: An Inside Perspective," Shalom Hartman Institute, April 11, 2013.

73. John Murphy, "Barack Obama, the Exodus Tradition and the Joshua Generation," *Quarterly Journal of Speech* 97, no. 4 (October 6, 2011): 387–410.

74. "Sabbath-Observant Jew Name Obama's New White House's Chief of State," *Haaretz*, October 1, 2010.

75. *New York Times*, September 4, 2009.

76. *New York*, September 19, 2011.

77. The seder is the Passover meal that celebrates the escape from Egypt and crossing to freedom. *RealClear Politics*, May 22, 2015; *Washington Times*, May 22, 2015.

78. *Washington Post*, January 28, 2016.

79. *Atlantic Review*, August 2009; *Huffington Post*, February 19, 2011.

80. *The Jew in Yellow*, November 13, 2008.

81. See "At Jewish Inaugural Gala, Axelrod 'Kvells,'" *Forward*, January 20, 2009; Marc Tracy, "Obama and the Jews," *Tablet*, August 23, 2010; "Oy Vey, Obama," *New York Times*, August 10, 2010, and Stuart Schwartz, "'Them Jews' of Obama: From Kvell to Kvetch," *American Thinker*, February 19, 2011.

82. "Rightwing Extremism: Current Economic and Political Climate Fueling Resurgence in Radicalization," Office of Intelligence and Analysis, U.S. Department of Homeland Security, April 7, 2009, 3–5.

83. Devin Burghart and Leonard Zeskind, *Tea Party Nationalism: A Critical Examination of the Tea Party Movement* (Kansas City: IREHR, 2010), 57 ff. See also Leonard Zeskind, *Blood and Politics: The History of the White Nationalist Movement from the Margins to the Mainstream* (New York: Farrar, Straus and Giroux, 2009).

84. Arlie Russell Hochschild, *Strangers in Their Own Land: Anger and Mourning on the American Right* (New York: New Press, 2018), 137–40 and 207.

85. Chip Berlet, "Taking Tea Parties Seriously: Corporate Globalization, Populism and Resentment," *Perspectives on Global Development and Technology* 10, no. 1 (2011): 17 ff. See also Kristin Haltinner, "Right-Wing Ideologies and Ideological Diversity in the Tea Party," *Sociological Quarterly* 59, no. 3 (2018): 458 ff.

86. Sarah Wildman, "There Were 7,000 Anti-Semitic Attacks Under Obama: That Doesn't Let Trump Off the Hook," *Vox*, March 13, 2017.

87. "Kansas City Shooting Suspect to Face Hate Crime Charges," *Chicago Tribune*, April 14, 2014.

88. Frazier Glenn Miller, "A White Man Speaks Out," 1999, available online (n.p.), https://archive.org/details/awmso.

89. USA v. Frazier Glenn Miller.

90. USA v. Frazier Glenn Miller.

91. Southern Poverty Law Center, "Frazier Glenn Miller," 2015.

92. Quoted in David Neiwert, *Alt-America: The Rise of the Radical Right in the Age of Trump* (London: Verso, 2018), 5.

93. Quoted in Neiwert, 270.

94. Quoted in Neiwert, 286.

95. Quoted in Neiwert, 292.

96. *Atlantic*, November 2016.

97. *New York Times*, December 11, 2019.

98. Christophe Mathias, "1 Neo-Nazi Group: 5 Murders in 8 Months," *Huffpost*, January 31, 2018.

99. Quoted in Wildman, "There Were 7,000 Anti-Semitic Attacks Under Obama."

100. Sarah Churchwell, "American Fascism: It Has Happened Here," *New York Review of Books*, June 22, 2020.

101. Chemi Shalev, "American Nazis, Then and Now," *Haaretz*, November 25, 2016.

102. "Hate in America," *Slate*, August 14, 2017.
103. Jeet Heer, "How the Southern Strategy Made Donald Trump Possible," *New Republic*, February 28, 2016.
104. There are many works on pro-violence white supremacist movements against people of color or Jews. See Kathleen Belew, *Bring the War Home: The White Power Movement and Paramilitary America* (Cambridge, Mass.: Harvard University Press, 2018).
105. Quoted in Emma Green, "Why the Charlottesville Marchers Were Obsessed with Jews," *Atlantic*, August 15, 2017.
106. Quoted in Green.
107. Erick Ward, "Skin in the Game: How Anti-Semitism Animates White Nationalism," *Political Research Associates*, June 29, 2017.
108. Al Sharpton, "In America Bias, Hate and Racism Move from the Margins to the Mainstream," *Guardian*, August 14, 2017.
109. Serge Ricard, "The Trump Phenomenon and the Racialization of American Politics," *LISA* 16, no. 2 (2018), doi: doi.org/10.4000/lisa.9832. See also Marie-Cécile Naves, *Trump, la revanche de l'homme blanc* (Paris: Textuel, 2017); and Evan Osnos, "Donald Trump and the Ku Klux Klan: A History," *New Yorker*, February 29, 2016.
110. Hochschild, *Strangers in Their Own Land*, 255 ff.
111. Southern Poverty Law Center, 2017.
112. Thomas Chatterton Williams, "The French Origins of 'You Will not Replace Us,'" *New Yorker*, November 27, 2017.
113. *Le Monde*, December 5, 2017 (my translation).
114. *Washington Post*, May 8, 2020.
115. https://twitter.com/brianschatz/status/897559129392168960?s=20&t=a2RMPQMzCHoSk944nISHEw.
116. *Le Monde*, August 15, 2017.
117. Thurman, "Philip Roth E-Mails on Trump."
118. Birnbaum, *Un mythe politique*.
119. *Haaretz*, April 28, 2017.
120. Ward, "Skin in the Game."
121. Anti-Defamation League, May 12, 2019.
122. Alexandra Schwartz, "The Tree of Life Shooting and the Return of Anti-Semitism to American Life," *New Yorker*, October 27, 2018.
123. Serwer, "White Nationalism's Deep American Roots."

124. Serwer.

125. Jonathan Chait, "Trump's Ideology Is Anti-Semitism Without Jews," *National Interest*, October 28, 2018; Taylor Lorenz, "The Pittsburgh Suspect Lived in the Web's Darkest Corners," *Atlantic*, October 27, 2018; "Deadly Shooting at Pittsburgh Synagogue," Anti-Defamation League, October 27, 2018; Julie Turkewitz, "Who Is Robert Bowers, the Suspect of Pittsburgh Synagogue Shooting?," *New York Times*, October 27, 2018.

126. Paul Berman, "Bowers Isn't Alone," *Tablet*, October 30, 2018.

127. US v. Robert Bowers.

128. Julie Hirsch David, "The Toxic Back Story to the Charge That Jews Have a Dual Loyalty," *New York Times*, August 21, 2019.

129. The American Presidency Project website, https://www.presidency.ucsb.edu/documents/remarks-the-israeli-american-council-national-summit-2019-hollywood-florida

130. *Le Monde*, December 12, 2019 (my translation).

131. See Christopher Caldwell, "What Does Steve Bannon Want?" *New York Times*, February 25, 2017.

132. Brett Stephens, "Steve Bannon Is Bad for the Jews," *New York Times*, November 16, 2017.

133. Ben Sales, "Stephen Bannon: Five Things Jews Need to Know," *Times of Israel*, November 14, 2016.

134. Sophie McBain, "What Steve Bannon Really Believes in," *New Statesman*, September 12, 2018.

135. Anti-Defamation League, "Steve Bannon: Five Things to Know," March 2, 2018.

136. *Washington Post*, April 27, 2019; *Los Angeles Times*, May 2, 2019.

137. *Daily Beast*, May 1, 2019; *News on 6*, November 4, 2019; AP News, November 5, 2019; *Jerusalem Post*, December 11, 2019; *Colorado Sun*, October 15, 2020; *New York Times*, October 15, 2020.

138. *New York Times*, December 15 and 19, 2019; *Jewish Journal*, September 20, 2019; *New Yorker*, April 29, 2019.

139. Danielle Ziri, "Four Anti-Semitic Hate Crimes Committed in New York City This Week," *Haaretz*, September 4, 2019. For more on these hostile acts, see Armin Rosen, "Everybody Knows," *Tablet*, July 16, 2019.

140. "New Report Say Coronavirus Pandemic Is Fueling Anti-Semitism," *Hill*, April 20, 2020.

141. Ed Kilgore, "The Lockdown Backlash May Be the New Tea Party Movement," *New York Times*, April 14, 2010; Kay Dervishi, "Why Have Anti-Semitic Hate Crimes Risen in New York?" *City and State New York*, January 29, 2020.

142. Flora Cassen, "Jews Control Chinese Labs That Created Coronavirus, White Supremacists' Dangerous New Conspiracy Theory," *Haaretz*, March 3, 2020.

143. Anti-Defamation League, "Extremists Use Coronavirus to Advance Racist, Conspiratorial Agendas," March 10, 2020.

144. Jonathan Greenblatt, "Fighting Hate in the Era of Coronavirus," *Horizons, Journal of International Relations and Sustainable Development*, no. 17 (Autumn 2020): 213.

145. "U.S. Extremist Blames 'Compliant' Jews for Holocaust in Idaho Protest," *Haaretz*, May 5, 2020.

146. "Covid-19 and Anti-Semitism: An Unseen Connection," *Jewish Boston*, May 7, 2020.

147. Aviya Kushner, "Pandemics Have Always Incited Anti-Semitism: Here's the History You Need to Know," *Forward*, May 4, 2020; Brian Schrauger, "COVID-19 and the Jews: Today's Black Plague," *Jerusalem Post*, April 6, 2020.

148. "Extremist Activity Is Growing in the Pandemic: How Worried Should Jews Be?," *Forward*, June 27, 2020.

149. Magda Teter, "The Pandemic, Anti-Semitism, and the Lachrymose Conception of Jewish History," *Jewish Social Studies* 26, no. 1 (Fall 2020): 21. Loyal to Baron's reasoning, Teter believes that, including in the case of the virus, there is too much emphasis placed on the idea of persecution, and the constant hate toward the Jews, by refusing analogies with the Middle Ages (22–26).

150. Anti-Defamation League, May 12, 2020; and Statista Research Department, May 12, 2020; *Le Monde*, November 18, 2020.

151. Emily Bruza, "American Extremism: White Supremacists," Homeland Security Digital Library, May 26, 2020.

152. Ben Sales, "Two Years After the Synagogue Shooting Pittsburgh Has Become a Hub for White Supremacists," *Forward*, November 19, 2020.

One head of the synagogue congregations stated in an interview: "I always fell into the camp of 'it can happen anywhere.'"

153. "Anti-Semitism in the United States," Jacob Blaustein Institute for the Advancement of Human Rights, New York, April 2019.

154. *L'ExPress*, September 30, 2020.

155. *Haaretz*, October 21, 2020.

156. *Haaretz*, November 24, 2020.

157. Jacob Korbluh, "Enough for a Minyan: A Jewish Who's Who of Biden's Cabinet-to-Be," *Forward*, January 18, 2021.

158. David Bateman, Ira Katznelson, and John Lapinski, *Southern Nation: Congress and White Supremacy After Reconstruction* (Princeton, N.J.: Princeton University Press, 2018), 402.

159. Jon Ossoff's "Letter to the Jewish Community," *Atlanta Jewish Times*, December 19, 2020.

160. "Five Jewish Things to Know About Jon Ossoff," *Forward*, November 6, 2020; "How Israel and Anti-Semitism Helped Shape Georgia's High Stake Senate Race," *Haaretz*, January 5, 2021; Jason Sokol, "Has Georgia Reached a Turning Point for Democrats?," *New York Times*, January 5, 2021; *Libération*, January 5, 2021; Bateman, Katznelson, and Lapinski, *Southern Nation*, 402.

161. For Guy Gerstle, a New Deal specialist, "Biden n'est pas encore Roosevelt et ne le sera peut-être jamais," interview with Guy Gerstle by Raphaël Bourgeois, *AOC*, May 8, 2021.

162. Neil MacFarquhar, "From the Past, a Chilling Warning About the Extremists of the Present," *New York Times*, May 1, 2021.

163. David Kirkpatrick, "Police Shrugged Off the Proud Boys, Until They Attacked the Capitol," *New York Times*, March 14, 2021.

164. Emma Green, "A Christian Insurrection," *Atlantic,* January 8, 2021.

165. Clint Smith, "The Whole Story in a Single Photo," *Atlantic*, January 8, 2021.

166. Jonathan Sarna, a specialist of American Judaism, underscores the influence of *The Turner Diaries* during the attack of the Capitol in "A Scholar of American Anti-Semitism Explains the Hate Symbols Present During the Capitol Riot," *Conversation*, January 9, 2021.

167. Larry Buchanan, "How a Pro-Trump Mob Stormed the U.S. Capitol," *New York Times*, January 7, 2021; Amir Tibon, "From Charlottesville

to Capitol Hill: This Is Trump's Legacy," *Haaretz*, January 6, 2021; Ben Samuel, "Republican Congresswoman Pro-Trump Rally Near U.S. Capitol: 'Hitler Was Right,'" *Haaretz*, January 6, 2021; Arnaud Parmentier, "Le Jour où des partisans de Donald Trump ont semé le chaos au Capitole," *Le Monde,* January 7, 2021, as well as "États-Unis: Les émeutiers du Capitole, reflet de la galaxie trumpiste," *Le Monde*, January 11, 2021. See also Florian Reynaud, Corentin Lamy and Gregor Brandy, "QAnon, Stop the Steal, d'où viennent les symboles et slogans brandis par les émeutiers du Capitole?," *Le Monde*, January 8, 2021; as well as Laura Adkins and Emily Burack, "Neo-Nazis, QAnon and Camp Auschwitz: A Guide to the Hate Symbols and Signs on Display at the Capital Riot," *Haaretz*, January 8, 2021; Marc-André Argentino, "QAnon et l'assaut du Capitole: L'effet réel des théories du complot en ligne," *La Conversation*, January 7, 2021; Luke Mogelson, "Among the Insurrectionists," *New Yorker*, January 15, 2021; Ursula Moffitt, "White Supremacists Who Stormed the U.S. Capitol Are Only the Most Visible Product of Racism," *Conversation*, January 15, 2021; Joel Rubin, "Supremacist Terrorism as a Transnational Threat," *Foreign Policy*, January 18, 2021. On QAnon extremists, the virus, and conspiracy theories, see Kellen Browning, "Extremists Find a Financial Lifeline on Twitch," *New York Times*, April 27, 2021.

168. Danielle Schulkin, "White Supremacist Infiltration of the U.S. Police Forces," *Just Security*, June 1, 2020; Loïs Beckett, "'FBI Must Target White Supremacists' Infiltration of Police Agencies' Congressman Says," *Guardian*, March 10, 2021. See also William Ramsay, "Identity Crisis: White Supremacist Racist American Cops Must Be Removed," *Justice in My Town*, April 11, 2021.

169. Ben Samuels, "AOC Offers Solidarity to Jewish Community Tied to NYC Holocaust Museum," *Haaretz*, January 9, 2021.

170. Cowen argues that fascism or nationalist populism could never prevail in such a society. See Tyler Cowen, "Could Fascism Come to America?," in *Can It Happen Here? Authoritarianism in America,* ed. Cass Sunstein (New York: HarpersCollins, 2009). On the other hand, see the ideas of the specialists of European fascism, for instance, Anne Appelbaum, "What Trump and His Mob Taught the World About

America," *Atlantic*, January 8, 2021; and Timothy Snyder, "The American Abyss," *New York Times*, January 9, 2021.

171. Steve Oney, "What Jon Ossoff Means for the South and Its Buried Jewish Past," *Washington Post*, January 18, 2021.

## CONCLUSION

1. Moses Rischin, *The Promised City: New York's Jews, 1870–1914* (Cambridge, Mass.: Harvard University Press, 1978), 229. Monty Noam Penkower, "The Kishinev Pogrom of 1903: A Turning Point in Jewish History," *Modern Judaism* 24, no. 3 (October 2004): 187–225.
2. Avishai Margalit, "The Exemplary Pogrom," *New York Review of Books*, May 23, 2019.
3. David Roskies, *Against the Apocalypse* (Cambridge, Mass.: Harvard University Press, 1984), 43 and 91.
4. See the special issue, "Kishinev and the Twentieth Century," *Prooftexts* 25 (Winter 2005).
5. Olga Litvak, "Khave and Her Sisters: Sholem-Aleichem and the Lost Girls of 1905," *Jewish Social Studies* 15, no. 3 (2009): 18. See, for example, the letters published in *Plurielles*, no. 16: 21–23. See also the comments by Roskies, *Against the Apocalypse*, 167 ff.
6. Abraham Cahan, *The Rise of David Levinsky*, introduction by John Higham (New York: Harper Torchbooks, 1960), 60.
7. Lamed Shapiro, *The Cross and Other Jewish Stories* (New Haven: Yale University Press, 1987). See, for example, many short stories such as "The Kiss," "White Challa," or "In the Dead Town." See Daniel Oppenheim, "Lamed Shapiro de Kichinev 1903 à New York 1930," in *Plurielles*, no. 16: 18–24.
8. Saul Bellow, "Mr Katz, Mr Cohen and Cosmology," *Retort: A Quarterly of Social Philosophy* 1, no. 2 (1942): 14–20.
9. Bernard Malamud, *The Fixer* (New York: Farrar, Straus and Giroux, 2004), 300. A few pages later, Yacov Bok's attorney tells his client, who has been suffering for two years in a prison cell: "If you feel bad think of Dreyfus. He went through the same thing with the script in French. We're persecuted in the most civilized languages." To which Yacov replies: "I've thought of him. It doesn't help" (306). Again, and in

surprising ways, as in Atlanta, the Dreyfus affair is entangled with the memory of the pogroms.

10. Henry Roth, *Mercy of a Rude Stream*, vol. 1: *A Star Shines Over Mt. Morris Park* (New York: St. Martin's, 1994), 71.

11. Henry Roth, *Mercy of a Rude Stream*, vol. 2: *A Diving Rock on the Hudson* (New York: St. Martin's, 1995), 367–68. Again, like Atlanta Jews, Ira's parents also remember Dreyfus's fate.

12. On the theme of Jewish novels in the United States and their transformations, see Rachel Ertel, *Le Roman juif américain: Une écriture minoritaire* (Paris: Payot, 1980).

13. Mary Antin leaves Russia in 1891 and in 1912 publishes her famous autobiography, *The Promised Land*, in which her successful assimilation into American society is in stark contrast with the Russian pogroms of the turn of the century, mentioned multiple times. She writes: "I never was in an actual pogrom but there were times when it threatened us, even in Polotzk; and in all my fearful imaginings, as I hid in dark corners, thinking of the horrible things the Gentiles were going to do to me, I saw the cross, the cruel cross." Mary Antin, *The Promised Land* (New York: Houghton Mifflin, 1912), 9. See, for example, Nancy Miller, "I Killed My Grandmother: Mary Antin, Amoz Oz and the Autobiography of a Name," *Biography* 30, no. 3 (Summer 2007): 319–41. See also Jana Pohl "Looking Forward, Looking Back: Images of Eastern European Jewish Migration to America in Contemporary American Children Literature," *Studia Imagologica* 19 (January 2011).

14. Karen Brodkin, *How Jews Became White Folks and What That Says About Race in America* (New Brunswick, N.J.: Rutgers University Press, 2004).

15. Matthew Friedman, "American Pogrom," *Politics Letter*, November 5, 2018. See also Ezra Gershanok, "A Pogrom in Pittsburgh," *PennState Presidential Leadership Academy*, October 27, 2018.

16. Philip Roth, *The Plot Against America* (New York: Random House, 2004), 18.

17. Paul Starr, "The Message of the Synagogue Slaughter," *American Prospect*, October 29, 2018.

18. *Forward*, October 30, 2018. A resident declares: "We Jews have always politicized tragedy; politicization is the engine of Jewish survival, the

process by which we take responsibility for our destinies. It is, for instance, exactly what the writer Hayyim Nahman Bialik did after the Kishinev Pogrom in 1903."

19. For Corwin Berman, "American Jews always believed the U.S. was exceptional. We were wrong," *Washington Post*, February 11, 2018.

20. Adam Teller, *Rescue the Surviving Souls. The Great Jewish Refugee Crisis of the Seventeenth Century* (Princeton, N.J.: Princeton University Press, 2020), 8.

21. Arno Mayer, *Why Did the Heavens not Darken?: The "Final Solution" in History* (New York: Pantheon, 1988), 25.

22. In 1096, during the first Crusade, Jews were massacred in great numbers at Worms and also at Mainz, in Rhineland.

23. Hasia Diner, *The Jews of the United States* (Berkeley: University of California Press, 2004), 86–87.

24. See Shlomo Eidelberg, *The Jews and the Crusades: The Hebrew Chronicles of the First and Second Crusades* (Jersey City, N.J.: Ktav, 1996). Jeremy Cohen, "A 1096 Complex? Constructing the First Crusade in Jewish Historical memory, Medieval and Modern," in *Jews and Christian in the Twelfth Century Europe*, ed. Michael Signer and John Van Engen (Notre Dame: Notre Dame University Press, 2000), 22–23.

25. Shmuel Shpkaru, "The Preaching of the First Crusade and the Persecutions of the Jews," *Medieval Encounters* 18 (2012): 93–135. See pages 10 ff.

26. Nathan Hannover, *Le Fond de l'abime*, ed. J.-P. Osier (Paris: Cerf, 1991). Gershon Bacon, "The House of Hanover: *Gezeirot Tah* in Modern Jewish Historical Writing," *Jewish History* 17, no. 2 (2003): 179–206. Frank Sysyn, "The Khmel'Nyts'kyi Uprising: A Characterization of the Ukrainian Revolt," *Jewish History* 17, no. 2 (2003): 115–39; and the recent reevaluation of the number of deaths by Jits van Straten, "Did Shmu'el Ben Nathan and Nathan Hannover Exaggerate Estimates of Jewish Casualties in the Ukraine During the Cossack Revolt in 1648?" *ZUTOT* 6, no. 1 (2009): 75–82.

27. Becka Alper, "70 Years After WWII, the Holocaust Is Still Important to American Jews," *Pew Research Center*, August 13, 2015. Regarding American's overall understanding of the Shoah, see "What American Know About the Holocaust," *Pew Research Center*, January 22, 2020. Indeed, 45 percent among them count the number of deaths to

be six million. See Hasia Diner, *We Remember with Reverence and Love* (New York: New York University Press, 2009).

28. See Peter Novick's book *The Holocaust in American Life* (New York: Houghton Mifflin, 1999), 201–2. See also the discussion about this book between Eli Lederhendler and Novick, who responded in *Jewish Social Studies* 7, no. 3 (Spring-Summer 2001): 169–79. In another review of Novick's book, Régine Azria concludes by claiming that "whatever may be the degree of institutionalization of the efforts undertaken, the Holocaust does not belong to American's collective memory. It does not provide any answers to American as to their identity," *Archives de Sciences sociales des religions* 45, no. 112 (October-December 2000): 117 (my translation). Françoise Ouzan believes that the Eichmann trial gives the Shoah "a central place in American popular culture." "La mémoire de la Shoah aux États-Unis," in *De la mémoire de la Shoah dans le monde juif*, ed. Françoise Ouzan and Dan Michman (Paris: CNRS, 2008), 311 (my translation).

29. Jonathan Woocher, *Sacred Survival: The Civil Religion of American Jews* (Bloomington: Indiana University Press, 1986).

30. David Engel, *Historians on the Jews and the Holocaust* (Stanford: Stanford University Press, 2010), 23.

31. Anthony Julius, "Before the Holocaust, Jewish Suffering Had One Name," *New York Times*, July 24, 2018.

32. David Nirenberg, "The Rhineland Massacres of Jews in the First Crusade: Memories Medieval and Modern," in *Medieval Concepts of the Past: Ritual, Memory, Historiography*, ed. Gerd Althoff (Cambridge: Cambridge University Press, 2002), 299 ff.

33. Nirenberg, 303.

34. Yitzhak Baer, *Galut* (Paris: Calmann-Lévy, 2000), 101 ff

35. Gary Rosenblatt, "Is It Still Safe to Be a Jew in America?," *Atlantic*, March 15, 2020. In a prescient article published in 1995, the sociologist Charles Liebman already believed that in this increasingly polarized society "we are likely to see rising levels of antisemitism in the United States over the course of the next decade or two." "Jewish Survival, Antisemitism and Negotiation with the Tradition," in *The Americanization of the Jews*, ed. Robert Selzter and Norman Cohen, 437.

36. Danielle Ziri, "Pittsburgh Jews Still Fear Far-Right Violence, Two Years After Massacre," *Haaretz,* October 27, 2020; as well as "A Year

from Deadly Attacks, New York Jews Fear Even Greater Antisemitism in 2021," *Haaretz*, December 24, 2020. See, in June of 2021, the poll from the Public Religion Research Institute showing that 15 percent of Americans are adherents of an extremist ideological current in this movement and approve the use of violence against "satanic" elites. Giovanni Russonello, "QAnon Now as Popular in U.S. as Some Major Religions, Poll Suggests," *New York Times*, May 27, 2021.

37. Fintan O'Toole, "The Trump Inheritance," *New York Review of Books*, February 25, 2021.

38. John Mearsheimer and Stephen Walt, *The Israel Lobby and U.S. Foreign Policy* (New York: Farrar, Straus and Giroux, 2007).

39. Sergio DellaPergola and L. Daniel Staetsky, *Jews in Europe at the Turn of the Millennium* (London: Institute for Jewish Policy Research, October 2020), 14–15.

40. Emptied of all Jews and Jewish life.

41. Pierre Birnbaum, *Les deux maisons. Essai sur la citoyenneté des Juifs en France et aux Etats-Unis* (Paris: Gallimard, 2012).

42. Thus immediately following the clashes between Hamas and Israel, synagogues are attacked, and passersby are assaulted to the point that Jews fear leaving their homes. Shanna Fuld, "U. S Victims of Anti-Semitism Attacks Worry That Things Are Only to Get Worst," *Haaretz*, May 26, 2021. See also Ben Samuels, "U.S. Jewish Groups Urge Biden to Confront Anti-Semitism Emerging from Israeli-Palestinian Flare-Up," *Haaretz*, May 22, 2021.

43. Yosef Hayim Yerushalmi, "Vers une histoire de l'espoir juif," *Esprit*, nos. 104/105 (1985): 27. See Pierre Birnbaum, *Geography of Hope: Exile, the Enlightenment, Disassimilation* (Stanford: Stanford University Press, 2008).

# INDEX

employment, ix, x, 16, 64, 86–87
Engel, David, 32, 179*n*52
Enlightenment, 5, 17, 18, 24, 37, 172
Esterhazy, Ferdinand Walsin, 96
Europe, xi, 31, 34, 48, 169–70
European Jews, 8, 15, 32, 53, 58, 163,
165, 167
exceptionalism, American, viii, xv,
8, 91, 111, 115, 207*n*19; romance
of, 34, 37, 38, 53, 159; violence
and, 155, 161–62, 170
executions, vii, 65, 84, 92, 119
exile (*galut*), 25, 43–45, 167–68
Exodus, 6, 35, 54, 128
expulsion, 18, 24, 31, 32, 38, 44, 159,
170

fake news, 91, 95–96, 98
far-right mobilization: alt-right,
xiii, xvi, *xvi*, 91, 121, 153–56;
with antisemitic violence, 125,
126, 127; at Charlottesville, xiii,
*xiv*, 137–42, 144; extremism, 8,
53, 130–31, 152–53; growth,
152–53, 168–69; political
antisemitism and, 140–42,
152–55; Trump with, xii–xiii,
128, 134, 137–41, 147, 151. *See also*
white supremacists
fascism, xiv, 107, 161, 204*n*170;
alt-right and, 121; Trump and,
108, 136
FBI, xv–xvi, 123, 124, 148, 153, 154
Feinstein, Dianne, 142
Fields, James, 139
First Amendment, 7

*Fixer, The* (Malamud), 158–59,
205*n*9
Ford, Henry, ix, 115, 133
*Fortune* (magazine), 112, 113
*Forty Days of Musa Dagh, The*
(Werfel), 157
*Forverts/Forward* (newspaper), 58,
118
France, 3, 19, 21, 31, 61, 164, 169;
antisemitism in, xii, xv, 8, 92,
109–10, 114, 119, 139–40, 171;
Catholic Church and, 4, 5, 6;
state, 49, 98–99, 111–13, 171.
*See also* French Revolution
Francis (Pope), 145
Frank, Jerome, 112
Frank, Leo, 67, 68, 93, 105, 115.
*See also* Leo Frank affair
Frank, Lucille Selig, 67, 71, 75, 99
Frankfurter, Felix, x, 96, 112–13,
114, 115
Franklin, Benjamin, 54
Franklin, Joseph Paul (James
Clayton Vaughn), 119–20, 134
*Frank v. Mangum*, 83–84
*Fraynd* (newspaper), 56
French Revolution, 3, 15, 19, 26, 28,
31–32, 36–37; American
Revolution and, 35; with
assimilation of Jews, 20, 23;
Enlightenment and, 17, 18, 24
Friedman, Matthew, 160–61
*From Spanish Court to Italian Ghetto*
(Yerushalmi), 46, 48–49
Frug, Shimon, 56
Furrow, Buford, 126

*Mein Kampf* (Hitler), 117, 120, 132, 148

melting pot, 19–20, 56–57, 59, 92–93

*Melting Pot, The* (Zangwill), 56, 59, 92

memory, historical, 60, 75, 80, 92–93, 107, 116, 162–68

Mendelssohn, Moses, 17, 18

*Menorah Journal*, 13, 19, 42, 43

*Mercy of a Rude Stream* (Roth, H.), 159

Middle Ages, Jews in, 12, 18, 22, 34, 172; American Jewish history and, 38; emancipation compared to, 14–17, 23–28; lachrymose conception of history and, 28, 32, 33, 43; Nazism and, 29; with royal alliance, 26, 27, 28, 30, 41, 50–51, 177*n*31, 178*n*43; suffering of, 31, 32, 43–44; with violence, 25, 44

military: Confederate States Army, 63, 64, 137; conscription, 15, 27

Miller, Frazier Glenn, Jr., 132–34

Mishnah, 198*n*70

Montesquieu, 35

Morgenthau, Henry, Jr., 112

Muhammad, John Allen, 125

*Murder in Harlem* (film), 98

*Murder of Mary Phagan, The* (TV miniseries), 98

murders, vii–viii, 67, 68–69, 105. *See also* Leo Frank affair; lynchings; pogroms

"muscle Jews," 58, 185*n*15

Museum of Jewish Heritage, New York, 155

Myers, Jeffrey, 142

Namier, Lewis, 13–14

National Association for the Advancement of Colored People, 78

nationalism, viii, 8, 31, 39, 53, 107, 118

National Policy Institute, 135

National Socialist Party, 122, 139

National Socialist Party of America, 132

National States Rights Party, 120

Nation of Islam, 125

nation-state, 19, 21, 27, 34–35, 39, 41, 180*n*58

Native Americans, vii, 1, 2, 8, 10, 54

nativism, viii, 7, 67

Nazi National Alliance, 126

Nazi Party, 114, 117, 120, 132, 139, 144, 147

Nazism, 32, 34, 36, 91, 115, 126, 161; with January 6 Capitol attack, 153; Ku Klux Klan and, 120, 121, 128, 132, 137; Middle Ages and, 29; rise of, 45, 106, 117–18, 120, 137, 143–44; state and, 30; with threat minimized, 28; Trump and, 135–36, 141; violence and, 44, 119, 124

New Deal, 106, 108–10, 113–14, 128, 141, 167

Senate, U.S., 87, 90, 152
Sephardic Jews, 61, 65
September 11, 2001, 127
serfs, xi, 16, 22, 27, 40, 105, 164
*servie camerae* (servants of the
treasury), 22, 27, 47
Shalom Village, Kansas, 132, 133
Shapiro, Dan, 128
Shapiro, Lamed, 158
*Shevet Yehuda* (Ibn Verga), 26, 47,
178*n*43
Shoah (Holocaust), vii, 25, 28, 44,
162, 165; antisemitism and, 116,
117, 120, 121, 133, 135, 138, 148,
149, 153, 155; Auschwitz, 117, 153,
166, 167; S. Baron with, 29;
Crusades and, 168; Day of the
Shoah, 166; deaths, 207*n*27;
*Historians of the Jews and the
Holocaust*, 179*n*52; in historical
memory, 166–67; lachrymose
conception of history and,
30–31; state with role in, 178*n*43;
in U.S. popular culture, 208*n*28
shofar, 128, 154, 198*n*71
*Shylock* (film), 67
Silver Shirts, 114–15
Sixth Convention of the Federation
of American Zionists, 56
Sixth Zionist Congress, 56
Slaton, John, 66, 84–87, 93, 96–97,
98, 192*n*124
slavery, 102; African Americans
and, 1, 62, 63, 72, 152; Jews and,
17, 20, 39, 43, 165; Jews as slave
owners, 62, 63; white, 122–23

Small, Albion, 21–22
Smith, William, 101
sociability, 22, 33, 38, 171
*Social and Religious History of the
Jews, A* (Baron, S.), 20, 23–24, 49
social antisemitism, ix–xi, 7, 55, 64,
66, 92, 110–11, 173*n*5
socialism, 3, 10, 117
social justice, 91, 141
social sciences, 19, 21
sociology, 3, 21, 38
Sombart, Werner, 10
Sorkin, David, 179*n*48
Soros, George, 135, 144, 149, 153
South, the, viii, x, 54, 91, 114, 162;
antisemitism in, 64–65, 66,
117–20, 137–39, 144, 195*n*36;
Atlanta, 65–68, 72–73, 78–79,
115–16, 118, 152; Charlottesville,
xiii, xiv, 115, 137–42, 144, 155;
Confederate States Army, 63,
64, 137; Jews in, 61–73; political
antisemitism in, 131–34, 141,
153–55; supreme courts, 64, 81,
82, 120; xenophobia in, 67, 132.
*See also* Ku Klux Klan; Leo
Frank affair; slavery
Southern Poverty Law Center, 91,
139
Spain, 25, 42, 50, 172; *From From
Spanish Court to Italian Ghetto*,
46, 48–49; Inquisition, 6, 44,
53, 61
Spanish Jews, 45, 46
Spencer, Richard, 135–36
Springfield race riots (1908), 73

Stanislawski, Michael, 185*n*16
state: control over sociability with
    community, 22; French, 49,
    98–99, 111–13, 171; ghetto and,
    50; nation-state, 19, 21, 27, 34–35,
    39, 41, 180*n*58; Nazism and, 30;
    political antisemitism and,
    49–50, 51–52; *servie camerae* and,
    22, 47; Shoah and role of,
    178*n*43; U.S. with strengthened,
    112–13; U.S. with weak, xii, 40,
    41, 47, 48, 98–99, 110, 111;
    violence against, xvi, 2; welfare,
    xii, 113, 128
stereotypes, antisemitism, ix, xi,
    xii, xv, 164
Stoner, J. B., 120
*Stormfront* website, 126
*Strangers in the Land* (Higham),
    173*n*5
Straus, Oscar Solomon, 58, 110
suffering: antisemitism and, 39;
    *galut* with, 43–44; history of,
    150; Jewish happiness, 16, 21, 24,
    26, 33, 35, 44–45, 51–52; of Jews
    in Middle Ages, 31, 32, 43–44.
    *See also* history, lachrymose
    conception of
suicides, 164, 167, 178*n*42
Supreme Court, U.S., 96, 113, 118,
    120; *Brown v. Board of
    Education*, 90, 116; *Frank v.
    Mangum*, 83–84; Jewish justices
    on, x, 151–52; Leo Frank affair
    and, 82, 83, 99; on U.S. as
    "Christian Nation," 64

supreme courts: Georgia, 81,
    82; Missouri, 120; South
    Carolina, 64
synagogues, 138, 157; attacks on,
    125, 126, 209*n*42; attendance at,
    151; bombings, 115–16, 118–19,
    121, 127, 152; Jefferson at Mill
    Street, 6; mass murder in
    Pittsburgh, xii, xiii, 56, 60, 131,
    142–43, 144, 145, 146, 160–62,
    163, 202*n*152; shootings at,
    119–20, 126, 134, 142, 148; in the
    South, 65; Washington at
    Touro, 4, 5, 161

Talmud, 12, 23, 129, 142
Tarrant, Brenton, 148
Tartars, 165
Tea Party, 130–31, 134–35, 149
Teller, Adam, 178*n*42
Temple Beth Israel, Eugene, 126
Temple B'nai Israel bombing
    (2005), 127
Temple Emanuel in Pueblo,
    Colorado, 148
Tennessee Valley Authority, 112
Teter, Magda, 202*n*149
*They Won't Forget* (film), 98
Thompson, Franklin, 114
Tielsch, Steven, 121
Tocqueville, Alexis de, 1–4, 8, 18,
    34, 35, 42, 53–54, 91
Torah, 138, 198*n*70
*Toronto Mail Empire* (newspaper), 92
Touro synagogue, Newport, 4, 5, 161
trade, 16, 23, 111

William Breman Jewish Heritage
and Holocaust Museum (The
Breman Museum), 97
Williams, Thomas Chatterton, 140
Winn, Courtland, 66
Wirth, Louis, 38
Wise, Stephen, 12, 78–79
Wittmayer, Mina. *See* Baron, Mina
Wood, John, 90
*World of Our Fathers* (Howe), 8
Worms massacre (1096), 162,
207n22
Wrong, Dennis, 9

xenophobia, viii, 67, 107, 132

Yellen, Janet, 151
Yerushalmi, Yosef Hayim, 45–52,
172, 183n112
Yevtushenko, Yevgeny, 157
*Yidishe Gazen, Di* (newspaper), 58
Yom Kippur War (1973), 166

Zangwill, Israel, 19, 20, 39, 56–57,
59, 92
*Zion* (journal), 25, 44
Zionism, 10, 12, 41, 56, 68, 185n15
Zionist Occupational Government
(ZOG), 127
Zunz, Leopold, 13
Zweig, Stefan, 49–50, 52, 169

Printed and bound by CPI Group (UK) Ltd, Croydon, CR0 4YY

10/08/2023

03245594-0001